D1377224

NONCOMMUNICABLE DISEASES AND DISORDERS: SYMPTOMS, DIAGNOSIS, TREATMENT

MACMILLAN
HEALTH
ENCYCLOPEDIA

3

Noncommunicable Diseases and Disorders: Symptoms, Diagnosis, Treatment

MACMILLAN LIBRARY REFERENCE USA
Simon & Schuster Macmillan
NEW YORK

Simon & Schuster and Prentice Hall International
LONDON • MEXICO CITY • NEW DELHI • SINGAPORE • SYDNEY • TORONTO

MACMILLAN
HEALTH
ENCYCLOPEDIA

3

EDITORIAL CREDITS

Developed and produced by
Visual Education Corporation, Princeton, NJ

Project Editor: Darryl Kestler

Editors: Richard Bohlander, Susan Garver, Michael Gee, Emilie McCardell, Cynthia Mooney, Suzanne Murdico, Frances Wiser

Editorial Assistant: Carol Ciaston

Photo Editors: Maryellen Costa, Michael Gee

Photo Research: Cynthia Cappa, Sara Matthews

Production Supervisor: Anita Crandall

Proofreading Management: Amy Davis

Art Editors: Maureen Pancza, Mary Lyn Sodano

Advisor, Anatomical Illustrations:
David Seiden, Ph.D.
Robert Wood Johnson Medical School
Piscataway, New Jersey

Layout: Maxson Crandall, Lisa Evans

Word Processing: Cynthia Feldner

Design: Hespenheide Design

The information contained in the *Macmillan Health Encyclopedia* is not intended to take the place of the care and advice of a physician or health-care professional. Readers should obtain professional advice in making health-care decisions.

PHOTO CREDITS

Jacket: Howard Sochurek/The Stock Market

Armed Forces Institute of Pathology: 7, 8 (bottom), 59, 114

Arthritis Foundation: 15, 16

Centers for Disease Control: 51

Daemmrich: 66

Tom Dunham: 42, 56, 85, 89, 113

Ewing Galloway: 111

inStock: Sunstar, 47

Sara Matthews: 55

National Institutes of Health: 83

John Neubauer: 64 (left)

PhotoEdit: 10 (top), 62; Bill Aron, 18; Melanie Brown, 106; Jose Carrillo, 64 (middle); Paul Conklin, 50; Myrleen Ferguson, 23; Tony Freeman, 25, 46; Phil McCarten, 5; Alan Oddie, 95, 104; Elena Rooraid, 11; David Young-Wolff, 41, 65, 92, 116

Photo Researchers: David Leah/Science Photo Library, 96; SIU, 101

The Picture Cube: Spencer Grant, 105; MacDonald, 37; Phil Savoie, 33

Rainbow: Dan McCoy, 48, 73; Hank Morgan, 88, 97; Frank Siteman, 79

Martin M. Rotker: 13, 22, 26, 36, 39, 52, 54, 57, 64 (right), 86, 98, 99, 102, 103 (top), 109, 112, 118

Terry Wild Studio: 8 (top), 103 (bottom)

Unicorn Stock Photos: Batt Johnson, 100; Alon Reininger, 61; Aneal Vohra, 10 (bottom)

SIMON & SCHUSTER MACMILLAN
Macmillan Library Reference
1633 Broadway
New York, NY 10019-6785

Printed in the United States of America

printing number
10 9 8 7 6 5 4 3

Library of Congress Cataloging-in-Publication Data
Macmillan health encyclopedia.
v. <1– >
Includes index.
Contents: v. 1. Body systems—v. 2. Communicable diseases—v. 3. Noncommunicable diseases and disorders—v. 4 Nutrition and fitness—v. 5. Emotional and mental health—v. 6. Sexuality and reproduction—v. 7. Drugs, alcohol, and tobacco—v. 8. Safety and environmental health—v. 9. Health-care systems/cumulative index
ISBN 0-02-897439-5 (set).—ISBN 0-02-897431-X (v. 1).—ISBN 0-02-897432-8 (v. 2).
1. Health—Encyclopedias. I. Macmillan Publishing Company.
RA776.M174 1993
610′.3—dc20 92-28939
CIP

Volumes of the *Macmillan Health Encyclopedia*
1 *Body Systems* (ISBN 0-02-897431-X)
2 *Communicable Diseases* (ISBN 0-02-897432-8)
3 *Noncommunicable Diseases and Disorders* (ISBN 0-02-897433-6)
4 *Nutrition and Fitness* (ISBN 0-02-897434-4)
5 *Emotional and Mental Health* (ISBN 0-02-897435-2)
6 *Sexuality and Reproduction* (ISBN 0-02-897436-0)
7 *Drugs, Alcohol, and Tobacco* (ISBN 0-02-897437-9)
8 *Safety and Environmental Health* (ISBN 0-02-897438-7)
9 *Health-Care Systems/Cumulative Index* (ISBN 0-02-897453-0)

PREFACE

The *Macmillan Health Encyclopedia* is a nine-volume set that explains how the body works; describes the causes and treatment of hundreds of diseases and disorders; provides information on diet and exercise for a healthy lifestyle; discusses key issues in emotional, mental, and sexual health; covers problems relating to the use and abuse of legal and illegal drugs; outlines first-aid procedures; and provides up-to-date information on current health issues.

Written with the support of a distinguished panel of editorial advisors, the encyclopedia puts considerable emphasis on the idea of wellness. It discusses measures an individual can take to prevent illness and provides information about healthy lifestyle choices.

The *Macmillan Health Encyclopedia* is organized topically. Each of the nine volumes relates to an area covered in the school health curriculum. The encyclopedia also supplements course work in biology, psychology, home economics, and physical education. The volumes are organized as follows: 1. *Body Systems: Anatomy and Physiology;* 2. *Communicable Diseases: Symptoms, Diagnosis, Treatment;* 3. *Noncommunicable Diseases and Disorders: Symptoms, Diagnosis, Treatment;* 4. *Nutrition and Fitness;* 5. *Emotional and Mental Health;* 6. *Sexuality and Reproduction;* 7. *Drugs, Alcohol, and Tobacco;* 8. *Safety and Environmental Health;* 9. *Health-Care Systems/Cumulative Index.*

The information in the *Macmillan Health Encyclopedia* is clearly presented and easy to find. Entries are arranged in alphabetical order within each volume. An extensive system of cross-referencing directs the reader from a synonym to the main entry (GERMAN MEASLES see RUBELLA) and from one entry to additional information in other entries. Words printed in SMALL CAPITALS ("These substances, found in a number of NONPRESCRIPTION DRUGS . . .") indicate that there is an entry of that name in the volume. Most entries end with a list of "see also" cross-references to related topics. Entries within the same volume have no number (See also ANTI-INFLAMMATORY DRUGS); entries located in another volume include the volume number (See also HYPERTENSION, **3**). All topics covered in a volume can be found in the index at the back of the book. There is also a comprehensive index to the set in Volume 9.

The extensive use of illustration includes colorful drawings, photographs, charts, and graphs to supplement and enrich the information presented in the text.

Questions of particular concern to the reader—When should I see a doctor? What are the risk factors? What can I do to prevent an illness?—are indicated by the following marginal notations: Consult a Physician, Risk Factors, and Healthy Choices.

Although difficult terms are explained within the context of the entry, each volume of the encyclopedia also has its own GLOSSARY. Located in the front of the book, the glossary provides brief definitions of medical or technical terms with which the reader may not be familiar.

A SUPPLEMENTARY SOURCES section at the back of the book contains a listing of suggested reading material, as well as organizations from which additional information can be obtained.

GLOSSARY

acute Refers to a symptom or disease that begins suddenly, is usually severe, and generally lasts a short time.

anticoagulant A substance used to prevent and treat abnormal blood clotting.

antihistamine A drug that relieves allergy symptoms by blocking the action of histamine, a chemical released during an allergic reaction.

artery A blood vessel that carries blood away from the heart.

atrophy The shrinking or wasting away of tissue or organs, which may be caused by disuse, inadequate cell nutrition, or disease.

behavior The way a person acts and responds to the environment.

benign Refers to a condition or growth, such as a tumor, that is not cancerous.

blood vessels A general term for the arteries, veins, and capillaries through which blood circulates in the body.

cartilage Strong, dense, elastic tissue found in the nose, ears, and joints (see CONNECTIVE TISSUE, **1**).

cerebral Of or pertaining to a part of the brain.

chronic Refers to a disorder or set of symptoms that persists over a period of time or recurs frequently. Asthma and hypertension are chronic conditions.

concussion Disruption of brain function due to a blow or fall, causing brief unconsciousness.

congenital Refers to a characteristic or condition that is present before or at birth but is not necessarily inherited from parents.

contagious Refers to the time period when an infected person is able to pass an infectious disease to another person by direct or indirect contact; also used to describe the person who is spreading the disease.

convalescence Recovery period after an illness or surgery when a patient regains health and strength before returning to normal activities.

cyst An abnormal lump or swelling, filled with fluid, gas, or semisolid material, that can occur in the body and on the skin.

degenerative disease A long-term disease that involves a gradual breakdown of the structure and function of tissues and organs. It is a condition that usually worsens with time.

disease, disorder An abnormal change in the structure or functioning of an organ or system in the body that produces a set of symptoms. The change may be caused by infection, heredity, environment, or lifestyle or by a combination of these.

embolism An obstruction of a blood vessel by material—such as a blood clot or air mass—floating in the bloodstream.

enzyme A type of protein produced in the cells that causes specific chemical processes that take place in the body. Some enzymes, for example, help break down food.

genes Structures in cells that are inherited from parents; they determine an individual's physical and mental characteristics.

genetic Refers to a characteristic, condition, or disease that is transmitted to an individual through the genes of one or both parents (see GENETICS, **6**).

hemorrhage Severe, uncontrolled bleeding, either internal or external.

heredity The traits—physical, mental, and emotional—that children receive from both of their parents by means of genes; also, the process by which such traits are transmitted by genes.

immunity The body's ability to protect itself from disease.

inflammation Redness, swelling, pain, and heat in a body tissue due to physical injury, infection, or irritation.

lifestyle The way a person lives, as shown by attitudes, habits, and behavior.

lumbar Refers to the part of the back between the lowest pair of ribs and the pelvis.

lymphocyte A type of white blood cell that fights invading organisms as part of the body's immune system.

malignant Refers to an abnormal and dangerous condition, usually a tumor, that can spread uncontrollably and cause death.

metabolism The physical and chemical processes of the body that convert food into energy and body tissue.

metastasis The spreading of a disease, usually cancer, from its original location.

mutation A sudden, permanent change or alteration in a genetic characteristic.

pathogen A microorganism, such as a bacterium or a virus, that can cause disease.

plaque Deposits of cholesterol and other substances that can build up on the inner walls of a blood vessel, reducing blood flow and contributing to heart disease; also refers to a buildup of bacteria and other material on the teeth.

prognosis The medical assessment of the probable course and outcome of a disease.

prosthesis Artificial replacement for a missing part of the body, such as an organ or a limb.

pulmonary Pertaining to the lungs.

remission Temporary lessening or disappearance of the symptoms of a disease.

seizure A sudden attack, usually marked by convulsions and loss of consciousness, such as occurs with epilepsy.

spasm Involuntary and abnormal muscular contraction.

stress The body's response to any physical or mental demand made on it.

syndrome A group of symptoms that characterizes a particular disease or disorder.

tendon A tough, flexible, fibrous cord that joins muscle to bone or muscle to muscle in the body.

tremor Involuntary trembling or shaking.

ulcer An open sore on the skin or mucous membrane.

vascular Pertaining to the blood vessels and the circulation of blood through the body.

vertebrae (sing. *vertebra*) The bony segments of the spinal column.

virus The smallest known living infectious agent (see MICROORGANISMS, **2**).

Acne

Acne is a common skin disorder of adolescence. It is caused by increased production of *sebum*, an oil that lubricates the skin, which leads to blocked *hair follicles* and inflammation of *sebaceous* (si BAY shus) *glands* (the glands that produce sebum). As many as four out of five teenagers have acne, and it is considered a normal part of growth and development. Acne can occur in adults, too, particularly in women as a result of hormonal changes before their menstrual periods.

Acne generally develops on the face, neck, chest, upper back, or shoulders—skin areas that contain many sebaceous glands. In teenagers, acne may last for a few weeks, or it may linger into early adulthood. Although most cases of acne clear up without serious physical effects such as scarring, the disorder can affect an individual's self-confidence and self-esteem.

Symptoms Blocked hair follicles can result in blackheads, whiteheads, pustules, or cysts, firm swellings below the skin (see illustration: Development of Acne). *Blackheads,* the mildest form of acne, develop when increased amounts of sebum combine with dead skin cells to form a plug in the *pore,* the follicle opening on the skin's surface. *Whiteheads* form when the sebum collects below the skin, forming a plug that closes off the pore. *Pustules* are infections that occur when the follicle wall ruptures and bacteria invade the skin. When the sebaceous gland continues to produce sebum that does not break through the skin, a *cyst* may form.

Causes and Treatment The exact cause of acne is unknown, but it is related to the increased production during puberty of androgen, the male sex hormone. Heredity seems to play an important role in whether a person develops acne. Teenagers whose parents had moderate or severe acne are more likely to develop it. Certain drugs, including corticosteroids, those containing androgens, and oil-based skin products, can increase oil production in the skin and aggravate existing acne.

Mild acne can be treated by keeping the skin as free of oil as possible by gentle and thorough cleansing two or three times a day and by frequent shampooing. Over-the-counter creams, lotions, and gels may help dry the skin and promote healing. If these measures are not effective, a physician may prescribe antibiotic creams, vitamin A acid creams,

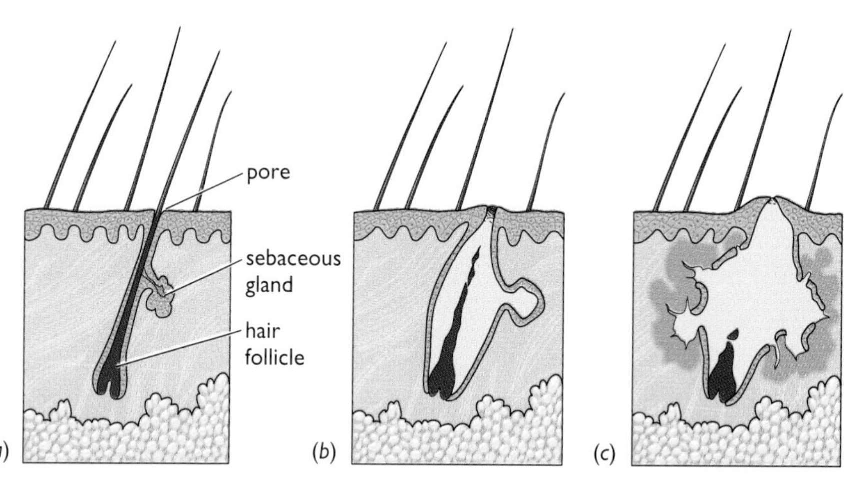

Development of Acne. (a) *Normal hair follicle and sebaceous gland.* (b) *A blackhead forms when sebum and dead skin cells collect in the hair follicle, causing the follicle to deteriorate.* (c) *Pustules form when the follicle wall ruptures and bacteria spread under the skin.*

a peeling agent, or even oral antibiotics. Minor surgery is sometimes performed to remove cysts. To prevent infection and scarring, avoid picking or squeezing the skin.

HEALTHY CHOICES

Prevention Most experts agree that acne can be minimized by cleaning the skin thoroughly and by avoiding oil-based cosmetics, suntan lotions, and moisturizing products. Avoiding certain foods, however, has generally been abandoned as a way of treating this condition. No connection has been found between acne and foods such as chocolate with high fat or sugar content. (See also SKIN, **1**; PUBERTY, **6**; PHYSICIANS (M.D.'s)—DERMATOLOGIST, **9**.)

ACUPUNCTURE

Acupuncture is a form of *alternative medicine* that involves the insertion of needles into the body to treat disease and relieve pain. The technique has been practiced for 2,500 years in China and other parts of Asia but has only recently been introduced in Western countries.

Acupuncturists believe that life forces flow through the body along 14 meridians, or pathways. In a healthy person, the life forces are in perfect balance; in an unhealthy person, the life forces are disturbed. The acupuncturist seeks to restore balance by inserting needles along the meridians at specific points corresponding to organs and body parts (see illustration: Acupuncture).

Acupuncture has been used as an anesthetic in dental procedures, childbirth, and surgery. It has also been used to treat migraine headaches, asthma, arthritis, anxiety, and addictions such as smoking, alcoholism, and overeating. Depending on the disorder, the acupuncturist may heat the needles or pass a mild electrical charge through them. The needles are inserted at specific angles and then twisted, vibrated, or simply left in place. No one knows exactly how acupuncture works, but researchers theorize that it interferes with neurological functions and may stimulate the brain to release *endorphins,* a natural sedative and painkiller produced by the body.

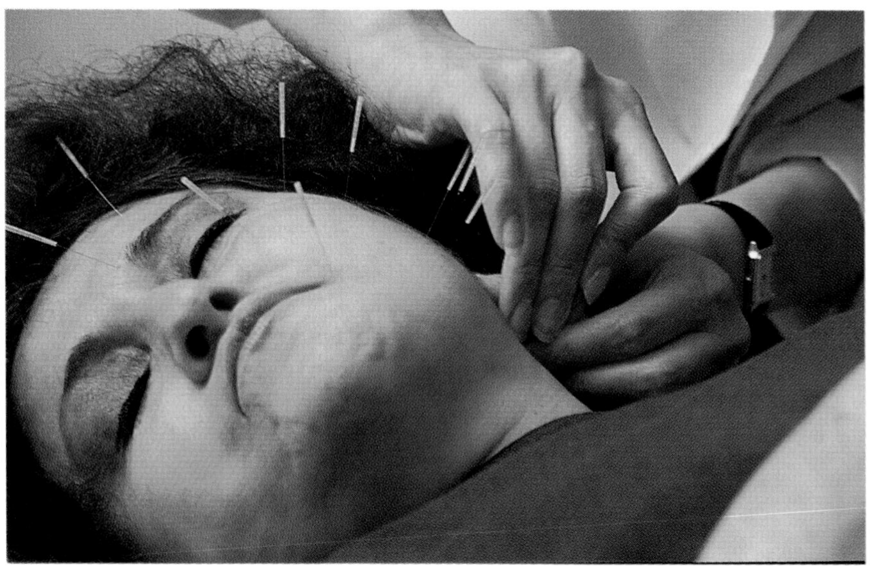

Acupuncture. *An acupuncturist inserts needles along meridian lines at points that are believed to affect a particular organ or part of the body.*

In the United States, some health insurers are beginning to cover acupuncture therapy for certain illnesses. Many acupuncturists use disposable needles now to avoid the possibility of infection. Standards for regulating acupuncturists vary widely from state to state. (See also ENDORPHINS, 1; ALTERNATIVE HEALTH CARE, 9.)

Allergies

An allergy is an overreaction of the immune system to a normally harmless foreign substance. The *immune system* is designed to mobilize forces to fight the invasion of disease-causing microorganisms. Millions of people, however, find that their immune systems also attempt to destroy substances—such as pollen, venom from insect bites, and even certain foods and drugs—that are harmless to other people. An otherwise harmless substance that causes an allergic reaction is an *allergen*. Allergens trigger the immune system to produce *histamines,* which cause the allergic symptoms, such as a runny nose, itchy eyes, a rash, or stomach cramps.

Allergies are among the most common disorders, affecting as many as 40 million Americans. Most allergy attacks are uncomfortable but not life-threatening. Occasionally, however, an allergic reaction results in *anaphylactic shock,* a potentially fatal reaction that requires immediate medical treatment.

Allergies are among the most common disorders, affecting as many as 40 million Americans. Most allergy attacks are uncomfortable but not life-threatening.

Types of Allergies Allergies are often categorized by the type of allergen involved. Some allergies are caused by airborne allergens—such as pollen, house dust, mold spores, and animal dander (flakes of dried skin from animals)—that are inhaled into the nose and lungs. Airborne allergens are responsible for HAY FEVER (allergic rhinitis), an allergy to pollen that causes sneezing, a runny nose, and itching eyes. They also can cause ASTHMA, a serious respiratory disorder characterized by wheezing, difficulty in breathing, and tightness in the chest.

Allergies to certain foods—most often berries, shellfish, nuts, eggs, milk, corn, beans, or wheat—can produce symptoms such as stomach cramps, diarrhea, nausea, vomiting, wheezing, nasal congestion, a rash, and hives. *Hives* (urticaria) are raised, itchy welts that can develop within minutes after a person has eaten a food allergen (see illustration: Hives).

Allergic reactions can also be caused by certain drugs or by the venom present in the sting of wasps or other insects. The most common drug allergies are to penicillin and aspirin. Drug allergy symptoms include a rash or hives; venom allergies most often cause hives, a constricted throat and chest, or itchy eyes. In rare cases, a sting can result in anaphylactic shock.

The most common skin allergy (*contact dermatitis*) is triggered by the residue from poison ivy, poison oak, and poison sumac plants. Within a day or two after the plant's resin comes in contact with the skin, itchy red bumps develop that turn into watery blisters. Skin allergies may also be caused by contact with chemicals found in substances such as hair dyes, cosmetics, and printing inks. ECZEMA is a kind of contact dermatitis that causes itchy, red, flaky skin.

An unusual condition that has been reported more frequently in recent years is an allergic reaction to a number of different elements in

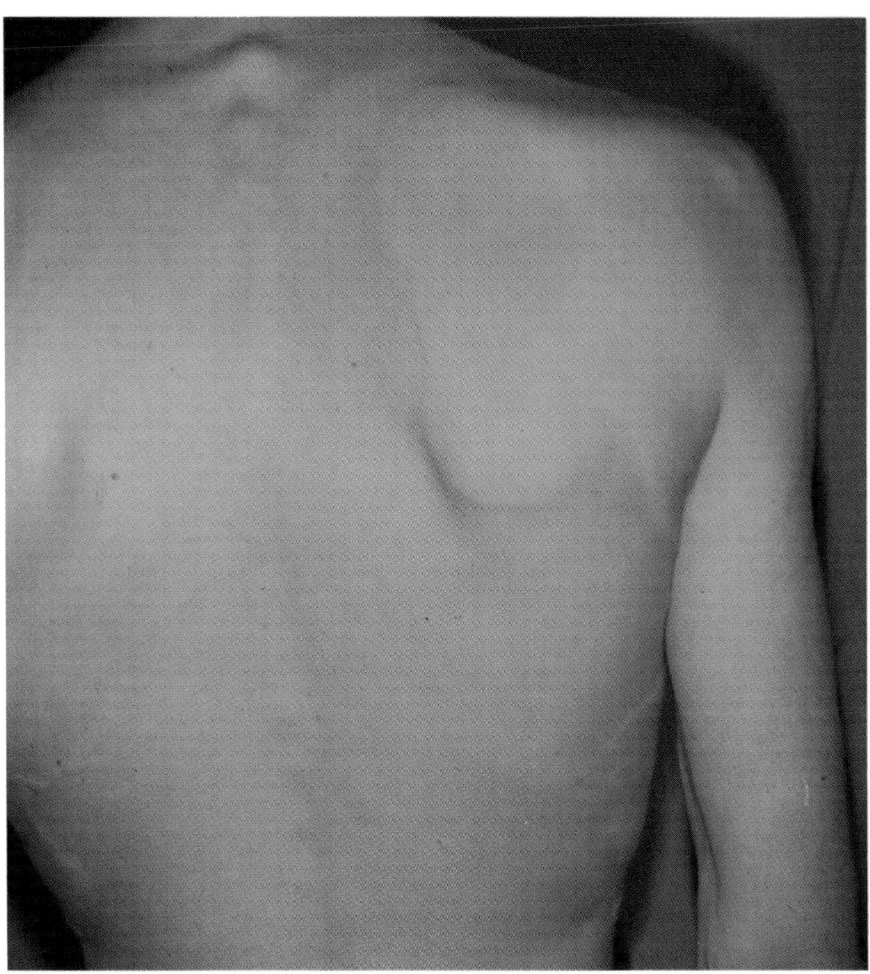

Hives. *These itchy, swollen red blotches can last for minutes or days. Scratching them will cause new hives to develop.*

one's environment—especially carpeting, upholstery, common household chemicals, fabrics, and pollution in the air. Some people call this the "twentieth-century disease." Symptoms include headaches, fatigue, a stuffy nose, rashes, insomnia, and abdominal pain. There is some doubt among physicians as to whether this is a true allergy or a psychological disorder. Nevertheless, a small number of people claim to be completely disabled by the condition, and a few have chosen to live in bare wooden houses in the desert to escape the symptoms.

Allergies can be treated by avoiding the allergen, taking medication to relieve the symptoms, or undergoing immunotherapy. Avoiding the allergen may involve replacing feather pillows with foam ones, avoiding contact with or giving away pets, staying indoors during hay fever season, or avoiding certain foods, chemicals, or drugs.

Allergy attacks may occur despite attempts to avoid an allergen. When allergy symptoms flare up, physicians usually prescribe *antihistamines,* drugs that suppress the production of histamine. In more severe cases, physicians also prescribe steroid nasal sprays or oral steroids to shrink tissues inflamed by histamine. A third method of treating allergies is IMMUNOTHERAPY, a long-term program of injections to gradually desensitize the body to the allergen.

Medic Alert Bracelet.

HEALTHY CHOICES

People who have severe reactions to drugs or insect bites must take special precautions. Special medical identification should be worn to inform others of drug allergies in case of a medical emergency. In addition, people who are severely allergic to insect stings should carry emergency kits containing *epinephrine* (adrenaline) in a syringe so that they can treat themselves immediately after the sting occurs. These precautions can save lives. (See also ALLERGY TESTS; IMMUNE SYSTEM, 1; RASH, 2; ANTIHISTAMINES AND DECONGESTANTS, 7.)

Allergy Tests

An allergy test is a procedure designed to identify *allergens,* substances that cause allergic reactions. The most common allergy tests are the skin test, the double-blind food allergy test, and the radioallergosorbent test (RAST).

Skin Test The skin test is used primarily to test for airborne and skin ALLERGIES. Small amounts of suspected allergens are inserted under the skin of the forearm or upper arm. If the individual is sensitive to any of the substances, raised, often itchy bumps will develop on the arm within 15 or 20 minutes (see illustration: The Skin Test). The skin test, however,

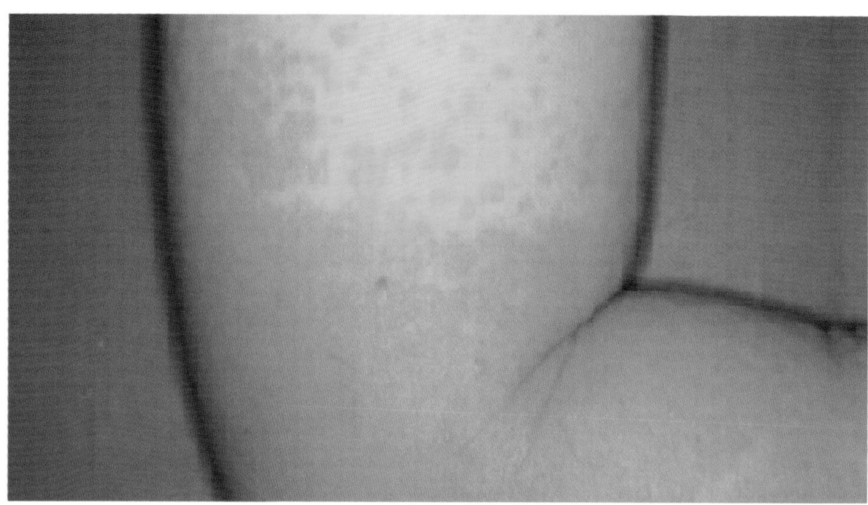

The Skin Test. *Raised, reddish areas at the site where a substance was injected into the body may indicate an allergic reaction to that substance.*

is not completely reliable. Some substances test positive but are not true allergens; on the other hand, some allergens may cause no reaction during a skin test.

Double-Blind Food Allergy Test In the double-blind food allergy test, capsules are prepared containing either the suspected allergen or a *placebo,* a harmless, inactive substance. Neither the physician nor the person being tested knows whether a particular capsule contains the allergen or the placebo. This ensures that the person is not influenced by psychological factors. If the person reacts more than once to the allergen-filled capsules, a food allergy is diagnosed.

RAST The RAST is a new laboratory test in which a sample of the patient's blood is analyzed to measure the amount of a specific type of antibody. High levels of the antibody indicate an allergic reaction. Although safer than skin testing, the RAST cannot be used to test as many allergens. (See also ASTHMA; PHYSICIANS (M.D.'S)—ALLERGIST, **9**.)

ALZHEIMER'S DISEASE

Alzheimer's disease causes brain cells to degenerate, causing loss of memory and mental ability. It is a progressive disease that occurs primarily in people over 65, although it can also occur in middle-aged people. It takes 3 to 15 years to run its course. No one knows what causes Alzheimer's disease, and there is no cure. Alzheimer's disease is often confused with *senility,* the loss of mental functioning due to age. Unlike Alzheimer's disease, however, some causes of senility are treatable.

Alzheimer's disease was first described at the turn of the century by a German neurologist, Dr. Alois Alzheimer. He identified certain characteristic changes in the brain of a person with the disease who had died. The patient's brain had shrunken and had developed a tangled mass of threadlike bundles of nerve fibers.

Many theories have been advanced on the cause of Alzheimer's disease. In recent years, research has pointed to heredity.

Many theories have been advanced on the cause of Alzheimer's disease. In recent years, research has pointed to heredity: Alzheimer's disease develops in 15 percent of those who have a family history of the disease. Researchers looking for a cause have noted the presence of a protein that attacks nerve cells in the brain. The protein seems to damage only those areas of the brain that are responsible for learning, memory, and reasoning.

Symptoms and Diagnosis Physicians still cannot make a definite diagnosis of Alzheimer's disease except by examining a sample of brain tissue taken in a biopsy or after death. Most physicians, however, rely on clinical diagnosis—observing the patient's behavior for symptoms of the disease. The first symptom is usually forgetfulness. Next, the patient's ability to concentrate, recall appropriate words, and perform numerical calculations all decline. As the disease progresses, the patient will develop symptoms of DEMENTIA. These include anxiety, personality changes, and loss of memory of recent events. In the last stages of the disease, the patient becomes severely disoriented and may suffer from delusions. Eventually, the patient also becomes physically incapacitated and must be cleaned, fed, and cared for by others.

Alzheimer's Disease. *In the later stages of the disease, it is often necessary to place the patient in a hospital or nursing home.*

Treatment Treatment for Alzheimer's disease involves keeping the patient clean, comfortable, and safe. Medication can help the patient rest and relieve some feelings of anxiety. Most Alzheimer's disease patients can be cared for at home for some time, but this can become extremely difficult and cause enormous stress for family members. Support groups, counseling, and day-care programs are helpful in relieving some of the stress. Eventually, the patient will require constant care and may have to be placed in a nursing home or other health-care facility. (See also BRAIN, **1**; SENILITY, **5**.)

AMPUTATION

Artificial Limb. *Modern artificial limbs allow for movement that is near normal. They are controlled by brain impulses that are picked up by electronic circuitry in the artificial limb.*

Amputation is the removal of a body part, such as a finger or a foot. Automobile and industrial accidents are major causes of accidental amputation. Surgical amputation is sometimes required to halt the spread of disease or to remove a limb that has been damaged beyond repair.

Accidental Amputation In accidental amputation, the greatest risk is loss of blood, which may cause death. Any accidental amputation requires immediate medical attention. In some cases, severed limbs can be reattached through microsurgery.

Surgical Amputation Before the discovery of antibiotics, amputation was a common operation. Today surgical amputation is used primarily as a last resort to halt the spread of bone cancer and to treat incurable ulcers and GANGRENE in people with DIABETES or circulatory diseases. In performing the amputation, the surgeon leaves extra tissue, including skin and muscle with which to form a stump so that a *prosthesis,* or artificial limb, can be comfortably attached after the surgery heals (see illustration: Artificial Limb).

Amputation is a traumatic event. Patients must adjust to the loss of a limb both physically and psychologically. They must go through weeks or months of physical therapy to learn how to function without the limb. Many suffer from *phantom limb pain,* tingling sensations or pain that seems to be coming from the amputated limb. In addition, the patient may require treatment for depression. Therapists can do much to help amputation patients through these difficulties. Modern artificial limbs also enable many amputation patients to lead normal lives. (See also SHOCK.)

ANEMIA

Anemia is the most common disorder of the blood. It occurs when blood does not have enough *hemoglobin* (the part of the blood that carries oxygen) in red blood cells to transport oxygen from the lungs to tissues throughout the body. Anemia results when the body does not produce a sufficient supply of red blood cells or when the red blood cells produced are defective.

There are many types of anemia, but the symptoms of each type are similar: fatigue, weakness, dizziness, headaches, pale skin, shortness of breath, and rapid heartbeat. Severe anemia may be accompanied by chest pain or heart failure. Physicians diagnose anemia by evaluating a patient's symptoms and checking blood tests. In some cases a sample of bone marrow (the substance that produces red blood cells) is also analyzed.

Iron-Deficiency Anemia The most common type of anemia results from insufficient reserves of iron, which the body needs to make hemoglobin. Bleeding is the most common cause of iron-deficiency anemia, and women of childbearing age are particularly prone to iron deficiency because of monthly menstrual bleeding. Bleeding in the gastrointestinal tract—from an ulcer, polyp in the colon, or stomach or intestinal cancer—can also be responsible for anemia. In addition, iron-deficiency anemia may be caused by the body's inability to absorb iron and, occasionally, by an insufficient amount of iron in the diet.

To treat iron-deficiency anemia, the underlying cause must be corrected. For example, the cause of gastrointestinal bleeding must be diagnosed and treated to cure the anemia. Iron supplements or even changes in diet can correct deficiency due to menstrual bleeding or related to pregnancy. Iron supplements should not be taken without a physician's

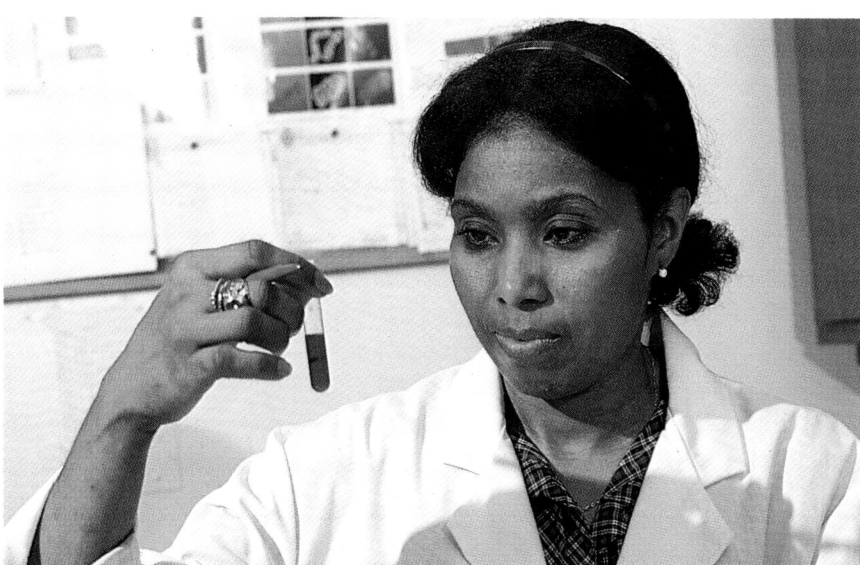

Blood Tests. *A sample of blood is tested to determine if an individual has anemia.*

advice, however, because too much iron can also cause serious health problems. Foods such as fruit, whole-grain breads, beans, lean meat, and green vegetables are rich sources of dietary iron.

Vitamin B_{12} Anemia Vitamin B_{12} anemia, also called *pernicious anemia,* is caused by a deficiency of vitamin B_{12}, which is needed to produce red blood cells. Usually the deficiency is caused by failure to absorb the vitamin properly through the digestive tract. It is particularly common among people who have had part of the stomach or intestine removed. Treatment involves injections of vitamin B_{12}.

Folic Acid Anemia A deficiency of folic acid, a member of the vitamin B group, interferes with the body's ability to produce red blood cells. Folic acid anemia occurs when the diet is low in folic acid or when the intestines cannot absorb the vitamin. Treatment depends on the cause. A physician may prescribe tablets of folic acid if diet is the cause; injections are given if the problem is in the intestinal tract.

Hemolytic anemia develops when old red blood cells are broken down in the spleen faster than new ones are produced by the bone marrow.

Hemolytic Anemia Hemolytic anemia develops when old red blood cells are broken down in the *spleen* (the organ that destroys old blood cells) faster than new ones are produced by the bone marrow. The disease can be inherited or acquired. SICKLE CELL ANEMIA is an inherited form of the disease. Acquired cases can be caused by infections, diseases of the spleen, or immune system disorders. Treatment may involve corticosteroid drugs or surgical removal of the spleen.

Other Types of Anemia *Aplastic anemia,* a disease of the bone marrow that results in too few red blood cells, may be caused by exposure to chemicals or radiation or by antibiotics or other drugs. A bone marrow transplant is required to treat this anemia. *Sideroblastic anemia* is a rare disorder that results from red blood cells that contain too much iron. *Thalassemia* is an inherited disorder that causes abnormal hemoglobin production; it strikes mainly people from the Mediterranean region and the Middle East and their descendants. Occasionally, anemia develops as a symptom of a chronic disease such as rheumatoid arthritis, kidney disease, and liver disease. (See also BLOOD TEST, **1**; BONE MARROW, **1**; IRON, **4**; VITAMIN B COMPLEX, **4**.)

ANESTHESIA

Anesthesia means the absence of all sensation. In medical terms, it refers to the use of drugs that deaden sensation in patients about to undergo surgery, childbirth, or other medical procedures. The purpose of anesthesia is to prevent pain during a medical procedure, making it safer and easier for the patient. The two main types of anesthetic are local anesthetic and general anesthetic.

Local Anesthesia Under a local anesthetic, the patient remains conscious, and the loss of sensation is limited to a particular area of the body. For minor procedures, such as the stitching of small wounds or drilling for dental fillings, anesthetic drugs are injected directly into the area to be treated. Local anesthetics can also be given in the form of sprays, creams, gels, lozenges, and suppositories.

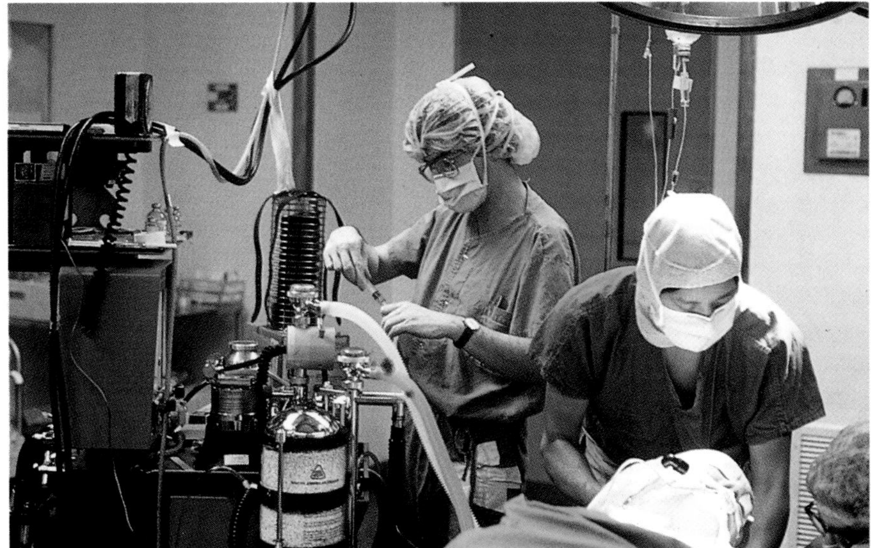

Administration of Anesthetic. *The anesthesiologist and nurse anesthetist closely monitor the patient's vital signs—blood pressure, heart function, breathing, and temperature—during a surgical procedure.*

When it is necessary to anesthetize a larger area or an area that is deep within the body tissues, *nerve blocks* may be used. In these cases, the anesthetic is injected into the fluid-filled space surrounding the spinal cord or at a point through which the major nerve serving the area to be operated on passes. Nerve blocks are widely used for surgery of the arms, legs, and lower abdomen.

General Anesthesia Under a general anesthetic, which is inhaled or injected, the patient is rendered unconscious and kept in this state throughout the operation. General anesthetics are used for most major surgical procedures. An *anesthesiologist,* a physician trained in the use of anesthetics, administers the drugs that induce and sustain unconsciousness and monitors the patient's condition throughout the operation.

The risk of complications from anesthesia depends on the patient's health before the operation, the type of anesthetic used, and the operation performed. Because the patient remains conscious, local anesthetic is generally considered the safest. With general anesthetic, side effects such as nausea, vomiting, and muscle aches are common but usually temporary and easily managed. (See also PAIN; SURGERY; ANESTHETIC DRUGS, 7; ANESTHESIOLOGIST, 9.)

ANEURYSM

An aneurysm is a swelling in the wall of a blood vessel. It develops when a weakened section of an artery fills with blood and bulges outward. Aneurysms can occur anywhere in the body but are most commonly found in the aorta (the main blood vessel carrying blood from the heart), the arteries in the abdomen, and the arteries that supply blood to the brain (see illustration: Aneurysm). An emergency medical condition results when an aneurysm ruptures.

Symptoms and Diagnosis An aneurysm may be caused by a congenital weakness in the wall of the blood vessel, HYPERTENSION (high blood pressure), ARTERIOSCLEROSIS, injury, or infection. Symptoms will vary on

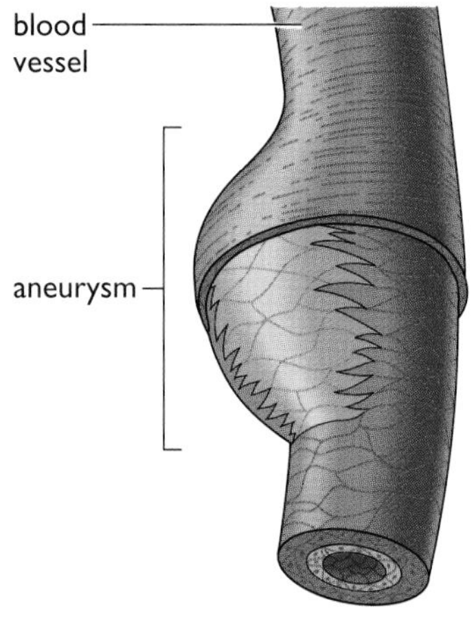

Aneurysm.

its size and location; a pulsing sensation and pain are common symptoms. An aneurysm in the aorta, for example, may be accompanied by chest pain, difficulty in swallowing, and hoarseness due to pressure on nerves that control vocal cords. Aneurysms can also develop without any symptoms.

Sometimes an aneurysm forms a BLOOD CLOT. A blood clot that breaks away and travels through the bloodstream is called an *embolus;* an embolus can cause a sudden obstruction of a blood vessel, an *embolism,* in another part of the body. A ruptured aneurysm produces sudden, severe pain and may result in extremely low blood pressure and SHOCK, loss of consciousness, or death.

An aneurysm of a large blood vessel can be seen in an X ray. More detailed information is revealed by *angiography* (a diagnostic procedure that involves injecting a dyelike substance into the vessels), a CAT SCAN, or MAGNETIC RESONANCE IMAGING.

Treatment Treatment to prevent an aneurysm from rupturing involves surgery to replace the weakened portion of the blood vessel with a section of artificial artery made from synthetic material. Once an aneurysm has ruptured, prompt surgical treatment is required to control bleeding and repair damage. (See also CARDIOVASCULAR DISEASE; HEART DISEASE.)

ANGIOPLASTY

see HEART SURGERY

APPENDICITIS

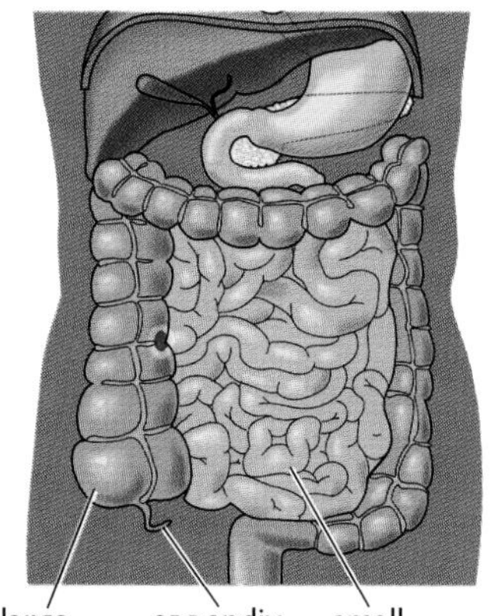

The Appendix. *Located in the abdomen at the beginning of the large intestine, the appendix can become swollen and filled with pus.*

Appendicitis is an inflammation of the appendix, the small, worm-shaped structure attached to the large intestine (see illustration: The Appendix). It is characterized by severe abdominal pain, fever, nausea, and vomiting. Appendicitis is a relatively common disorder but one that needs to be taken seriously. If not treated promptly, the inflamed appendix may burst, resulting in PERITONITIS, a serious infection of the abdominal lining. Appendicitis occurs most frequently in children, teenagers, and young adults.

The first symptom of appendicitis is usually pain in the area around the navel. Within a few hours, the pain becomes sharper and moves to the lower right side of the abdomen. Other possible symptoms include fever, nausea, vomiting, constipation, foul-smelling breath, a coating on the tongue, and loss of appetite. Because the symptoms of appendicitis are similar to those of many other abdominal disorders, the condition can be difficult to diagnose. Careful abdominal and rectal examinations as well as blood and urine tests are often necessary to confirm the diagnosis.

The cause of appendicitis is not always clear. Possible causes include obstruction of the appendix or bacterial infection. The usual treatment for acute appendicitis is an *appendectomy,* the surgical removal of the appendix, and antibiotic treatment. If appendicitis is suspected, it is important to seek immediate medical advice. (See also APPENDIX, **1.**)

Arteriosclerosis

Arteriosclerosis is a group of disorders that cause thickening and hardening of the walls of the *arteries,* the blood vessels that carry oxygen-rich blood away from the heart. The result is a decrease or loss of blood flow to the tissues and organs of the body, and an increase in blood pressure, leading to HYPERTENSION (high blood pressure). The most common type of arteriosclerosis is ATHEROSCLEROSIS, which occurs when fatty deposits narrow the arteries.

The symptoms and severity of arteriosclerosis depend on the arteries affected. For example, arteriosclerosis of the extremities decreases the supply of blood to the feet and legs, causing complications ranging from pain and cramping to infection and GANGRENE. Severe narrowing of the arteries that supply blood to the heart can cause a HEART ATTACK. Decreased levels of blood to the brain can cause a STROKE.

RISK FACTORS

Although arteriosclerosis is thought to be part of the aging process, certain risk factors increase its likelihood. These are hypertension, cigarette smoking, high levels of cholesterol in the blood, a family history of arteriosclerosis, and certain diseases such as DIABETES. (See also ARTERY, **1**; CHOLESTEROL, **4**.)

Arthritis

Arthritis is a term used to describe more than 100 inflammatory joint disorders. All are characterized by pain, swelling, and limited movement. The inflammation may affect one joint or many, and symptoms may vary in severity from a mild ache and stiffness to disabling pain. In some cases, arthritis can lead to permanent deformities. The three most common forms of arthritis are *osteoarthritis, rheumatoid arthritis,* and *gout.* A number of infectious diseases also produce arthritic symptoms.

RISK FACTORS

Osteoarthritis Osteoarthritis, which results from wear and tear on a joint, is the most common type of arthritis. Also known as degenerative joint disease, it appears most frequently in older people.

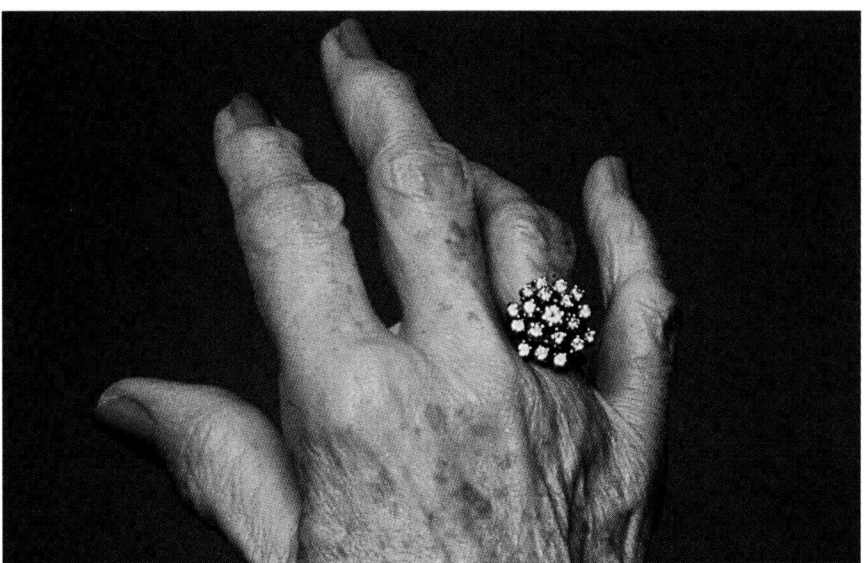

Osteoarthritis. *In people with osteoarthritis, bony lumps called Heberden's nodes often develop on the end joints of the fingers.*

The ends of the bones that meet in a joint are cushioned with a layer of cartilage. Over time, this cartilage deteriorates, causing the surfaces of the joint to become rough. Eventually, bony bumps develop around the joint (see illustration: Osteoarthritis). Pain occurs in both stages of joint degeneration. People whose joints have been damaged by an injury are at greater risk of developing osteoarthritis later in life.

RISK FACTORS

Symptoms of osteoarthritis include periodic bouts of pain, swelling, and stiffness in a joint. These symptoms may be brought on by using a particular joint or by a change in the weather. The hips, knees, fingers, neck, and back are the joints most often affected. A number of anti-inflammatory drugs, including aspirin, provide effective relief for the symptoms of osteoarthritis. Weight control is also an important part of therapy, since excess weight places an additional strain on the knees, hips, and spine.

Rheumatoid Arthritis Rheumatoid arthritis is the most disabling of all the inflammatory joint disorders. It generally appears as tenderness, swelling, and stiffness in the smaller joints of the hands and feet on both sides of the body. Larger joints such as the hips and knees can be affected as well. Small lumps, known as rheumatoid nodules, often develop on the joints and bones just under the skin. Attacks of rheumatoid arthritis are sometimes accompanied by a general feeling of being sick—achiness, weakness, and fatigue. Although these symptoms may subside, they can flare up again and again throughout the life of an affected person.

Unlike osteoarthritis, rheumatoid arthritis affects more than the musculoskeletal system. The disease can also damage the heart, lungs, eyes, and other organs. Although its cause is unknown, it is thought to be an AUTOIMMUNE DISORDER, a disease in which the body's immune system attacks itself. Rheumatoid arthritis strikes first against the *synovium,* the membrane lining each joint. During an attack, the synovium becomes red and swollen. The disease extends to the cartilage cushioning the joint, causing inflammation and gradual destruction of the cartilage. Over time the affected joints can become loose or deformed (see illustration: Rheumatoid Arthritis).

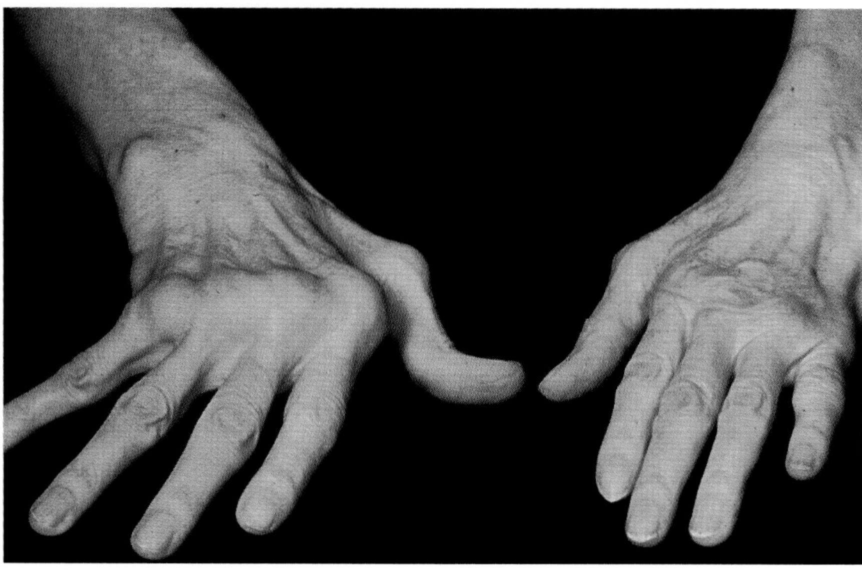

Rheumatoid Arthritis. *One common characteristic of rheumatoid arthritis is enlarged and bent joints in the hands.*

The severity of rheumatoid arthritis varies greatly from person to person. It is usually treated with a combination of rest, physical therapy, and anti-inflammatory drugs. In some cases, badly damaged joints are replaced with artificial joints made of plastic or steel.

RISK FACTORS

Rheumatoid arthritis can occur at any time, although it usually appears between the ages of 20 and 50 and affects women more often than men. *Juvenile rheumatoid arthritis,* or *Still's disease,* which has symptoms similar to those of rheumatoid arthritis, affects young children. It usually clears up after several years but sometimes leaves permanent disabilities.

Gout Gout, also called crystal-induced arthritis, is marked by a sudden outbreak of severe pain in a single joint. The base of the big toe is the place most often affected. The joint becomes red and swollen and remains very painful for several days. After 1 or 2 weeks, the pain and swelling disappear. Gout is caused by a buildup in the body of uric acid (one of the body's waste products). The uric acid forms crystals that cause the inflammation. Almost all people with gout are men over the age of 40. People who are obese or have HYPERTENSION are at a greater risk of developing gout, as are those with a family history of the disorder. A variety of drugs are used to treat acute attacks of gout and to control the level of uric acid in the body.

RISK FACTORS

Infectious Arthritis Pain and inflammation in the joints can also be caused by bacterial, viral, or fungal infections. In most cases, the infecting agent enters the body and spreads to the joints through the bloodstream. The pain and stiffness are usually limited to one joint, such as a knee, shoulder, elbow, or wrist. Other symptoms of infectious arthritis include fever, chills, and weakness. Antibiotics and physical therapy generally provide effective treatment. (See also BACK PROBLEMS; AGING, **1**; CONNECTIVE TISSUE, **1**; JOINT, **1**; LYME DISEASE, **2**.)

ASTHMA

Asthma, also called bronchial asthma, is a chronic respiratory disorder that causes narrowing of the bronchial passages and difficulty in breathing. It is caused by ALLERGIES to pollens, mold spores, animals, ingredients in house dust, and other irritants. Asthma affects approximately 10 million Americans, most of whom are children. The first symptoms typically appear before the age of 5, but many children outgrow the condition. Although asthma can be controlled by medication, it cannot be cured.

Cardiac asthma shares some symptoms with bronchial asthma, including wheezing and difficulty in breathing, but it is much more serious. It is caused by a buildup of fluid in the lungs and accompanies congestive heart failure. Cardiac asthma is a life-threatening condition that requires swift medical attention. (See also HEART ATTACK.)

Symptoms and Diagnosis The main symptoms of asthma are difficulty in breathing, wheezing, tightness in the chest, and a dry cough. During an asthma attack the bronchial tubes become swollen, the muscles surrounding them tighten, and mucus production increases. Airflow through swollen, mucus-clogged bronchial tubes is restricted. The person tries to draw more air into the lungs but cannot because stale air is not being completely expelled. The characteristic wheezing of asthma occurs when air is expelled with force through the narrowed air passages.

If the oxygen level in the blood falls too low during a severe asthma attack, a dangerous condition called *cyanosis* (purple-blue discoloration of the skin) may occur. A serious long-term complication of asthma is eventual loss of elasticity in the lungs, which can lead to EMPHYSEMA. In addition, if mucus secretions associated with asthma do not drain properly, *bronchitis* or *pneumonia* can result.

A number of different substances or conditions can trigger an asthma attack, including airborne allergens (such as pollen or mold spores), weather conditions (cold air or high humidity), certain foods, physical exertion, emotional distress, or respiratory infections such as colds. Physicians diagnose asthma through a complete physical examination, chest X rays, and special lung tests.

Treatment and Prevention Asthma attacks are treated with *bronchodilators,* drugs that help relax and widen air passages and relieve difficult breathing once an attack has begun. These drugs are often administered by a small, hand-held inhaler that allows the user to inhale the exact dosage of medication into the lungs (see illustration: Controlling Asthma with Medication).

Controlling Asthma with Medication. *People who have asthma can participate in sports. Taking medication before exercising can help prevent an asthma attack.*

The most important step in treating asthma, however, is preventing an attack. People who have asthma caused by allergies should avoid those things that may cause an attack, including lung irritants such as smoke or chemical fumes. ALLERGY TESTS can help asthma patients pinpoint specific substances that trigger their attacks. People with asthma should also take special care when exercising. Taking medication before exercising and wearing a scarf or a cold-air mask while outdoors in cold weather can help prevent attacks. Physicians may also prescribe medications that will help to prevent asthma attacks. (See also IMMUNOTHERAPY; LUNG, **1**; BRONCHITIS, **2**; PNEUMONIA, **2**; BRONCHODILATOR, **7**.)

ATHEROSCLEROSIS

Atherosclerosis (ath uh roh skluh ROH sis) is a disease of the inner walls of the arteries. It is caused by the gradual buildup of fatty deposits, called *plaques,* which are composed largely of *cholesterol* deposited from the bloodstream (see illustration: Arteries). Plaques restrict the flow of blood through the arteries. The result is that the tissues and organs supplied by the arteries—the heart and leg muscles, for example—may not receive the blood they need to function properly. Another result is elevated blood pressure. As atherosclerosis progresses and the arteries become more obstructed with plaques, there is increased risk of HEART ATTACK, STROKE, and other serious diseases. Atherosclerosis, which is a common form of ARTERIOSCLEROSIS, is a major cause of death in the United States.

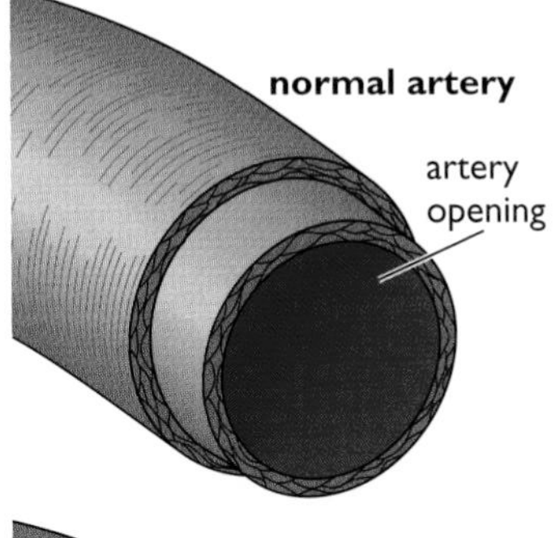

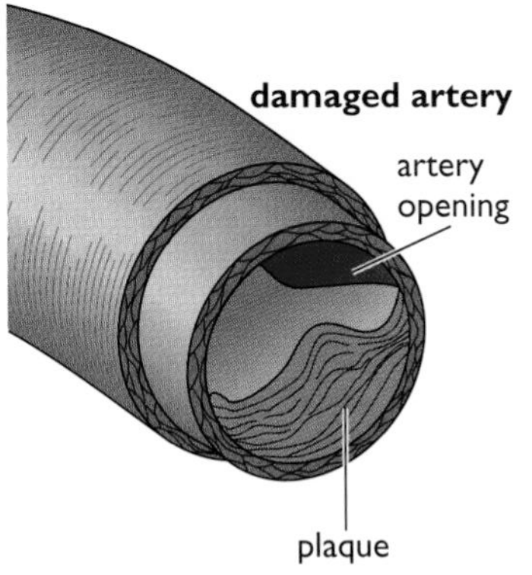

Arteries. *In a normal artery, there are no obstructions to restrict blood flow. However, in a damaged artery, plaques reduce the circulation of blood, increasing the risk of heart disease and stroke.*

Symptoms and Diagnosis In the early stages, atherosclerosis has no symptoms. However, when blood flow to a particular organ (such as the heart) is diminished, pain may be felt in that organ. A physician may also discover the disease during a routine physical exam. While using a stethoscope to examine the neck, abdomen, or groin areas, the physician may hear a blowing sound characteristic of blood flow through narrowed arteries. Another indication of atherosclerosis is decreased blood pulsations in the wrists, legs, and feet.

When atherosclerosis is suspected, *angiography* (X rays that reveal dye injected into the arteries) or tests using sound waves can help measure the degree of artery blockage. In many cases, atherosclerosis cannot be diagnosed until the artery is completely blocked and the patient has experienced a stroke, heart attack, or arterial *embolism* (a blood clot that blocks an artery).

Causes and Risk Factors Atherosclerosis develops over a period of many years, and the risk of getting the disease increases with age. Risk factors that may contribute to its development include diabetes, obesity, sedentary lifestyle, and smoking (see chart: Atherosclerosis Risk Factors).

Treatment Anticoagulant drugs help prevent the formation of BLOOD CLOTS in narrowed arteries, and *vasodilator* drugs help ease symptoms by dilating the arteries. However, neither type of drug reverses the progress of atherosclerosis. A surgical treatment, called balloon *angioplasty,* can help open up narrowed blood vessels. It is sometimes combined with a high-temperature laser technique that dissolves plaque deposits. In some cases, atherosclerosis is treated with coronary artery bypass surgery or the

ATHEROSCLEROSIS RISK FACTORS

Risk factor	How it contributes
Diabetes	Increased blood sugar level often is accompanied by increased fat level.
Family history	Atherosclerosis tends to run in families.
High blood cholesterol levels	Excess cholesterol deposits form on the lining of the blood vessels.
Hypertension (high blood pressure)	Damages artery walls, causing them to thicken and harden.
Obesity	Affects other risk factors because it may contribute to high blood cholesterol levels, high blood pressure, and diabetes.
Sedentary lifestyle	Affects other risk factors because it may contribute to high blood cholesterol levels, high blood pressure, and obesity.
Smoking	Encourages clumping of blood platelets, which seems to stimulate the formation of cholesterol deposits in the arteries.

replacement of blocked arteries with plastic tubes. New drugs that may help shrink plaques and lower blood cholesterol levels are now being used.

Preventing Atherosclerosis Individuals can reduce or eliminate many of the risk factors that increase the chances of developing atherosclerosis. People who have a family history of atherosclerosis should inform their physician of this fact. (See also HEART DISEASE; HEART SURGERY; HYPERTENSION; ARTERY, 1; CHOLESTEROL, 4; RISK FACTORS, 4.)

AUTOIMMUNE DISORDER

An autoimmune disorder is a disease in which the body attacks its own cells or tissues as if they were foreign substances. An *immune system* that is functioning properly can distinguish between the body's components and foreign substances. When a dangerous foreign substance invades the body, the immune system responds by producing antibodies that attack the invader. In a normally functioning body, built-in mechanisms keep the immune system from attacking the body's own cells. In an autoimmune disorder, however, these mechanisms are disrupted, and antibodies attack the body's cells.

Causes and Types of Autoimmune Disorders The causes of autoimmune disorders are unclear. Researchers believe that the tendency to disorders of the immune system may be inherited and that a viral or bacterial infection may activate the disorder. The most common autoimmune disorders are MULTIPLE SCLEROSIS (MS), *mononucleosis,* LUPUS ERYTHEMATOSUS, rheumatoid ARTHRITIS, and pernicious ANEMIA. Autoimmune diseases may involve only one organ or may be generalized. Addison's disease, for example, affects only the adrenal glands, but rheumatoid arthritis can affect the entire body.

Treatment Physicians usually treat autoimmune disorders by administering drugs that suppress the immune system. These drugs must be carefully monitored because they can reduce the body's ability to fight off other diseases. (See also IMMUNE SYSTEM, 1.)

Back Problems

Back problems are among the most common physical disorders affecting adults. Problems range from a muscle strain to the crippling pain of chronic joint disease. In most cases, pain is located in the lumbar, or lower, region of the spine and the surrounding tissues. People whose jobs involve repeated heavy lifting and carrying, overweight people, and those who spend long periods sitting in one position are the most likely to experience back pain. The most common back disorders are muscle strains, herniated disks, and osteoarthritis.

RISK FACTORS ▶ ▶ ▶ ▶ ▶ ▶ ▶

Muscle Strains Muscle strains are usually felt in the lower back. Symptoms may vary from stiffness in the morning and difficulty in getting out of a chair to sudden pain in the sides. The injured area is often tender to the touch, and the pain increases with movement. Lower back pain may be the result of lifting something heavy or exercising too strenuously. The exertion can strain or tear muscles, tendons, and ligaments.

The treatment for muscle strains depends on the severity of the problem. Painkilling drugs, such as aspirin or acetaminophen, usually help relieve the discomfort. Stronger anti-inflammatory drugs and muscle relaxants may be necessary. Treatment may also include resting in bed on a firm mattress, applications of heat, physical therapy, and exercise. If lower back pain is not treated, it can become a chronic problem.

Herniated Disk A herniated or "slipped" disk occurs when one of the disks in the spine slips out of place and presses on a spinal nerve and surrounding ligaments. If the injury affects the lumbar disks and presses on the *sciatic nerve* (the main nerve in each leg), it can result in sciatica. *Sciatica* is pain that starts in one of the buttocks and runs down the back of one leg into the foot. The pain is often so severe that it prevents the person from moving.

Tips for Avoiding Back Problems.

Lift with the back straight and the knees bent.

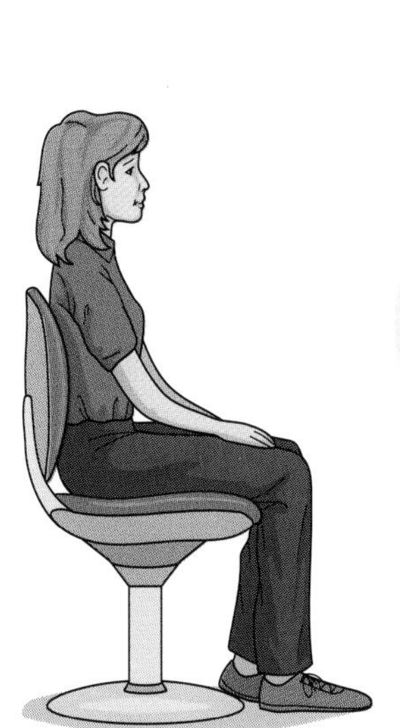

Sit up straight and rest the spine against the back of the chair.

Push heavy objects backward.

If a work surface is not at waist level, put your weight on one leg at a time.

Like strains, herniated disks are usually caused by lifting a heavy object or exercising too vigorously. The treatment for a herniated disk is similar to that for a muscle strain—rest, anti-inflammatory drugs, and physical therapy.

Osteoarthritis Osteoarthritis is a joint disease that occurs to some extent in almost all people over age 60. Symptoms of the disease include pain, swelling, and stiffness in one or more of the joints. Joints in the neck, lower back, and knees are often affected. Osteoarthritis often interferes with walking and other normal activities. The disease cannot be cured, but painkillers and anti-inflammatory drugs provide some relief.

HEALTHY CHOICES

Preventing Back Problems The key to preventing back problems is a sensible exercise routine that includes exercises for strengthening abdominal muscles and improving flexibility. Maintaining correct posture is also important (see illustration: Tips for Avoiding Back Problems). A person whose job involves long periods of sitting in one position should get up once in a while to walk around. Finally, maintain a recommended weight. (See also ARTHRITIS; MUSCULOSKELETAL SYSTEM, **1**; SPINE, **1**.)

BALDNESS

see HAIR LOSS

BIOPSY

A biopsy is a procedure in which a small specimen of cells or tissue is removed and examined in the laboratory. Biopsies are particularly helpful in diagnosing certain types of CANCER, such as breast cancer and skin cancer, and determining if a tumor is *malignant* (growing uncontrollably). A biopsy may be performed before surgery or during surgery to help the surgeon decide how to proceed.

Biopsies are performed in several different ways. In a *needle biopsy,* a long needle is guided to the organ and a sample of cells drawn out through the needle. An *endoscopic biopsy* involves inserting a long, flexible

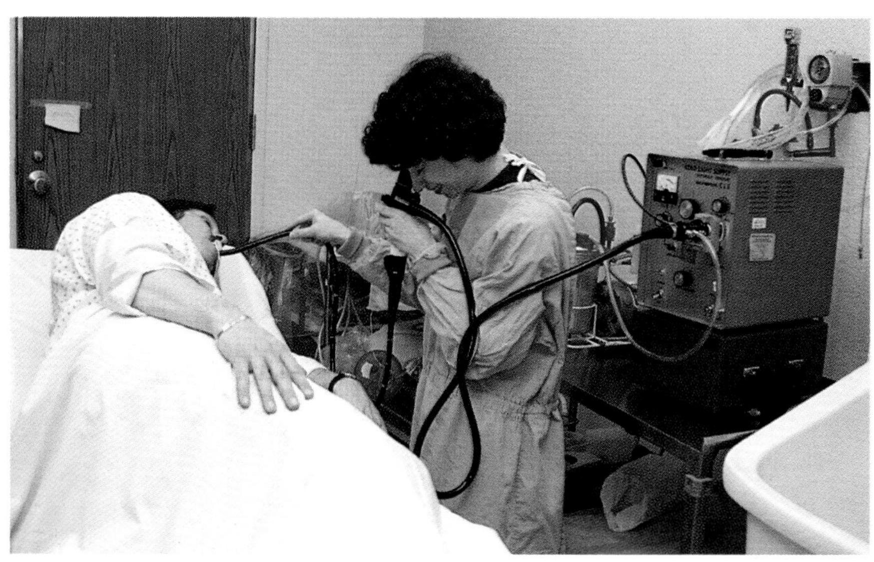

Endoscope. *An endoscope is inserted through a body opening or an incision in the skin to view an area of abnormal tissue. A forceps attachment is passed through the instrument to pinch off a piece of tissue.*

instrument through an opening in the body and into an organ (see illustration: Endoscope). Forceps are passed through the instrument to remove a piece of tissue. *Skin or muscle biopsy* is performed by scraping or cutting away a small piece of tissue for testing.

Blister

A blister is a puffy, raised area of skin containing fluid. Blisters are caused by injury to the skin or as a result of disease. They develop when serum (a colorless part of the blood) leaks from the blood vessels in underlying layers of the skin. The covering of the blister provides valuable protection to the damaged tissue below. Sharp pinching of the skin may result in *blood blisters,* in which blood from broken vessels (rather than serum) collects beneath the skin.

Causes and Treatment Burns, scalds, exposure to certain chemicals, contact with poisonous plants, pinching, and friction from badly fitting shoes can all result in blisters (see illustration: Sunburn Blisters). Blistering is also a symptom of many skin diseases, including ECZEMA, and certain bacterial or viral infections, such as *impetigo, chicken pox,* or *herpes* infections. These blisters contain infectious bacterial or viral particles and, if burst, may spread the infection elsewhere or to another person.

Sunburn Blisters. *Sunburn can result in blisters and severe damage to the skin. A sunscreen will help protect your skin from such damage.*

Because the covering of a blister protects wounded tissues from infection, it should not be opened. If a blister opens accidentally, it should be disinfected with a mild antiseptic and covered with a sterile bandage. If blisters are large or painful, or show signs of infection, a physician should be consulted. (See also CHICKEN POX, **2**; HERPES INFECTIONS, **2**; IMPETIGO, **2**.)

CONSULT A PHYSICIAN

Blood Clot

A blood clot is a mass of congealed blood. Forming a blood clot is the body's natural response to an injury. However, a blood clot can be harmful when it forms within a blood vessel and blocks the flow of blood (see illustration: Blood Clots in the Bloodstream). This condition, called *thrombosis*, can be fatal.

Blood clots form in different locations in the body. A blood clot that blocks an artery leading to the heart can cause a HEART ATTACK. A clot in an artery leading to the brain can cause a STROKE. A clot that blocks an artery supplying the kidneys, intestines, or other organ will result in damage to the tissues and loss of normal function. A blood clot can also form in a vein. If the clot is accompanied by inflammation of the vein, the condition is called thrombophlebitis (sometimes called phlebitis). It affects both deep veins and veins close to the surface, causing pain, tenderness, and swelling.

An *embolus* (pl. *emboli*) is a blood clot that breaks away from the site at which it formed and travels through the bloodstream to create a blockage (called an *embolism*) in another part of the body. Emboli are usually blood clots but can also be made up of fat cells, cancer cells, bacteria, or air bubbles. If an embolus suddenly obstructs an artery leading to the lungs, heart, brain, or kidneys, it is a medical emergency and can be fatal.

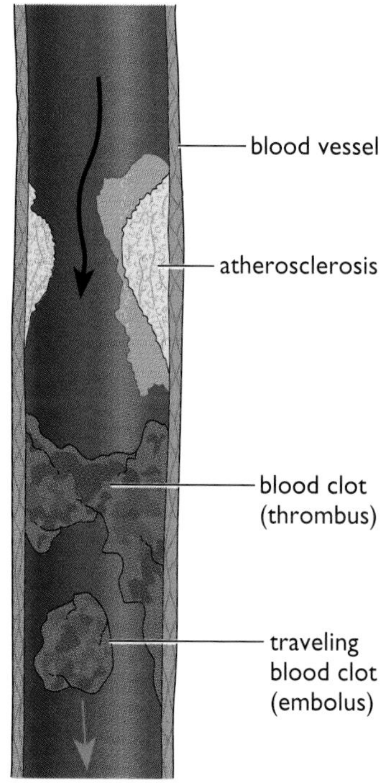

Blood Clots in the Bloodstream. *Two types of blood clots develop within a blood vessel. A thrombus is a clot that forms along a vessel wall, and an embolus is a clot that forms in one part of the body and breaks away, traveling through the bloodstream.*

Causes and Risk Factors Blood clots usually do not form within healthy blood vessels. Certain conditions, including damage to blood vessel walls occurring in ARTERIOSCLEROSIS and ATHEROSCLEROSIS, VARICOSE VEINS, and slow blood circulation, make it more likely that clots will form. Other factors that increase the risk of blood clots are smoking, prolonged bed rest, and long-term use of birth-control pills.

Treatment Treatment may include drugs that break up the blood clot and blood-thinning drugs (anticoagulants) that prevent the formation of new clots. Surgery may also be performed to remove the clot or to create a bypass for the blocked artery.

Prevention Anyone susceptible to blood clots should try to minimize the risk factors that can be controlled, especially those associated with the development of atherosclerosis. (See also ANEURYSM; CARDIOVASCULAR DISEASE; HEART DISEASE; CIRCULATORY SYSTEM, **1**.)

Blood Poisoning

Blood poisoning is the presence of microscopic organisms such as bacteria or, more rarely, fungi in the bloodstream. Bacteria may invade the body through a wound or during a surgical procedure and produce toxins (poisons).

The symptoms of blood poisoning include fever, chills, fatigue, and red stripes radiating from the site of the infection. Blood poisoning is serious. When it goes untreated, it can result in *septic shock,* a potentially fatal condition causing damage to organs and tissues. The usual treatment for blood poisoning is to drain or remove the infection site and inject large doses of antibiotics into the bloodstream. (See also SHOCK.)

Blood Transfusion

A blood transfusion is the process of transferring blood from one person to another. It is often prescribed for people who have lost a lot of blood after an accident or during surgery. People with serious illnesses or blood disorders may also need transfusions.

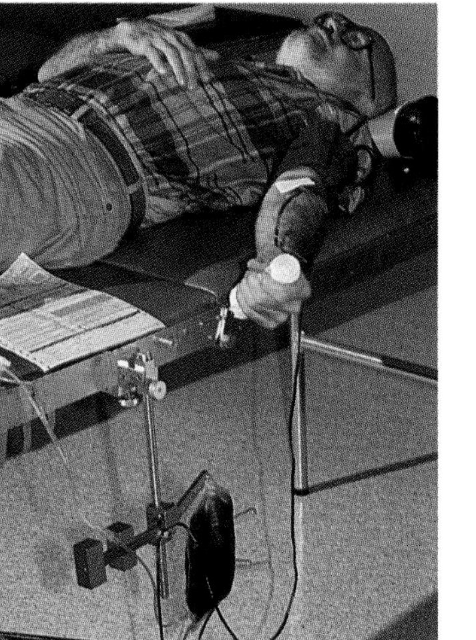

Blood Transfusion. *Blood transfusions would not be possible without people who donate blood. It does not take long to donate blood, and there is no risk of getting a disease while donating.*

How a Transfusion Works Most blood used in transfusions is provided by anonymous donors and stored under refrigeration in a blood bank. Before transfusion, a sample of the recipient's blood is mixed, or cross matched, with a sample of donor blood to be sure that the two are compatible. If they are, the donor blood is transfused into a vein in the recipient's arm. The amount of blood given depends on how much has been lost or on the severity of the person's blood disorder. Throughout the procedure, the patient's pulse rate, blood pressure, and temperature are carefully monitored.

Transfusion Problems Blood that has not been properly cross matched before transfusion may cause reactions such as fever, chills, chest pain, and shortness of breath in the recipient or serious problems such as kidney failure or SHOCK. Improperly screened donor blood can spread diseases, including hepatitis B, syphilis, malaria, and AIDS.

Keeping the Blood Supply Safe To minimize the risk of infection, various tests, including mandatory screening for antibodies to HIV (the AIDS virus), are performed on all donated blood. In recent years, the threat of AIDS has prompted many people to store their own blood ahead of time for use during elective surgery. However, the improved screening techniques in use today have made the risk of spreading AIDS through transfusion extremely small. (See also BLOOD, **1**; BLOOD BANK, **1**; BLOOD TYPE, **1**; AIDS, **2**; HIV, **2**; IMMUNITY, **2**.)

Brain Tumor

A brain TUMOR is an abnormal growth in or around the brain. Although not all brain tumors are *malignant* (cancerous), all are dangerous. As they grow, they press on brain tissue, disturbing normal functions and causing damage to the nervous system. The two major categories of brain tumors are *primary tumors,* those that develop in the brain itself, and *secondary tumors (metastatic tumors),* which originate elsewhere in the body (most often in the lungs or breasts) but spread to the brain.

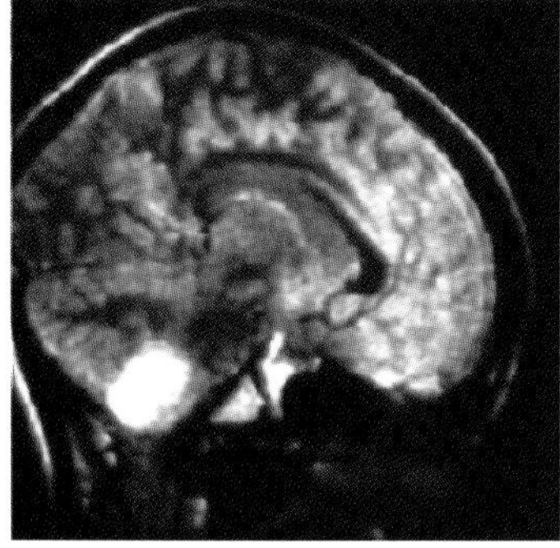

MRI Image of a Brain Tumor. *Magnetic resonance imaging can show brain structures as well as tumors, as seen in the lower part of the image, in great detail.*

Symptoms and Diagnosis The symptoms of a brain tumor are caused by the tumor's compression of brain and surrounding tissues. They include headaches, vomiting, muscle weakness, blurred vision, difficulty with speech or coordination, and changes in personality or behavior. A thorough physical examination combined with one or more special diagnostic techniques, including CAT SCAN (computerized axial tomography) and MAGNETIC RESONANCE IMAGING (MRI), may be needed to determine the location, type, and extent of the tumor.

Treatment Treatment of a brain tumor depends on its type, size, and location. Whenever possible, brain tumors are removed by SURGERY. The location or extent of some tumors, however, makes this impossible. In these cases, the surgeon removes as much of the tumor as possible to relieve pressure on the brain. Surgery is usually followed by RADIATION THERAPY and CHEMOTHERAPY (anticancer drugs) to slow the spread of the disease. (See also CANCER.)

BREAST CANCER

Breast cancer is the most common form of CANCER among women. One out of every nine women will develop breast cancer in her lifetime. The disease is characterized by the appearance of a lump, or TUMOR, in the breast. Breast cancer treatment is generally successful if the condition is caught early; untreated, however, cancer cells can *metastasize* (muh TASS tuh size), or spread, to other parts of the body and cause death.

Symptoms The first noticeable symptom of breast cancer is usually a lump or thickening in the breast. The lump is easier to feel than to see, and it is rarely painful. Other symptoms include a clear or bloody discharge from the nipple, scaliness or retraction (indentation) of the nipple, and a change in the shape of the breast. The skin over the lump may also become red, creased, or dimpled. Usually only one breast is affected.

Unfortunately, however, symptoms often do not appear until the tumor is at an advanced stage, when there are likely to be fewer treatment options and less chance for successful treatment. Early detection of breast cancer is vital.

Diagnosis Although most breast lumps are not cancerous, a woman who discovers a lump should see her physician. The physician will conduct a *clinical breast examination*—carefully examining the breast, the nipple, and the lymph nodes in the armpits—and order a *mammogram*—a special low-dose breast X ray. If the lump is merely a *cyst* (a fluid-filled sac), the fluid can be withdrawn with a thin needle and the lump may disappear completely. If, however, the physician suspects that the lump is a *malignant* (cancerous) tumor, a needle BIOPSY will be performed. During this procedure, a hollow needle is inserted into the lump to withdraw tissue or fluid that can be sent to a laboratory for analysis. If abnormal cells are present, a more extensive surgical biopsy may be required. This is usually done in the hospital under anesthesia and involves removal of all

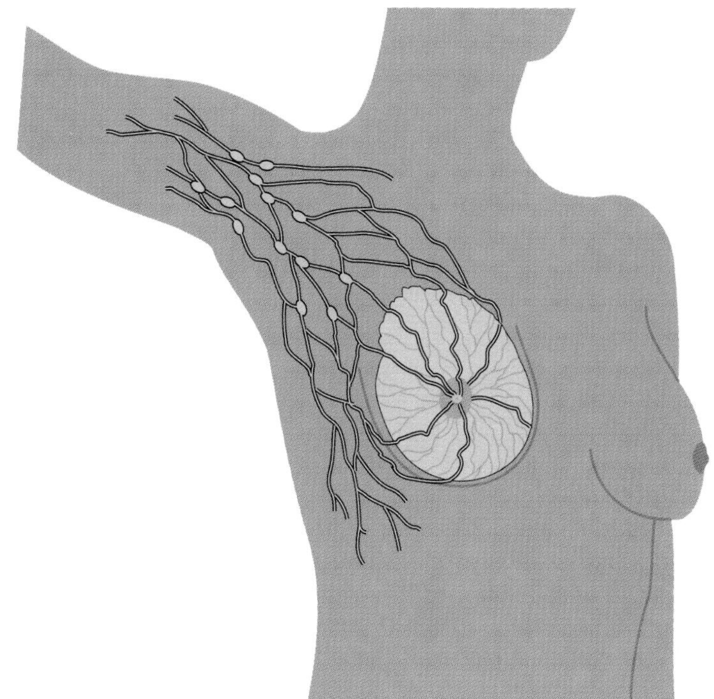

Metastasis of Breast Cancer. *Cancer cells from the breast may metastasize, or spread, through the lymph system. This illustration shows the lymph nodes in the armpit area through which cancer cells may travel to other parts of the body.*

or part of the lump and small amounts of surrounding tissues for laboratory analysis. If cancer cells are found, further tests will be performed to determine if the cancer has metastasized (see illustration: Metastasis of Breast Cancer).

Risk Factors It is not clear what causes breast cancer. However, scientists have identified a number of factors that may increase a woman's risk of developing the disease. These include women whose mothers, grandmothers, aunts, or sisters have had breast cancer, especially at a young age; women who have never had children; women who had their first child after the age of 30; and, possibly, a diet high in animal fats. The risk of getting the disease also increases with age.

Treatment and Prevention The choice of treatment for breast cancer depends on both the extent of the disease and the individual woman's preferences. If the cancer is discovered at an early stage, it can sometimes be treated with RADIATION THERAPY (high-energy doses of radiation from X rays or radioactive substances) alone. In most cases, however, surgery is necessary to remove a malignant tumor.

Until 10 years ago, a *radical mastectomy* (mast ECK tuh mee), the surgical removal of the breast, lymph nodes, and a layer of chest muscles, was considered the only reliable treatment. Today, however, a *simple mastectomy,* removal of the affected breast and lymph node tissue for testing, is more common and seems equally effective. If the cancer is confined to a small area, a *lumpectomy,* removal of the tumor and some lymph nodes, may be sufficient. The trend in recent years has been to follow up breast surgery with radiation therapy or *adjuvant therapy*—CHEMOTHERAPY (treatment with anticancer drugs), hormone therapy, or a combination of the two—to ensure that any remaining cancer cells are killed.

HEALTHY CHOICES

Early detection is the key to curing breast cancer. Physicians recommend that all women over the age of 20 examine their breasts on a monthly basis and undergo routine examinations by a physician. As an additional precaution, women age 40 and over should have a clinical breast examination and mammogram every 1 to 2 years. Women 50 and over should have a mammogram every year. By detecting tumors at an early stage, while they are still too small to be felt, mammograms increase the patient's chance of a complete cure. (See also MAMMOGRAM, 6.)

BURSITIS

Bursitis is the inflammation of a *bursa,* one of the fluid-filled sacs that cushion bones and tendons in many joints (see illustration: Bursas). Bursitis occurs most commonly in the elbow, knee, and shoulder joints. Depending on where it occurs, it is commonly called student's elbow or housemaid's knee. It is not a serious disease, but it can be very painful. Untreated bursitis in the shoulder can lead to a more severe condition called frozen shoulder.

RISK FACTORS

Causes and Treatment Often appearing suddenly, bursitis is characterized by swelling and pain in a joint area. The condition is most frequently associated with repeated physical activity, such as throwing a baseball, or stress or pressure on a joint. Housemaid's knee, for example, can develop from prolonged kneeling on a hard floor. Injury or infection can also cause bursitis, but in many cases the cause of an attack is unknown.

The most common treatment for bursitis is rest. The bursitis will usually clear up on its own after a few days. If the attack is severe, a physician may drain fluid from the bursa with a syringe to reduce the swelling. Ice packs, pressure bandages, anti-inflammatory drugs, and hydrocortisone injections are also used to reduce the swelling and speed healing. Bursitis tends to come back in the same place. Surgical removal of the bursa may be the only effective treatment for chronic or recurring bursitis.

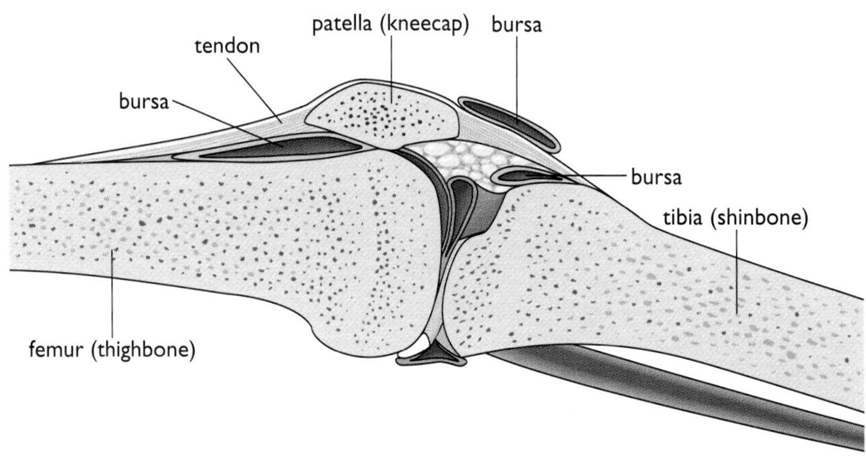

Bursas. *As shown here in the knee, bursas act as cushions between bones and tendons, protecting them from friction.*

CANCER

Cancer is any one of a group of more than 100 diseases characterized by the uncontrolled growth of abnormal cells in the tissues and organs of the body. The most common types are SKIN CANCER, BREAST CANCER, LUNG CANCER, COLORECTAL CANCER, and prostate cancer (see graph: Common Types of Cancer). Only HEART DISEASE causes more deaths among adults in the United States. Nevertheless, advances in care, detection, and treatment have significantly improved the long-term outlook for people with cancer. And every year, the extensive research in progress yields new understanding of the disease.

How Cancer Develops In order for the body to function properly, it must continually replace worn-out or injured cells. This takes place through a well-regulated process of cell division. When cell divisions are imperfect, abnormal cells develop. Many abnormal cells die on their own, but sometimes they survive and grow as cancer cells. (See also CELL, 1.)

Like normal cells, cancer cells reproduce by dividing. Unlike normal cells, cancer cells grow unrestrained. Cancer cells tend to live longer than normal cells and divide more frequently. As they grow in number, they compete with normal cells for space and nourishment, often killing them. The unrestrained cells form a mass of tissue, called a TUMOR, in one of the organs or tissues of the body. Some tumors made up of abnormal cells are *benign*, or noncancerous, and do not spread to other tissues of the body. Others are *malignant*, or cancerous; these tumors invade or destroy surrounding tissue. The rate at which tumors grow varies greatly

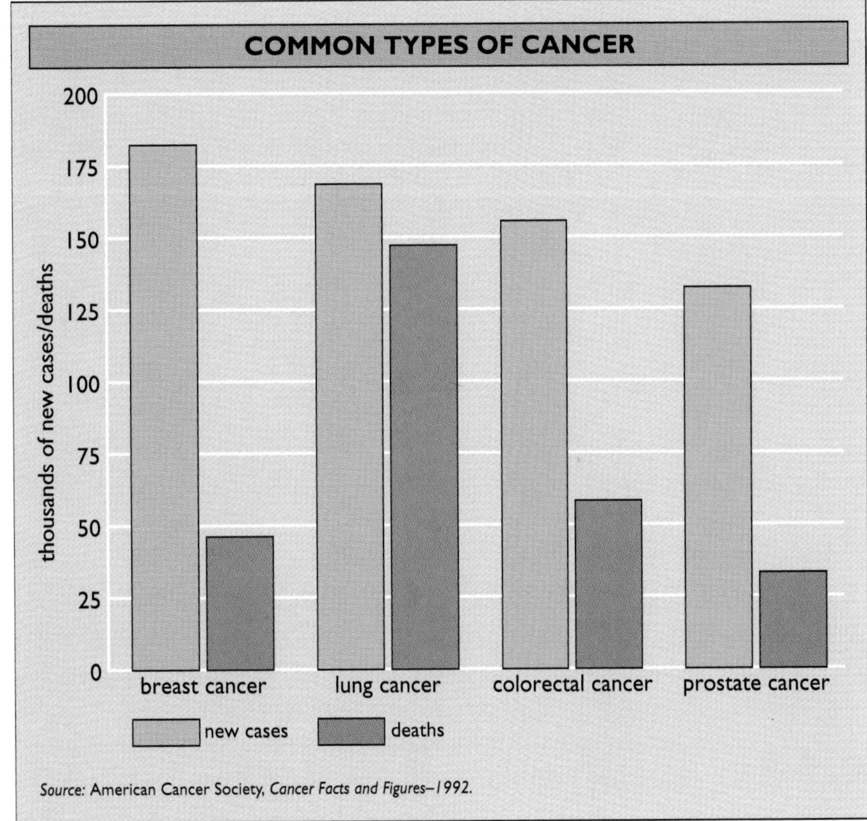

Common Types of Cancer. *These four types of cancer are the most common in the United States. (Skin cancer is not usually included in cancer statistics because of its high cure rate.) Although breast cancer had the highest number of new cases in 1992, deaths from lung cancer greatly outnumbered deaths from breast cancer.*

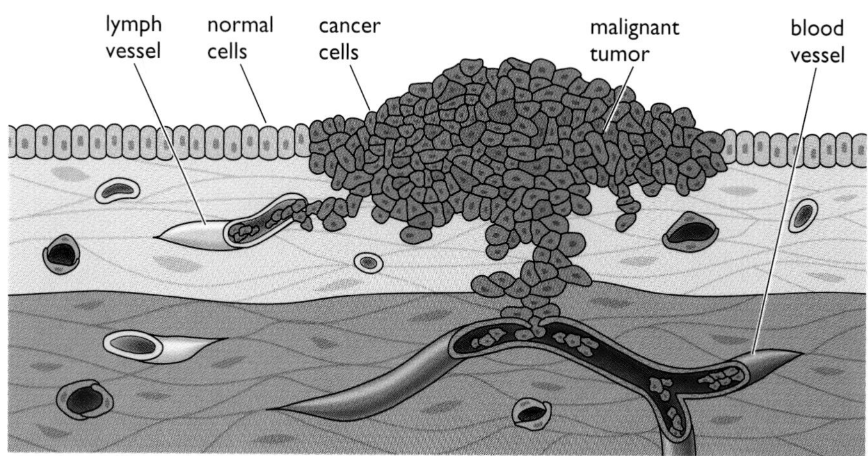

Metastasis of a Malignant Tumor. *Cancer cells can break away from a malignant tumor and get into the lymphatic system or bloodstream, which can carry the cells to other parts of the body. This process is called metastasis.*

from one form of cancer to another. Cancers may also develop in the bones, in the tissues of the bone marrow where blood cells are formed, and in the lymphatic system.

Cancer spreads when some cancer cells are shed from the malignant tumor and travel to other parts of the body through the *lymphatic system* or bloodstream. Such cells may invade other organs or tissues and form new tumors. This process is called *metastasis* (muh TASS tuh suss) (see illustration: Metastasis of a Malignant Tumor). Once cancer has metastasized, treatment is much more difficult, and the outlook is less favorable.

Cancers are often classified by the type of tissue in which the cancer begins. *Carcinoma,* the most common form, is cancer of the tissue that forms the skin and the lining of internal organs. Breast, lung, and skin cancer are examples of carcinoma. *Sarcoma* is cancer that develops in connective tissue (such as cartilage), muscle, or bone. Examples include bone cancer and KAPOSI'S SARCOMA. LEUKEMIA is cancer of blood-forming tissue; LYMPHOMAS begin in the lymphatic system.

Symptoms and Diagnosis The symptoms of cancer vary according to the type, location, and extent of the disease. In its earliest stages, it may produce no symptoms at all. The American Cancer Society has, however, identified seven major *warning signs,* any one of which may indicate the presence of cancer.

1. An unusual bleeding or discharge
2. A lump or thickening in the breast or elsewhere
3. A sore that does not heal
4. A change in bowel or bladder habits
5. Persistent hoarseness or a continuing cough
6. Indigestion or difficulty in swallowing
7. An obvious change in the appearance of a wart or mole

Other possible signs include rapid weight loss, persistent headaches accompanied by visual or behavior changes, continuing abdominal pain, prolonged tiredness, and excessive or unexplained bruising. These symptoms are not definite indications of cancer, but anyone experiencing one or more of them for more than a few days should consult a physician.

CONSULT A PHYSICIAN

Cancer may be diagnosed in several ways. Some forms of cancer appear as a lump that a patient or physician discovers. X rays and chemical tests may also be used to diagnose cancer. Sometimes a physician performs a BIOPSY, which involves taking a small piece of tissue from a tumor and examining it under a microscope. In this way the presence of cancer cells can be detected.

RISK FACTORS ▶▶▶▶▶▶

The Causes of Cancer Scientists believe that people develop cancer through repeated or prolonged contact with one or more cancer-causing agents, called CARCINOGENS. Suspected carcinogens include a number of natural and manufactured substances found in the environment. The tar in tobacco smoke, certain industrial chemicals, and ultraviolet radiation from the sun are all suspected carcinogens. By damaging body cells, carcinogens increase the possibility of abnormal (or cancerous) cell growth. However, many years may pass after exposure to a carcinogen before any evidence of the disease develops. Scientists also believe that heredity—a history of cancer in families—and certain kinds of bacterial and viral infections put some individuals at greater risk of developing cancer.

RISK FACTORS ▶▶▶▶▶▶

Methods of Treatment There are three main methods of treating cancer: surgery, radiation therapy, and chemotherapy. The choice of therapy depends on the type of cancer; the stage to which the disease has developed; and the person's age, sex, and general health.

SURGERY may be performed to remove a tumor or tumors and to repair the affected organ. It may also be used to determine whether a tumor is malignant or to find out if malignant cells have spread to other parts of the body. Surgery is widely used to treat cancers of the breast and intestines. Some BRAIN TUMORS can also be removed surgically. Sometimes a surgeon must remove healthy tissue along with a tumor to help prevent the further spread of the disease. Surgery is most successful if performed at an early stage, when cancer is confined to a limited area.

Some forms of cancer are treated with RADIATION THERAPY. In radiation therapy, the diseased part of the body is exposed to high-energy radiation from X rays or radioactive substances. Like surgery, radiation therapy is effective against certain localized cancers but does not affect cancer cells that have spread outside the area of radiation. Because it kills normal cells as well as cancerous ones, radiation therapy must be used with caution.

A third method of treating cancer is CHEMOTHERAPY, the use of one or more anticancer drugs to destroy malignant cells. Unlike surgery or radiation, anticancer drugs travel throughout the bloodstream to attack cancer cells wherever they are. Chemotherapy is the first line of treatment in leukemia and lymphoma, but it is used against other forms of cancer as well. Like radiation, however, chemotherapy also kills normal cells, and can produce unpleasant side effects such as nausea and hair loss.

One of the latest developments in treating cancer is the use of hormones. Artificial hormones such as tamoxifen citrate have been effective in *adjuvant therapy,* the use of drugs to kill cancer cells that might remain after surgery. IMMUNOTHERAPY involves the use of hormones and other biological agents to stimulate the body's immune system to attack malignant cells. These treatments are still in the experimental stage, but scientists believe that further research may eventually lead to better cancer-fighting techniques.

Today, almost half of all cancers can be cured completely through surgery, radiation therapy, or chemotherapy. In recent years, combinations of treatments have been particularly effective. These provide a higher rate of cure and minimize the unpleasant side effects of a single therapy. New surgical techniques, improved methods of administering radiation, and new, safer cancer-fighting drugs have all helped reduce side effects and improve the outlook for cancer patients.

Preventing Cancer A key factor in controlling cancer is the early detection of precancerous conditions through regular self-examinations and routine clinical screening tests (such as the Pap test for women, which is used to detect cervical cancer). Because most cancers in the United States are believed to be linked to *risk factors* that are part of a person's lifestyle or environment, everyone can take certain steps to reduce the risk of developing the disease. The single most important means of preventing cancer is to stop smoking, or avoid starting. About 30 percent of all cancer deaths are caused by cigarette smoking. Limiting exposure to the sun, particularly if you are fair-skinned, is important. Unnecessary X rays should also be avoided. What you eat is important, too. Studies indicate that eating fatty foods increases the likelihood of developing colon, breast, and prostate cancer. On the other hand, foods that are rich in vitamins A and C (such as broccoli, spinach, carrots, peaches, and citrus fruits) or high in fiber (fruits, vegetables, and whole-grain breads and cereals) may lower the risk of developing certain cancers. Intake of alcoholic drinks and salt-cured, smoked, or nitrate-cured foods should be limited. (See also HODGKIN'S DISEASE; LYMPHATIC SYSTEM, **1**; CANCERS OF THE SEX ORGANS, **6**; PHYSICIANS (M.D.'S)—ONCOLOGIST, **9**.)

RISK FACTORS

HEALTHY CHOICES

CANKER SORE

A canker sore is a small, painful *ulcer* that occurs in the mouth or on the lips. Canker sores tend to recur: Some people may have one or two a year, while others have continuously recurring ulcers.

A tingling or burning sensation in the mouth or on the lips may signal the onset of a canker sore. Then an ulcerous sore with a gray center and red, inflamed border appears and lasts for 1 to 2 weeks.

Causes The cause of canker sores is unclear. They may be caused by a virus that normally resides in the body, or they may occur in reaction to bacteria. Minor injuries, such as biting the inside of the mouth, also may cause a sore to appear.

Treatment Although canker sores usually heal without help, a physician may prescribe ointments and mouth rinses to help reduce pain and speed healing. For severe attacks, corticosteroids, antibiotics, or antihistamines may be prescribed. To reduce discomfort, it's a good idea to avoid spicy or acidic foods until the canker sore has healed. (See also COLD SORE, **2**; HERPES INFECTIONS, **2**.)

CARCINOGENS

Carcinogens (car SIN uh junz) are substances known to cause CANCER. Some are natural substances found in the environment; others are substances manufactured by human beings. Certain viruses have also been identified as causing cancer.

Environmental and Chemical Carcinogens Excessive exposure to X rays, radioactive materials, or ultraviolet radiation from sunlight may cause abnormal changes in body cells that lead to cancer. Exposure to asbestos fibers—used in some insulation—has also been linked to cancer, especially cancer of the lungs.

The largest group of carcinogens are the type of chemicals found in tobacco smoke, tar, and soot. Certain workplace chemicals, such as vinyl chloride (in plastics) and benzene (in rubber), and the naturally occurring gas radon may also be carcinogens. Prolonged exposure to fumes or physical contact with these chemicals over a long period of time has been known to cause cancers in some individuals. Alcohol and food additives such as nitrites (used in ham and bacon) are also thought by some researchers to be carcinogenic.

Biological Carcinogens Only a few viruses or other biological agents have been definitely linked to cancer in humans. Researchers have identified two such factors that can play a role in liver cancer—a fungus that contaminates stored grain and the hepatitis B virus. In addition, HIV (the human immunodeficiency virus that causes AIDS) destroys the immune system, allowing many diseases, including a cancer called KAPOSI'S SARCOMA, to develop.

Reducing Exposure to Carcinogens The federal government, labor unions, and certain industries have instituted programs to test for carcinogens in the workplace or in products that the public buys or comes in contact with. In industry, any substance that is identified as a carcinogen may be used only if its use is essential, exposure to it is strictly controlled, and workers exposed to the substance are monitored medically.

Asbestos Removal. *Workers who remove asbestos insulation from old buildings must protect themselves carefully, since breathing in asbestos fibers is associated with certain kinds of lung cancer.*

CARDIOVASCULAR DISEASE

Cardiovascular disease is a broad term covering many disorders of the blood vessels—the arteries and veins—and the heart. In the United States, nearly 1 million deaths are attributed to cardiovascular disease every year. Although this number is significant, it is important to keep in mind that more than 69 million Americans have some form of cardiovascular disease yet are able to lead active lives. The major types of cardiovascular disease are discussed below.

Diseases of the Arteries The two major types of cardiovascular disease that affect the arteries are ARTERIOSCLEROSIS, hardening or thickening of artery walls, and ATHEROSCLEROSIS, narrowing of arteries because of fatty deposits called *plaque*. HYPERTENSION (high blood pressure) can damage artery walls and accelerate the development of arteriosclerosis. Arteries that are narrowed by disease are more likely than are normal arteries to become blocked by BLOOD CLOTS or other material. If an artery leading to the heart becomes blocked, the result is a HEART ATTACK. If a blockage forms in an artery leading to the brain, a STROKE occurs. Other artery disorders include ANEURYSM, the weakening and swelling of an artery wall, and arteritis, the inflammation of artery walls.

Diseases of the Veins VARICOSE VEINS, the most common vein disorder, is a swelling and twisting of the veins. It usually affects the legs but can occur in the veins in the lower part of the esophagus and the anus (HEMORRHOIDS). Inflammation of a vein is called *phlebitis*. When there is also a tendency to form blood clots in the inflamed vein, it is called thrombophlebitis.

Diseases of the Heart HEART DISEASE includes a wide variety of disorders. Among these are coronary artery disease, which occurs when the heart muscle does not receive an adequate supply of blood. This condition can lead to heart attack. Hypertensive heart disease results from the long-term effects of hypertension. Diseases of the heart valves can result in a number of problems, including reduced blood flow, enlargement of a heart chamber, and congestive heart failure. In congestive heart failure, the heart's pumping ability becomes increasingly inefficient, and the heart cannot maintain adequate circulation of the blood. A HEART MURMUR is an unusual noise in the heart that may indicate an abnormal flow of blood through the heart's chambers and valves. (See also HEART SURGERY; CIRCULATORY SYSTEM, 1; HEART, 1; ENDOCARDITIS, 2; RHEUMATIC FEVER, 2.)

CARPAL TUNNEL SYNDROME

Carpal tunnel syndrome is a condition that causes pain in the wrist and numbness and tingling in the thumb, index finger, and two middle fingers. One or both wrists may be affected, and symptoms may be worse at night. The syndrome occurs when ligaments in the wrist become swollen and compress the median nerve where it passes into the hand through the carpal tunnel (see illustration: The Hand). The *median nerve* provides sensation to the affected fingers.

Carpal tunnel syndrome is related to jobs and activities that require excessive, repetitive use of the wrist, such as typing, carpentry, and golfing. It usually develops in middle age and affects women more often than men.

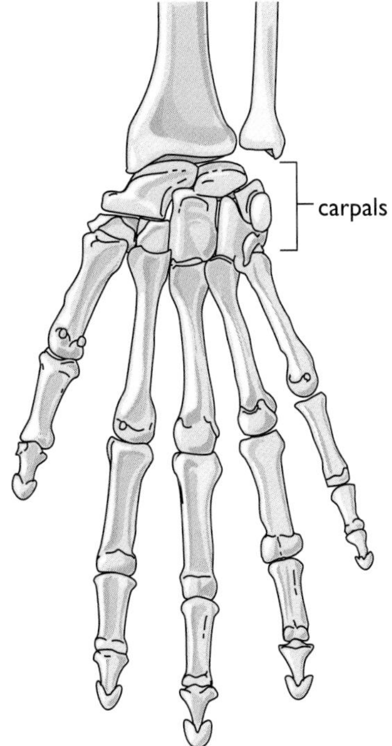

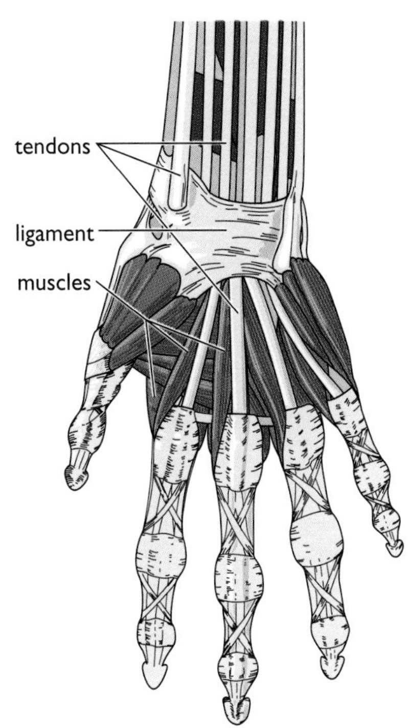

The Hand. *The carpal tunnel is a narrow opening between the carpal bones and the wrist ligament on the palm side of the wrist. Nerves, including the median nerve, and tendons responsible for helping to bend the wrist pass through this tunnel.*

Treatment involves resting the wrist, taking anti-inflammatory drugs, or using a splint. Physical therapy may also be helpful. In severe cases, corticosteroid drugs may be injected into the ligament or minor surgery may be performed to reduce pressure on the nerve. (See also HAND, **1**.)

Cataracts

Cataracts. *Cataracts may be located anywhere on the lens, but most develop in the center or around the edges of the lens. Much less light is able to enter an eye with a cataract than enters a healthy eye.*

A cataract is clouding of the lens of the eye. The lens is normally transparent; clouding blocks the light needed for sight, causing a gradual loss of vision (see illustration: Cataracts). Almost 25 million people in the United States experience vision loss because of cataracts. However, cataracts are easily treatable with surgery, and more than a million cataract operations are performed in this country each year.

Symptoms Cataracts are painless, and their first symptoms may be slightly blurred vision, less acute vision in very dim or bright light, or halos around lights at night. The progress of symptoms is so gradual that patients may not discover that they have cataracts until they have a regular EYE TEST. Usually cataracts develop in both eyes, but one eye is nearly always more seriously affected than the other.

Causes The development of cataracts is a normal process of aging, and most people over 60 have some degree of cataract formation. Age is the cause of approximately 75 percent of all cataracts. Diseases and other factors also contribute to cataract development. These include eye injury, DIABETES, the taking of corticosteroid drugs over a period of years, and exposure of the eyes to large amounts of radiation from X rays, microwaves, or sunlight. In addition, congenital (present at birth) cataracts can develop in babies whose mothers have had *rubella* during pregnancy.

In all cases, the whitish, clouded appearance of the lens is caused by changes in protein fibers within the lens.

Treatment Cataracts may be treated in the early stages with eyedrops that widen the pupil. The most effective treatment, however, is surgical removal of the clouded lens and replacement with an artificial plastic lens. This type of surgery results in improved vision for 95 percent of cataract patients. Lens implants are not suitable for people with other eye diseases or for young people. For these patients, special contact lenses or eyeglasses are used.

Today's surgical techniques make the cataract operation painless and relatively simple. The procedure takes about an hour and is usually performed on an outpatient basis under local anesthetic. Patients can return to their normal activities soon after leaving the hospital. (See also EYE DISORDERS; EYE, **1**.)

CAT Scan

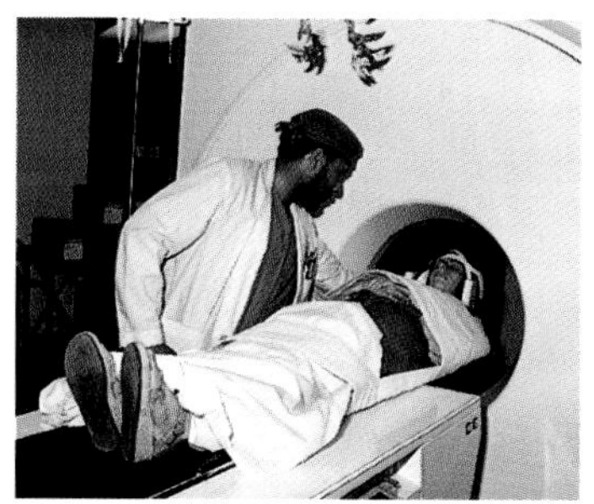

CAT Scan. *During a CAT scan, the cylindrical scanner rotates around the person, passing X-ray beams through the body at different angles.*

A CAT (computerized axial tomography) scan is a diagnostic tool that combines *X rays* and computers to produce clear images of cross sections of body tissues. In use since 1972, the CAT scan (also called CT scan) exposes people to less radiation than conventional X rays and is 100 times more accurate. CAT scans are very useful for detecting injuries, TUMORS, hemorrhages, and other disorders in the soft tissues of the body.

A person having a CAT scan must lie still on a table inside a large metal cylinder (see illustration: CAT Scan). The cylinder passes X rays through the person's body from thousands of different angles. The resulting information is then sent to a computer that produces a cross-sectional view of the part of the body that is under study. These two-dimensional "slices" can be combined and rotated to produce a three-dimensional image. A CAT scan is a painless procedure that is completed in about 20 minutes. (See also MAGNETIC RESONANCE IMAGING; X-RAY EXAMINATION.)

Cerebral Palsy

Cerebral palsy is a group of physical disorders caused by brain damage that occurs before, during, or shortly after birth or in early childhood. Symptoms can range from slightly awkward or jerky movements to various degrees of paralysis. Mental retardation occurs in about 75 percent of cerebral palsy cases. The disease is permanent and nonprogressive—that is, it cannot be cured, but it will not get any worse.

Causes Most cerebral palsy cases develop before or at birth. A variety of causes have been identified. Among these are an infection, such as rubella, in the mother during pregnancy and malnutrition in the mother. Cerebral palsy can also be caused by a difficult birth during which the fetus is deprived of blood or oxygen. After birth, a head injury or infection, such as meningitis or encephalitis, can result in cerebral palsy. It affects as many as 6 out of every 1,000 children.

Symptoms Cerebral palsy is usually diagnosed when the child is between 1 and 2 years old, and it is classified according to the symptoms. The three main categories are spastic, dyskinetic, and ataxic. *Spastic cerebral palsy* is characterized by stiff, contracted muscles in the arms and legs and some degree of paralysis. In some cases, the legs may be more severely paralyzed than the arms, or the limbs on only one side of the body may be affected, or all four limbs may be affected. *Dyskinetic cerebral palsy* is characterized by clumsy, jerky movements and by involuntary writhing and twitching. *Ataxic cerebral palsy* usually involves jerky movements of the head and neck, trembling, and lack of coordination and control over voluntary movements.

Treatment Because there is no cure for cerebral palsy, the primary goal of all treatment is to help the person with cerebral palsy achieve the best quality of life possible. Physical therapy can help train muscles and loosen stiff limbs, while medications can relax and control sudden and violent muscle contractions. Speech therapy can help improve speech problems or teach alternative ways to communicate. Children with mild cases of cerebral palsy are generally encouraged to attend a regular school. Those with more severe symptoms may require special schooling.

CHEMOTHERAPY

Chemotherapy (kee moh THEHR uh pee) is the use of medications to treat disease. It is usually used to treat CANCER. The term *chemotherapy* comes from two words that mean "chemical" and "treatment." Cancer chemotherapy involves the use of one or more anticancer drugs as part of a treatment plan that may also include SURGERY or RADIATION THERAPY.

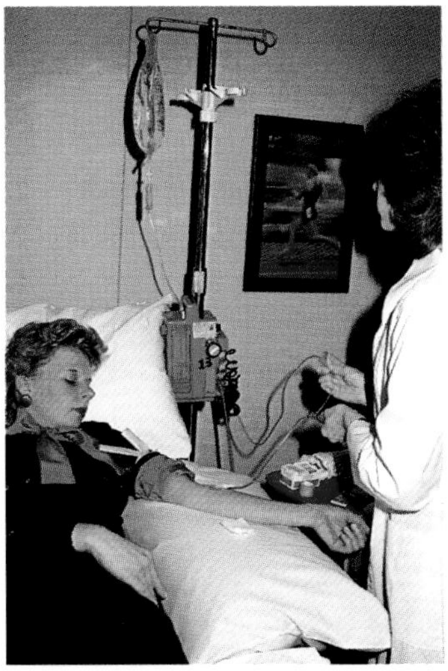

Chemotherapy. *Chemotherapy treatments are usually given by injection or through an intravenous drip.*

How It Works As cancer cells multiply rapidly, they sometimes break loose from a TUMOR (a mass of abnormal tissue) and spread throughout the body. This makes it difficult to treat them with surgery or radiation therapy. The drugs used in chemotherapy, however, spread throughout the body to affect as many cancer cells as possible. Anticancer drugs are chosen specifically because of their ability to halt or slow the rapid reproduction of cancer cells.

Side Effects Unfortunately, chemotherapy affects not only rapidly multiplying cancer cells but also normal cells. This results in unpleasant side effects that frequently include nausea, vomiting, fatigue, and hair loss. Not everyone receiving chemotherapy experiences these side effects, however, and the side effects can be reduced significantly through adjustment of the schedule of treatments, modification of the diet, and medication. Once the treatments have been stopped, the side effects usually disappear and healthy cells have a chance to grow normally.

Chronic Fatigue Syndrome

Chronic fatigue syndrome (CFS) is characterized by flulike symptoms that include fatigue, weakness, muscle and joint pain, and swollen lymph glands. In addition to physical symptoms, patients may also experience problems of concentration, sleep disturbances, memory loss, and depression. Symptoms last six months or more and may be mild or severe. Some patients are bedridden, while others are able to continue working.

RISK FACTORS

Although it affects people of all ages, CFS seems to strike young adults with active lifestyles most frequently. The number of people suffering from chronic fatigue syndrome is still unknown because there is no laboratory test to diagnose it. In 1990, the national Centers for Disease Control initiated a research program to study the prevalence of CFS.

The nature and cause of chronic fatigue syndrome are also under investigation. In the past, it was believed that emotional and psychological factors caused the syndrome. However, recent research indicates that CFS may be a disorder of the *immune system,* which makes it difficult for the body to fight common viral infections. Researchers have suggested a number of causes, including long-term stress and exposure to the *Epstein-Barr virus* (the virus that causes infectious *mononucleosis*) or to an animal virus transmitted through meat or milk. A recent study has found that people with chronic fatigue syndrome may have lower-than-normal amounts of certain hormones in their brains and endocrine glands. (See also IMMUNE SYSTEM, **1**; MONONUCLEOSIS, **2**.)

Cirrhosis

Cirrhosis (suh ROH suss) is a progressive, irreversible disease of the liver in which healthy liver cells are replaced by scar tissue. As the disease progresses, large areas of scars surround healthy liver cells, cutting off the blood supply and reducing the liver's ability to remove toxins (harmful substances) from the bloodstream (see illustration: Cirrhosis of the Liver). If the progression is not stopped, the liver will eventually fail, causing death.

Causes In the United States and other developed countries, the most common cause of cirrhosis is alcohol abuse. Some forms of hepatitis and two hereditary diseases, hemochromatosis (excessive iron retention) and Wilson's disease (excessive copper retention), can also result in cirrhosis.

Symptoms and Effects Symptoms are seldom apparent in the early stages of cirrhosis. Symptoms of later stages may include enlargement of the liver and spleen, JAUNDICE (a yellowing of the skin and eyes), pain and swelling in the abdomen, vomiting of blood, and mental confusion. Physicians diagnose cirrhosis through a blood test and an examination of a sample of liver cells in a liver BIOPSY.

Several serious complications may also develop in cases of cirrhosis, because the liver is no longer efficient in cleansing the blood of toxins. These include *portal hypertension,* high blood pressure in the veins leading to the liver. Portal hypertension can damage veins in the esophagus,

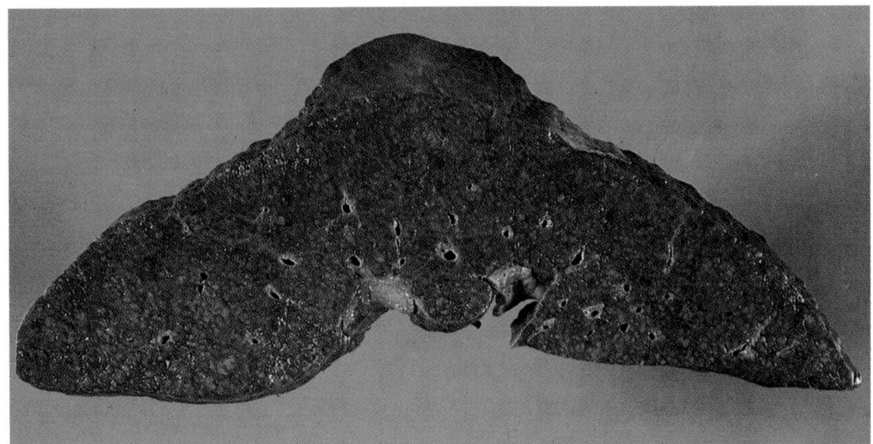

Cirrhosis of the Liver. *Cirrhosis results in extensive scar tissue surrounding areas of healthy cells. The liver's ability to filter blood is restricted by the scar tissue.*

and if the veins rupture, internal bleeding and vomiting of blood will result. In addition, fluid retained in the abdomen can cause PERITONITIS.

Treatment There is no cure for cirrhosis, but its progression can be slowed or halted by treating the underlying cause. In alcoholics, abstinence from alcohol can halt the disease and prolong the patient's life. Many of the complications can also be treated. Ultimately, however, the patient may need a liver transplant. (See also LIVER, **1**; HEPATITIS, **2**; ALCOHOLISM, **7**.)

Colitis

Colitis is an inflammation of the colon (large intestine), which usually causes diarrhea and other symptoms. Two serious, chronic types of colitis, ulcerative colitis and Crohn's disease, are also known as inflammatory bowel disease. *Ulcerative colitis* is marked by ulcers in the lining of the rectum and colon. *Crohn's disease* (also called ileitis) involves chronic inflammation of the intestines, usually in the colon and lower part of the small intestines. Both diseases can produce many complications, including pain, bleeding, infection, and undernourishment.

Symptoms and Diagnosis The symptoms of colitis include persistent diarrhea that may contain blood or mucus, abdominal pain, fever, fatigue, and weight loss. To diagnose the condition, a physician may perform a *sigmoidoscopy* (examination of the rectum and colon with a special viewing tube), or administer a *barium enema* (used with an X ray), or take a BIOPSY of tissue from the affected area.

RISK FACTORS ▶ ▶ ▶ ▶ ▶ ▶

Causes and Treatment The causes of ulcerative colitis and Crohn's disease are not known, but it is believed that heredity and stress play a role. Both diseases usually appear first in young adults. The symptoms may recede after the first few attacks, or they may periodically recur or become progressively worse.

Both types of inflammatory bowel disease are treated with anti-inflammatory drugs and aspirin derivatives. A physician may recommend a special diet with vitamin supplements. When severe symptoms of the disease persist, surgery may be required to remove damaged sections of the intestine.

Colorectal Cancer

Colorectal cancer is a malignant TUMOR in the large intestine (the colon) or rectum. It is one of the most common types of CANCER in the United States, affecting mostly people between the ages of 50 and 75. If untreated, colorectal cancer may lead to an intestinal blockage or may spread to other organs, causing death.

Symptoms and Diagnosis The earliest sign of colorectal cancer is an unexplainable change in the type or frequency of bowel movements. Other symptoms are blood in the feces, rectal bleeding, and pain in the lower abdomen. Often, however, no symptoms occur until the tumor obstructs the bowel. Chemical tests can detect blood in the feces. Other diagnostic tests include *barium X rays* and a *proctosigmoidoscopy* (PRAHK toh SIG moi DAHS kuh pee), an examination of the rectum and lower colon with a flexible lighted tube.

Causes, Treatment, and Prevention A number of factors seem to increase the risk of developing colorectal cancer. One factor is a diet high in fat and low in fiber. Other factors are heredity and a history of certain colon disorders, such as COLITIS and polyps (growths) in the colon.

RISK FACTORS

Treatment of colorectal cancer usually involves a partial *colectomy,* or surgical removal of the diseased portion of the intestine and surrounding tissue. In some cases a *colostomy*—an artificial opening in the abdomen for the elimination of feces—may be necessary. RADIATION THERAPY or CHEMOTHERAPY may be used instead of or in combination with surgery. New studies suggest that aspirin and other anti-inflammatory drugs may also be helpful in fighting colon cancer.

HEALTHY CHOICES

The American Cancer Society recommends that everyone over the age of 50—especially those with a family history of colorectal disorders—undergo annual screening tests. Early detection provides the best chance for successful treatment. (See also FATS, **4**; FIBER, **4**.)

Coma

A coma is a deep unconscious state. Someone in a coma will generally not respond to external stimulation, such as pinching or shouting, or to internal stimulation such as hunger. Depending on the cause of the coma, it may last for hours, days, weeks, or even years.

Symptoms Coma symptoms vary depending on the depth of unconsciousness. *Automatic responses,* including breathing, coughing, yawning, and eye movement, usually continue even in the deepest coma, indicating that the lower brain stem is functioning. However, a person in a deep coma will not respond to repeated stimuli, such as light slapping or a pinprick. A person in a less severe coma may react to vigorous stimuli with body movement or by mumbling.

Causes and Treatment A coma results from damage or disturbance to areas of the brain that play a role in maintaining consciousness. Any condition that restricts blood flow to the brain may result in coma. Possible causes include head injury, BRAIN TUMOR, STROKE, and diseases such as *meningitis, encephalitis,* or EPILEPSY. A coma may also occur when brain

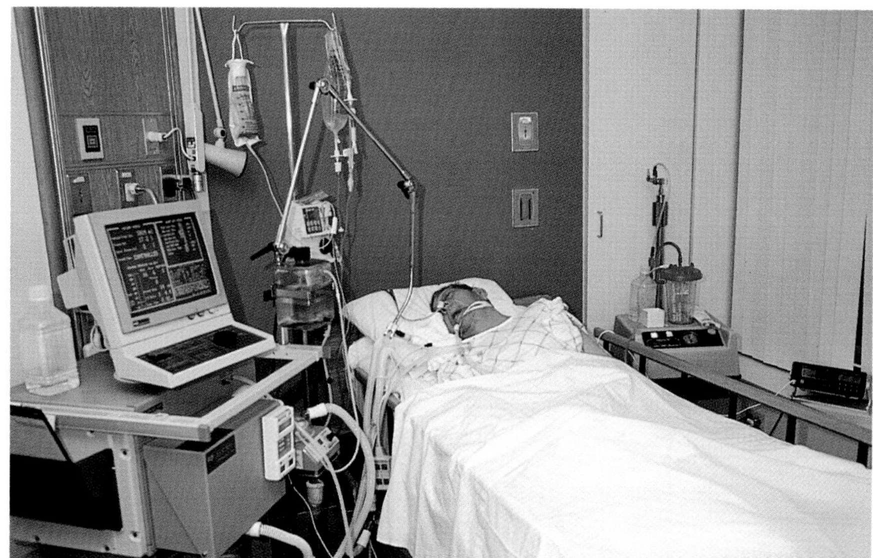

Comatose Patient. *Life-support systems such as a respirator and intravenous feeding tubes are necessary to keep patients in deep comas alive.*

tissues are overwhelmed by toxic substances—for example, drugs or alcohol or poisons released as a result of advanced liver or kidney disease.

CONSULT A PHYSICIAN

When a person is unconscious, it is essential to keep air passages clear and get immediate medical attention. Do not attempt to get the person to drink anything. Treatment of a coma will depend on its cause and severity. If the damage extends to the lower brain stem, life-support systems are necessary to help the patient with breathing and blood circulation. (See also BRAIN, 1; MEDICAL ETHICS, 9.)

CONSTIPATION

Constipation is difficulty in passing feces (semisolid body wastes) or the infrequent passing of feces. It is characterized by dry, hard feces, sometimes accompanied by abdominal bloating and discomfort. Many people believe that not having a bowel movement every day indicates constipation, but this is incorrect. The "normal" frequency of bowel movements varies by individual from three times daily to three times weekly. Constipation is experienced more frequently by older people and those with sedentary lifestyles.

RISK FACTORS

Although constipation itself is not an illness, it is sometimes a sign of a more serious disorder, such as COLORECTAL CANCER. A physical checkup is recommended, especially when the condition persists or reflects a sudden change in bowel habits.

Causes Constipation is most often caused by lack of *fiber* in the diet or regularly ignoring the urge to defecate. Additional causes include a major change in diet, certain drugs, and the effects of hormones produced during pregnancy.

Treatment and Prevention The cause of constipation must first be identified and resolved. The use of *laxatives* to treat constipation should be limited. Regular laxative use may create other problems and actually worsen constipation.

Foods Rich in Fiber. *These include fresh fruits and vegetables, whole-grain breads and cereals, bran, and dried beans and peas. High-fiber foods can help prevent constipation.*

HEALTHY CHOICES

The following steps can help prevent constipation: Eat plenty of high-fiber foods, drink plenty of water, exercise regularly, and try to establish regular eating habits and times for bowel movements. (See also FIBER, 4; LAXATIVES, 7.)

CYSTIC FIBROSIS

Cystic fibrosis is an inherited disease affecting the lungs and pancreas that makes it difficult to breathe or to digest food. Until recently, most babies with cystic fibrosis died before adulthood, but today more effective treatment enables many with the disease to live into their twenties and thirties. Cystic fibrosis affects about 1 in every 2,000 white children; it is very rare among blacks and Asians.

RISK FACTORS

Cystic fibrosis is caused by a defective gene, which is *recessive.* This means that both the mother and father must carry the gene for the disease to be inherited by the child. If both parents carry the gene, their children have a 50 percent chance of becoming carriers, a 25 percent chance of having cystic fibrosis, and a 25 percent chance of being free of the disease. Genetic tests are used to check for cystic fibrosis when there is a family history of the disease.

Symptoms and Diagnosis In a person with cystic fibrosis, the lungs produce a thick, sticky mucus that clogs breathing passages and encourages the growth of disease-causing microorganisms. Common symptoms include recurrent respiratory infections, chronic cough, breathlessness, and wheezing. Malnutrition, chronic diarrhea, and pale, foul-smelling bowel movements are also common. These occur because the pancreas fails to produce certain enzymes that break down fat and nutrients. In addition, the sweat glands of people with cystic fibrosis produce extremely salty sweat that can lead to heat exhaustion in hot weather. Cystic fibrosis is usually diagnosed shortly after birth. Infants may develop an intestinal blockage or fail to gain weight. In older children, the disease is diagnosed by a test to determine if the sweat is excessively salty.

Treatment There is no cure for cystic fibrosis, so treatment is directed at the symptoms. Antibiotics will help prevent the buildup of bacteria in the lungs, and special exercises will help loosen and drain the mucus. Replacement enzymes taken with each meal will promote fat digestion. Salt supplements will replace the excess sodium lost in sweat. In severe cases, the patient may benefit from a lung or heart-lung transplant. (See also LUNG, **1**; PANCREAS, **1**; GENETIC SCREENING, **6**; GENETIC COUNSELOR, **9**.)

DANDRUFF

Dandruff is a common condition caused by the shedding of large flakes of dead skin from the scalp. Dandruff is harmless and does not cause hair loss, but it can be unsightly and annoying. It can usually be controlled by using dandruff shampoos.

No one knows what causes dandruff. The body is always shedding its outer layers of dead skin. However, on some people the dead skin on the scalp mixes with dirt and oil and becomes dandruff. Dandruff is also associated with *seborrheic dermatitis,* a scaly, itchy rash of the scalp, face, and chest. Nonprescription dandruff shampoos that contain zinc pyrithione, salicylic acid, selenium sulfide, or coal tar can usually clear up the condition within 1 or 2 weeks. It is important to follow the directions on the shampoo bottle carefully. To avoid a buildup of shampoo residue, rinse the hair thoroughly, and alternate the use of the dandruff shampoo with other shampoos.

CONSULT A PHYSICIAN

If dandruff seems to be severe or does not respond to over-the-counter dandruff shampoos, consult a dermatologist, a physician specializing in skin disorders. The dermatologist may prescribe a corticosteroid cream or other lotion to treat the dandruff.

DEAFNESS

see HEARING LOSS

DEMENTIA

Dementia is a general term for the decline in mental functioning caused by a brain disorder. It is characterized by loss of memory, reasoning ability, judgment, and recall. The most common cause of dementia is ALZHEIMER'S DISEASE, but BRAIN TUMORS, hydrocephalus, multiple STROKES, brain injury, pernicious ANEMIA, alcoholism, and syphilis can also result in dementia.

RISK FACTORS ▶▶▶▶▶▶

Rare among people under 65, dementia in some form affects about 1 person in 10 over 65. Those with a history of strokes, HYPERTENSION, or ARTERIOSCLEROSIS are most susceptible.

Symptoms The onset of dementia usually occurs gradually. The person may forget names and dates, become lost in a familiar place, or become confused while performing a routine task. Individuals in the early stages of dementia often undergo personality changes or start to act inappropriately (for example, undressing in public). They may also suffer from depression.

The disease can be very difficult for care givers and family members. Delusions and episodes of paranoia (feelings of persecution) may develop as the disease progresses. In the final stages, the patients are unable to care for themselves and must be cleaned, fed, and dressed by others.

Treatment Dementia that is caused by brain tumor, brain injury, or a nutritional deficiency can be treated by surgery or medication. However, little can be done for people with irreversible dementia, especially those with Alzheimer's disease, beyond keeping the patients safe, clean, and comfortable. In some cases, physicians prescribe sedatives or antidepressant drugs to control restlessness and depression. People with severe dementia are often placed in a nursing home or hospital to receive the level of care they need. (See also SYPHILIS, **2**; ALCOHOLISM, **7**.)

DENTAL PROBLEMS

A wide variety of dental problems can cause pain, damage teeth and gums, and affect a person's health, appearance, speech, and ability to bite and chew food. Fortunately, most dental problems can be prevented or treated before they become severe. *Dentists* can usually repair damaged teeth and supporting tissues. Sometimes, however, it is necessary to extract, or remove, badly damaged teeth and replace them with natural-looking DENTURES. But a good dentist will try everything possible to save the tooth before considering extraction.

Tooth Decay Almost everyone suffers tooth decay, or dental caries, at some point in life. Tooth decay usually affects children and young adults but can occur at any age. It is caused by bacteria that mix with saliva and food particles to form a sticky paste called *plaque*. The plaque adheres to the surface of teeth, particularly the grooves and pits of the molars, and produces acids that erode the enamel of the teeth. This process causes a *cavity*. If treated promptly, however, the decay will not damage the dentin or the pulp (see illustration: Parts of a Tooth).

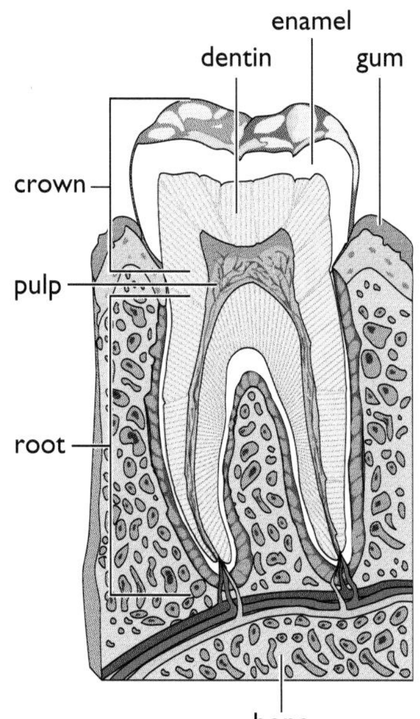

Parts of a Tooth.

The first symptom of tooth decay is usually pain in the tooth when eating something cold, hot, or sweet. In many cases, however, the dentist will detect tooth decay through examination and X rays before there is any pain.

Treatment consists of drilling a hole in the tooth to clean out the decay, then filling the hole with a material, called amalgam, that seals and protects the cavity from further decay. A badly decayed tooth may be capped with a *crown*, a metal or porcelain cover that is cemented in place over the tooth.

Abscess An abscess is a bacterial infection in the soft tissue and bone at the root of a tooth (see illustration: Abscessed Tooth). It is an advanced stage of tooth decay. The bacteria invade the pulp of a tooth through a cavity and slowly kill the pulp, making the tissues and blood vessels swell and throb painfully. The abscess forms a pus-filled sac at the

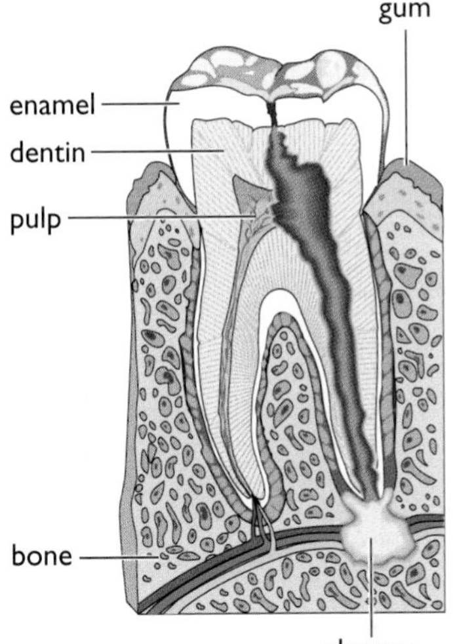

Abscessed Tooth. *An abscess is an advanced stage of tooth decay. Acids on the tooth gradually erode the enamel, creating a cavity through which bacteria enter. The bacteria slowly kill the pulp as they spread downward.*

root or in the gums. Sometimes the sac will burst, releasing foul-tasting pus into the mouth.

Treatment of an abscess involves drilling a hole in the tooth and cleaning and disinfecting the pulp chamber. This is called a *root canal* treatment. In addition, the dentist usually prescribes an antibiotic to kill the infection and keep it from spreading. Once the infection has cleared up, the dentist fills the cavity and caps the tooth with a crown.

Malocclusion and Impacted Teeth Malocclusion occurs when the upper and lower teeth fail to fit together in a normal bite. The teeth should meet so that the front upper teeth slightly overlap the front lower teeth, and the lower molars should fit into the hollows of the upper molars. Although a perfect bite is rare, only severe malocclusion requires professional treatment.

An *orthodontist* usually treats malocclusion with an ORTHODONTIC DEVICE that shifts the teeth into line. *Braces,* metal wires fastened to the teeth, are the most common orthodontic device. Many children and adolescents must wear braces for a period of 1 to 3 years to correct abnormal bites.

An impacted tooth is one that cannot emerge through the gum line because the jaw is too small or the tooth has grown in the wrong direction. Impaction usually affects the third molars, or *wisdom teeth,* which appear in the late teens or early twenties. An impacted tooth may partially emerge through the gum, providing an opening for bacteria to penetrate the gum line. Or it may remain below the surface, pressing painfully on the jaw or neighboring teeth. The standard treatment for impacted wisdom teeth is to extract them, either in the dentist's office or in a hospital.

HEALTHY CHOICES

Preventing Dental Problems Children should be taught to brush their teeth at least twice a day and to floss once a day. Brushing alone cannot remove all of the plaque that forms on teeth. Flossing helps remove plaque between teeth and also stimulates the gums to prevent GUM DISEASE. Poor dental hygiene may be the cause of *halitosis,* or bad breath. Everyone should visit their dentist regularly. Cleaning by a dentist or *dental hygienist* twice a year helps keep teeth healthy and attractive.

In recent years, tooth decay in children has declined dramatically because of the addition of fluoride to drinking water and toothpaste. Many dentists treat children with a fluoride rinse during their regular visits. Children and the elderly can also benefit greatly from a dental *sealant,* a clear plastic that coats the cracks and indentations of the teeth to protect them from plaque. (See also TOOTH, **1**; DENTAL CARE, **9**.)

DENTURES

Dentures are artificial teeth that replace lost teeth. The artificial teeth are set in a metal or plastic plate that is fitted to the gums and surrounding teeth. Dentures may be an entire set of teeth (full dentures) or may consist of only one tooth (partial denture). Dentures enable people to maintain their appearance and to chew food normally. In addition, dentures

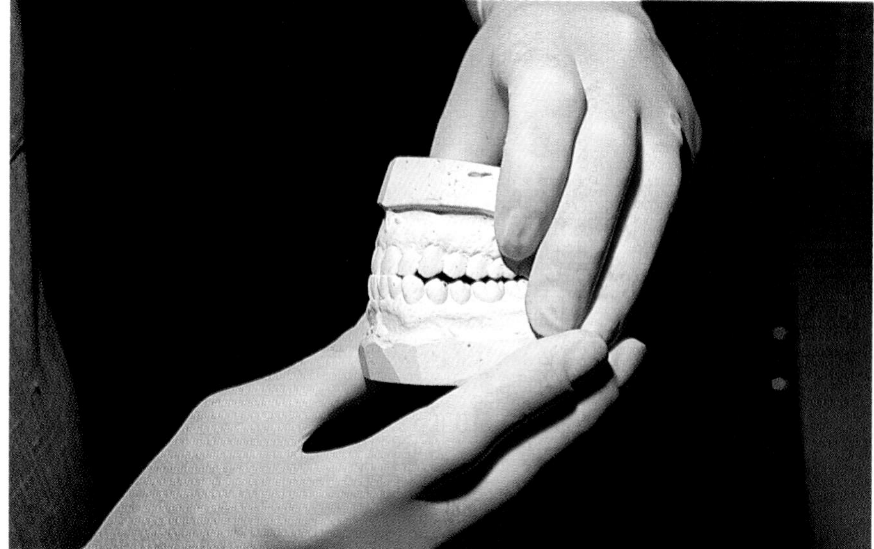

Denture Model. *A plaster of Paris model of the teeth is made from impressions taken of the mouth. Dentures are then made from the models.*

are used to hold neighboring teeth in place in the jaw, preventing the teeth on either side of a lost tooth from shifting toward the gap.

When a person has one or more teeth extracted, the dentist takes an impression of the gums and the remaining teeth. The dentist then makes the dentures, using the impression as a model (see illustration: Denture Model). The color, size, and shape of the dentures can be matched to the patient's real teeth. Usually several visits are necessary to adjust the new dentures until they fit comfortably. Partial dentures, called *bridges,* can be fixed permanently in place, or they can be removable.

People with dentures must brush and floss daily to keep their gums and remaining teeth in good condition and to provide a good supporting structure for the dentures. Removable dentures should be taken out nightly to clean them and to give the gums a rest. Loose dentures can cause mouth ulcers and interfere with chewing. (See also DENTAL PROBLEMS; DENTAL CARE, 9.)

DIABETES

Diabetes is a disorder of the pancreas that prevents the body from using sugars and starches properly. When the pancreas is functioning normally, it releases hormones (primarily insulin) to maintain correct levels of glucose (sugar) in the blood, help the muscle cells use glucose for energy, and aid in storing glucose in the liver and muscles. Without sufficient insulin, body cells are unable to use glucose properly and blood levels of glucose rise, producing *hyperglycemia,* the major symptom of diabetes. More than 10 million Americans have been diagnosed as having diabetes, and an estimated 5 million have the disease without knowing it.

There are two types of diabetes: *insulin-dependent diabetes mellitus,* or IDDM (also called type I, juvenile, or ketosis-prone diabetes), and *non-insulin-dependent diabetes mellitus,* or NIDDM (also called type II, adult-onset, or stable diabetes). The cause of diabetes is not known, although heredity is a factor. An immune system response following a viral

RISK FACTORS
▶ ▶ ▶ ▶ ▶ ▶

infection may also play a part in the development of IDDM. Obesity is a risk factor for developing NIDDM.

Insulin-Dependent Diabetes Mellitus IDDM affects just 1 in 10 people with diabetes. It generally develops in children and young adults and affects more males than females. Symptoms usually develop rapidly, sometimes within a few weeks. With IDDM the pancreas produces very little or no insulin and, as the name suggests, treatment requires insulin.

RISK FACTORS
▶ ▶ ▶ ▶ ▶ ▶

Non-Insulin-Dependent Diabetes Mellitus NIDDM affects people who are more than 40 years old and overweight or obese. With NIDDM the pancreas is producing insulin, but the body is resistant to insulin and greater amounts are needed to keep normal levels of glucose in the blood. NIDDM may have no symptoms for many years, and it may be discovered unexpectedly during a routine examination. Insulin is not always needed to treat NIDDM.

Symptoms and Diagnosis Diabetes has multiple symptoms, including persistent thirst, increased urination, weight loss, increased appetite, frequent vaginal and bladder infections, blurred vision, fatigue, nausea, and vomiting. Diagnosis of diabetes is based on the presence of characteristic symptoms as well as on tests that measure levels of glucose and other substances in the blood and urine.

Treatment The progress of both types of diabetes responds to changes in lifestyle, and the patient can assume significant responsibility for the day-to-day management of the disease. A physician will outline a diet that controls weight, establishes regular eating patterns, and helps control glucose concentrations in the blood. Generally, people with diabetes must limit alcohol intake, regulate consumption of carbohydrates, and eat plenty of fiber-rich foods. Regular exercise is also recommended because it reduces blood glucose levels, helps cells use glucose more efficiently, and strengthens the heart and blood vessels. For some people with NIDDM, diet modification and increased exercise may be enough to control the disease. Others may require oral medication.

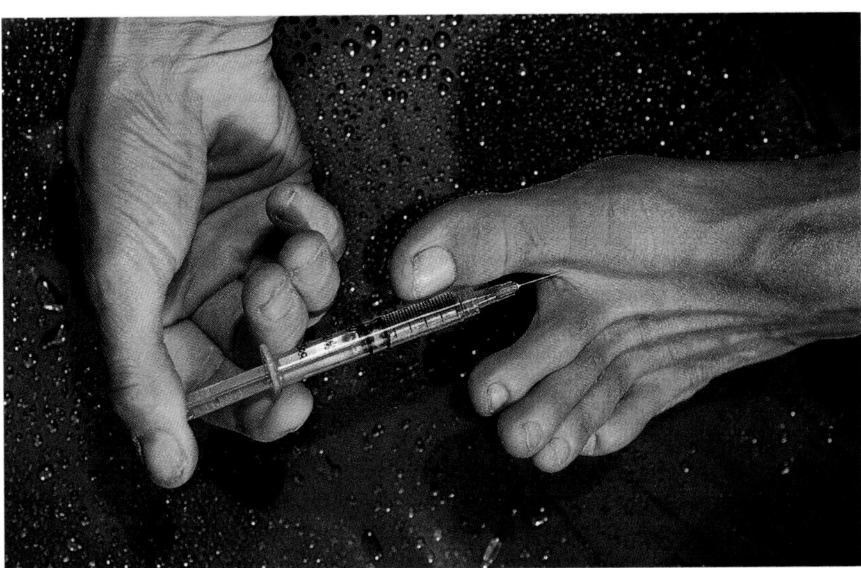

Administering Insulin. *People with diabetes often administer insulin themselves, using a syringe.*

For others with diabetes, including most of those under the age of 40, insulin treatments are generally prescribed. Insulin may be injected once or several times a day by the patient or administered continuously by a pump device on the abdomen. Insulin is obtained from the pancreases of hogs or cattle or produced synthetically.

Complications People with diabetes who are insulin-dependent can develop severe short-term complications when the balance between insulin and glucose is not properly maintained. Too little glucose (*hypoglycemia*) can result in weakness, dizziness, and unconsciousness. Excess levels of glucose and ketones (chemicals produced by the liver from fatty acids) can produce similar symptoms. Both conditions are temporary and reversible.

The long-term health effects of diabetes are more serious and progressive, more so when the disease is not well controlled. They result primarily from damage to blood vessels and nerves. Common circulatory complications include high blood pressure, hardening of the arteries, reduced circulation to the limbs, kidney problems, and damage to the retina of the eye, sometimes causing blindness. Nerve-related complications include numbness, pain, and impotence. People with diabetes also have a reduced ability to fight infection, and they heal less quickly than do other people.

HEALTHY CHOICES

Prevention The chances of developing NIDDM may be decreased by maintaining ideal body weight. Regular exercise may also help prevent the development of diabetes or lessen its severity. (See also PANCREAS, **1**; INSULIN, 7.)

DIALYSIS

Dialysis is a medical procedure in which an artificial kidney machine performs the kidneys' function of removing waste substances from a person's blood. It is used when injury or disease has caused *kidney failure.* In

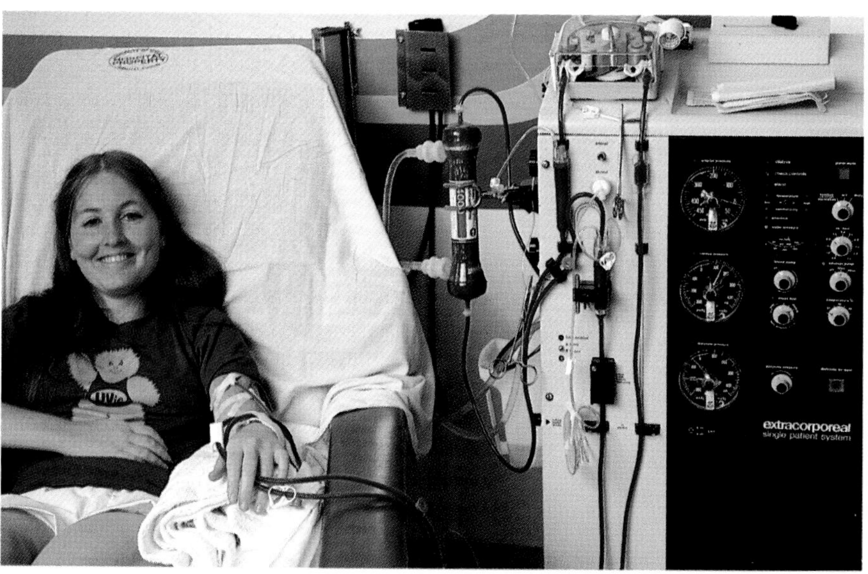

Dialysis. *Dialysis usually takes place at a hospital or special dialysis center.*

some cases, dialysis is a temporary measure used until the kidneys resume normal functioning. For people with chronic kidney failure, however, dialysis becomes a permanent part of their lives.

There are several types of dialysis. In the most common form, *hemodialysis,* a plastic tube is surgically inserted between a person's vein and artery. The tube is then connected to a dialysis machine for a period of 2 to 6 hours, several times a week. Blood flows from the artery to the machine, which filters out the impurities. The purified blood is then returned through the tube to the person's vein. Most people undergo dialysis as an outpatient at a hospital or in a special dialysis center. (See also KIDNEY DISORDERS; KIDNEY, **1**.)

DIVERTICULITIS

Diverticulitis is a disease of the colon (large intestine) caused by inflammation of small pouches on its walls. Many people develop these pouches, called *diverticula,* as they get older. This common condition, known as *diverticulosis,* generally causes no symptoms and does not become a medical problem. If, however, the diverticula become infected with bacteria, the condition turns into diverticulitis.

Symptoms The major symptoms of diverticulitis are nausea, fever, and mild or severe cramping, usually in the lower left part of the abdomen. CONSTIPATION or diarrhea are also common symptoms. In severe cases, the inflamed diverticula can rupture, sending infected material into the abdominal cavity. This results in PERITONITIS, a serious infection of the abdomen that is potentially fatal.

Treatment and Prevention Treatment for mild cases of diverticulitis includes bed rest, a stool softener, a low-fiber or liquid diet, and antibiotics to destroy the infection. People with ruptured or bleeding diverticula or recurring attacks of diverticulitis may need surgery to remove the affected portion of the colon.

HEALTHY CHOICES

CONSULT A PHYSICIAN

The best way to prevent diverticulitis is to maintain a high-fiber diet that includes plenty of whole grains and fresh fruits and vegetables. A physician should be consulted if there is any unexplained bleeding from the rectum or any prolonged cramping or stomach pain. (See also DIGESTIVE SYSTEM, **1**; DIARRHEA, **2**; FIBER, **4**.)

DOWN SYNDROME

Down syndrome is a condition marked by abnormal physical and mental development that is caused by a genetic defect. People with Down syndrome are born with 47 rather than the normal 46 chromosomes. The frequency of the disease is related to the age of the mother:

RISK FACTORS

At age 25, a woman's chance of having a Down syndrome baby is about 1 in 1,205, whereas at age 35, her chance increases to 1 in 365.

Down Syndrome. *Down syndrome, which is caused by the presence of an extra chromosome, is marked by characteristic facial features.*

Symptoms Down syndrome is usually recognized soon after birth because of characteristic facial features: flattened nose, skin folds over the inner corners of the eyes, upward slanting of the eyes, a large tongue that often protrudes from a small mouth, and a small, rounded head (see illustration: Down Syndrome). Babies with Down syndrome are usually very slow to develop motor skills such as crawling and walking.

Down syndrome children frequently are born with defects of the heart and digestive systems. They may also experience chronic respiratory illnesses, ear infections, visual or hearing problems, and acute leukemia. Mental retardation ranges from mild to severe.

Diagnosis Down syndrome is diagnosed by counting the chromosomes found in a sample of white blood cells. Women at risk of having a baby with the syndrome may undergo a test during pregnancy called amniocentesis, which examines fetal cells for the extra chromosome.

Treatment and Outlook Although many children with Down syndrome do not survive their first year because of their physical defects and susceptibility to infection, many others thrive in a warm, supportive environment with special education and quality medical care. Institutionalization may be necessary, however, to care for those affected most severely. Advances in medical treatment have increased the life expectancy of those with Down syndrome.

Although Down syndrome is rarely inherited, genetic counseling is suggested for women over 35 who plan to have children and for parents who already have a child with Down syndrome. (See also GENETIC SCREENING, 6; GENETIC COUNSELOR, 9.)

Eczema

Eczema is a red, itchy rash sometimes accompanied by scaling or blisters. It may appear at any age and is uncomfortable but not life-threatening.

Symptoms and Causes In children, eczema usually starts on the cheeks and in the folds of the elbows and knees. It often begins as a pink patch of scaly skin or reddish pimples. The skin may then become thick and crusty. Eczema is usually itchy, causing the child who has it to scratch, especially during sleep. The scratching can cause oozing blisters that may become infected.

Eczema in infants and children is believed to be an inherited allergic condition. Children with eczema often come from families in which other family members suffer from ALLERGIES such as ASTHMA, HAY FEVER, or hives.

RISK FACTORS

In adults, irritating chemicals, such as detergents, dishwashing liquid, and household cleaners, can trigger eczema, particularly on the hands.

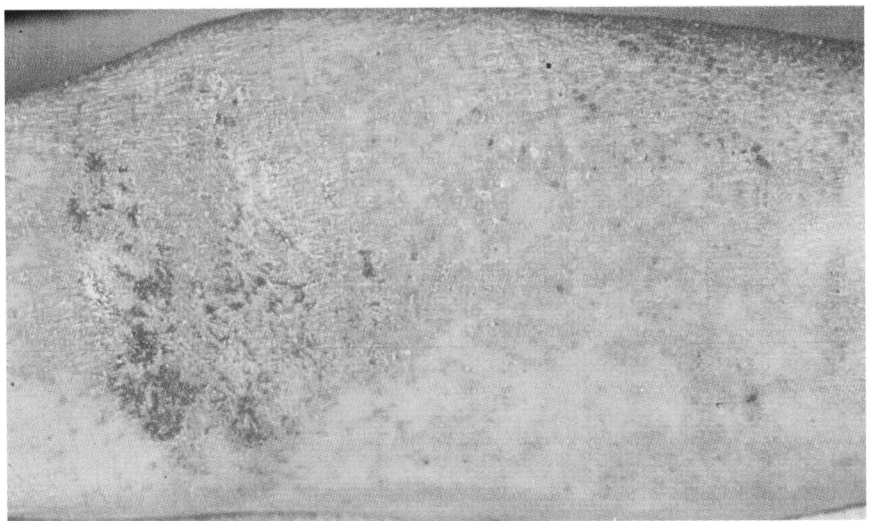

Eczema. *This patch of eczema shows the scaling and blisters that usually accompany this skin condition.*

Treatment and Prevention Treatment of eczema usually consists of soothing the rash to reduce the itchiness. Moisturizing cream and petroleum jelly can be used to keep the skin soft and moist. Antihistamines and corticosteroid creams may help reduce itching. If the rash becomes infected, a physician should be consulted. Babies with eczema should wear clothes that are 100 percent cotton, and their nails should be clipped short to minimize the effects of scratching. People with eczema should learn which substances irritate their skin and try to avoid them. (See also ANTIHISTAMINES AND DECONGESTANTS, 7; CORTICOSTEROIDS, 7.)

CONSULT A

Electrocardiogram

An electrocardiogram, also known as an ECG or an EKG, is a test that records the pattern of electrical activity within the heart. An ECG can reveal disorders of the heart, such as irregular rhythms or damage caused by a HEART ATTACK.

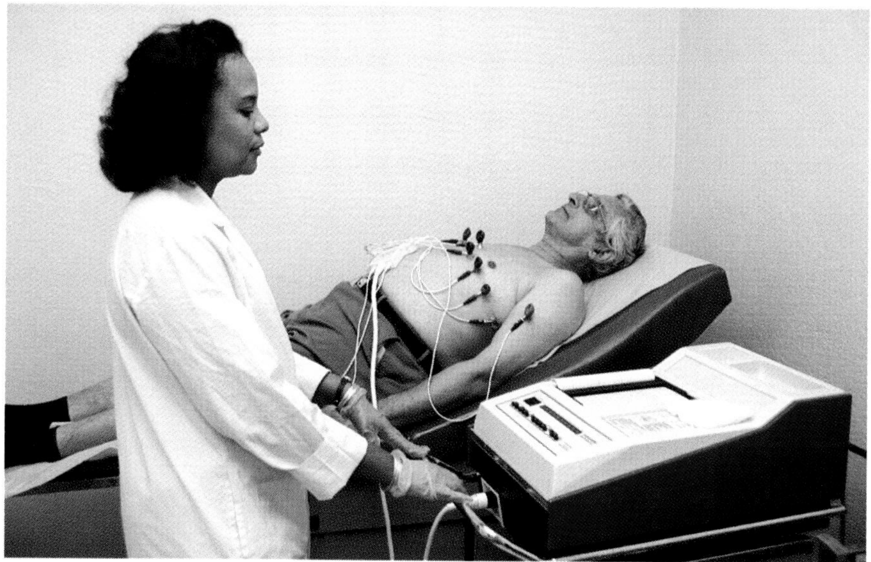

Electrocardiogram Test.

The procedure is painless and takes only a few minutes to complete. The patient is asked to lie down on a bed or examining table. Between 10 and 15 electrodes are attached with a jellylike substance to the chest, wrists, and ankles. During the minutes required to complete the procedure, the patient will be asked not to move or talk but will be allowed to breathe normally. The electrodes are attached to an *electrocardiograph*, which records the impulses and displays them as wavy lines on a television monitor or a long strip of paper continuously fed out of the machine (see illustration: Electrocardiogram Test). The test may also be done while performing normal activities or as part of a STRESS TEST, which measures the heart's activity during exercise. (See also HEART, **1**.)

ELECTROENCEPHALOGRAM

An electroencephalogram (ih lek troh en SEF uh luh gram), also called an EEG, is a diagnostic test that measures electrical activity in the brain. It is used to diagnose conditions such as EPILEPSY, BRAIN TUMORS, and some psychological disorders.

The test is performed using an electroencephalograph, a machine that records electrical impulses as irregular lines on a strip of paper. The test is painless and may be done during a short visit to a hospital or lab. A number of small electrodes are attached to the scalp. Changes in brain activity are measured while the person performs actions such as opening and closing the eyes or concentrating on a geometric pattern. Sometimes the test is performed during sleep. By examining the lines produced by the electroencephalograph, the physician can determine whether brain activity is normal or shows signs of disease.

EMBOLISM

see **BLOOD CLOT**

Emphysema

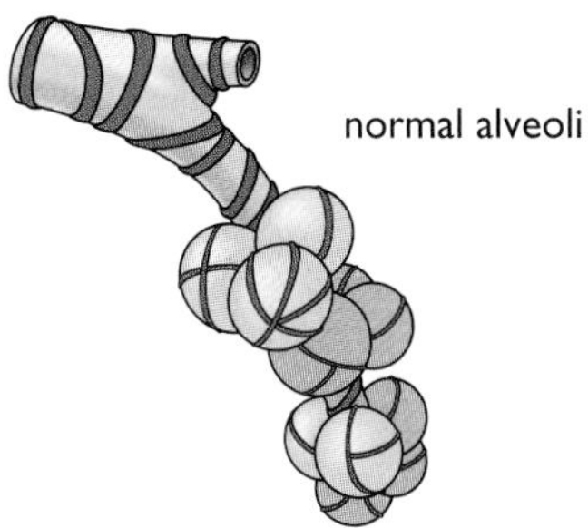

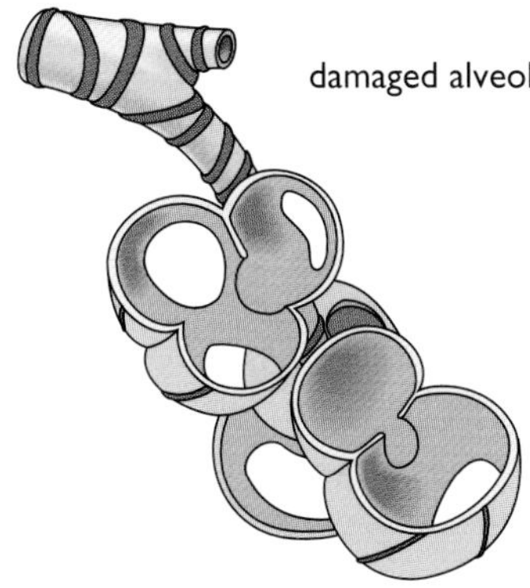

Effects of Emphysema. *In emphysema, the tiny air sacs (alveoli) in the lungs become enlarged and rupture as the result of repeated exposure to tobacco smoke. This severely impairs breathing efficiency.*

Emphysema is a chronic and irreversible lung disease, usually caused by smoking cigarettes over a long period. Emphysema affects more men than women, but as more women become smokers, their incidence of emphysema is increasing. In the United States several hundred people per 100,000 suffer from emphysema.

Symptoms and Diagnosis Emphysema develops slowly and may not be recognized for many years. The initial symptom is shortness of breath, which becomes worse over time. As the disease progresses, people with emphysema are less able to tolerate any exercise or exertion and eventually become unable to carry out normal activities. Chronic bronchitis and weight loss may accompany the disease. Eventually, emphysema leads to respiratory or heart failure.

A physician diagnoses emphysema by evaluating a patient's symptoms, medical history, lung X rays, and lung function tests. An enlarged chest is sometimes a characteristic of emphysema.

Causes and Treatment Emphysema develops when the walls of the *alveoli* (tiny air sacs) in the lungs are damaged. Eventually the alveoli burst open, forming larger air sacs with less surface area (see illustration: Effects of Emphysema). The lungs become less elastic, and their ability to exchange oxygen and carbon dioxide is reduced. The result is lowered levels of oxygen in the blood, enlargement of and strain on the heart, and the accumulation of fluid in the lungs. Exposure to cigarette smoke is the usual cause of emphysema, but tobacco smoke from cigars and pipes and marijuana smoke can also cause it.

No specific treatment exists for emphysema, but its progress can be stopped by giving up smoking. The efficiency of damaged lungs can be increased by regular exercise, drugs that dilate the air passages, and special exercises to improve inhalation and exhalation. A person with advanced emphysema may have to rely on oxygen therapy, which requires the use of an oxygen tank and a respirator at home.

HEALTHY CHOICES

Prevention Emphysema is a preventable disease if smoking is avoided. (See also LUNG DISEASE; LUNG, **1**; BRONCHITIS, **2**; SMOKING, **7**.)

Epilepsy

Epilepsy, also called seizure disorder, is a condition characterized by recurring seizures. It is not a disease but a set of symptoms caused by an irregularity in the brain's electrical function. Seizures occur when groups of *neurons* in the brain suddenly discharge uncontrolled electrical impulses. These impulses cause symptoms ranging from momentary lack of awareness to severe convulsions.

Symptoms and Diagnosis of Epilepsy Seizures are usually classified as partial or generalized. A *partial seizure* affects only a part of the brain. It may cause twitching of an arm or a leg, or lead to a sensory hallucination—for example, a visual image or a peculiar taste. This depends on the area of the brain that is involved.

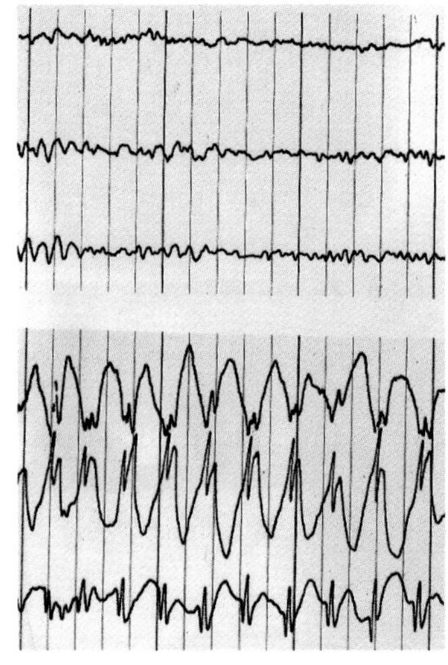

Normal and Abnormal EEG Readings. *An electroencephalograph is a machine that records the electrical activity of the brain on moving strips of paper. At the top is an EEG reading from a healthy brain. At the bottom is an EEG reading from a person who is experiencing a generalized epileptic seizure.*

A generalized seizure usually affects a wide area of the brain. It may be mild or severe. Mild seizures, once called *petit mal seizures,* are now called *absences* or, more formally, *generalized nonconvulsive seizures* (GNCS). They cause a person to freeze for a few seconds, staring or blinking repeatedly, unaware of what is going on. Absences may recur once or twice a month, or they may happen dozens of times during a day.

Severe seizures are known as *generalized convulsive seizures* (GCS), or *grand mal seizures.* They cause a person to lose consciousness, fall to the ground, and often to give a sharp cry. The person's body stiffens and then makes jerking movements. The tongue may be bitten and bowel or bladder control may be lost. After the jerking movements cease, the person may remain unconscious for a few more minutes and then on reviving is likely to be confused. Severe seizures may occur as often as once a day, or as rarely as once every few years.

Epilepsy can be diagnosed by performing an ELECTROENCEPHALOGRAM (EEG), a test that records electrical activity within the brain (see illustration: Normal and Abnormal EEG Readings).

Causes and Treatment of Epilepsy Sometimes epilepsy is caused by a brain injury—at birth, by an infection, in an accident, or as a result of a STROKE. But recurring seizures may also occur as a result of irregular body metabolism caused by disease or drug withdrawal. In many cases, the cause of epilepsy is unknown. Treatment with anticonvulsant drugs has been very successful in preventing or controlling epileptic seizures and has allowed most people with epilepsy to lead normal lives. Occasionally surgery is used to treat epilepsy.

CONSULT A PHYSICIAN

If you are with someone who experiences a severe seizure, you can help prevent injury. Clear the immediate area of any objects that could injure the person. Do not attempt to put anything into the person's mouth to prevent the tongue from being bitten. If the seizure continues for more than a few minutes, get medical help immediately. (See also BODY METABOLISM, **1**; NERVOUS SYSTEM, **1**; NEURON, **1**.)

EYE DISORDERS

Eye disorders are abnormal eye conditions that affect vision. They include color vision deficiency, night blindness, detached retina, macular degeneration, CATARACTS, and GLAUCOMA. VISION PROBLEMS are irregularities of the eye that can be corrected with glasses or contact lenses.

Color Vision Deficiency and Night Blindness Color vision deficiency, which is usually inherited, affects about 8 percent of males and 1 percent of females in the United States. People with color vision deficiency have difficulty distinguishing between red and green or, occasionally, between blue and yellow. Total "color blindness," in which everything is seen in shades of gray, is rare. EYE TESTS can diagnose color vision deficiency, but no treatment can reverse it.

Night blindness is the inability to see well in dim light. It can be caused by problems with the retina or by a lack of vitamin A. Some people with night blindness, however, show no signs of eye disease.

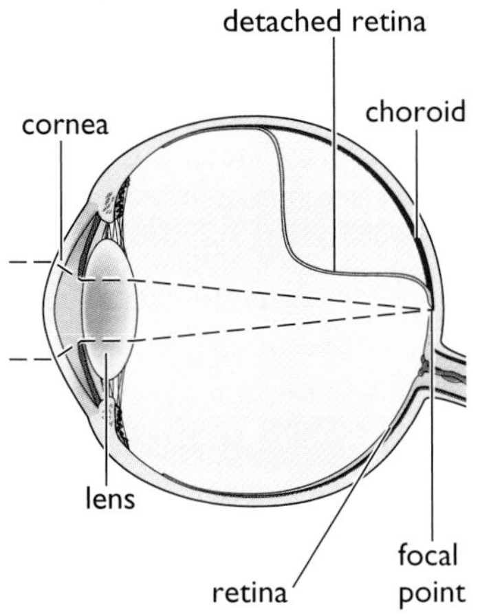

Detached Retina. *This disorder occurs when the retina peels away from the choroid layer.*

Detached Retina A detached retina occurs when the retina, the light-sensitive area at the back of the eye, peels away from the nourishing layer of tissue that lies behind it. Symptoms include floating specks, flashes of light, and—later—shadows that obscure vision. Most cases of detached retina occur because of degenerative changes in the retina, a condition most common in nearsighted people. Detachment of the retina may also be caused by a blow to the eye. This condition requires immediate treatment, which may involve using lasers to reattach the retina.

Macular Degeneration The leading cause of vision impairment in the elderly is macular degeneration. The macula is the area of the retina that helps you see details in the center of your field of vision. When macular degeneration occurs, the tissue in this area gradually breaks down. Although central vision is impaired, the outer part of the field of vision, called *peripheral vision,* is unchanged. This condition is generally untreatable, but with early diagnosis, lasers may be used to halt further degeneration. (See also THYROID DISORDERS; EYE, 1; EYE CARE, 9.)

EYE TEST

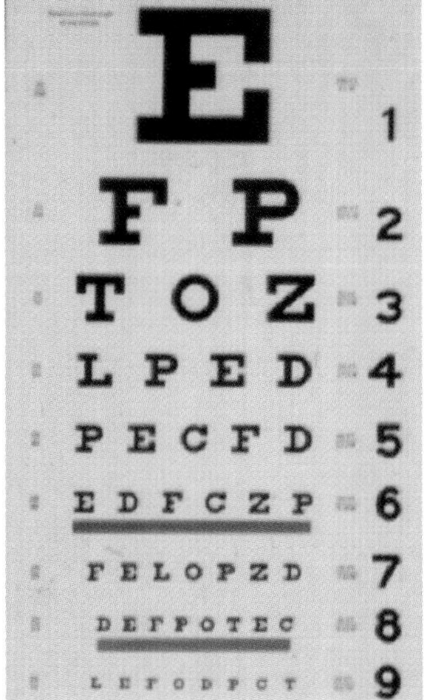

Snellen Chart.

An eye test, also called an eye examination, checks for problems and determines whether glasses or contact lenses are needed to correct vision. An eye test may be done as a routine checkup or to diagnose and treat a specific EYE DISORDER or VISION PROBLEM.

The eye specialist, an *ophthalmologist* or an *optometrist,* may begin by asking about the patient's family and personal medical history and about any eye problems and will then carefully examine the patient's eyes to look for signs of injury or disease. An *ophthalmoscope* is used to look at the back of the eye, where the examiner checks for detachment of the retina and inspects the eye's tiny blood vessels for damage caused by high blood pressure or diabetes.

The patient will be asked to read letters of different sizes on a chart, called a Snellen chart, while looking through a device into which different lenses can be placed. Additional tests measure color vision and *peripheral vision* (what can be seen around the edges of the field of vision). A test for GLAUCOMA, which measures the pressure within the eye, is usually given to people over 40.

Eye tests are recommended every 3 to 5 years for people who have no eye problems. For people who wear glasses or contact lenses, more frequent checkups are advised. (See also EYE CARE—OPHTHALMOLOGIST, OPTOMETRIST, 9.)

FAINTING

Fainting is a loss of consciousness resulting from a temporary disruption of the blood supply to the brain. The medical term for fainting is *syncope* (SING kuh pee). People sometimes feel weak, dizzy, or nauseous immediately before a fainting episode.

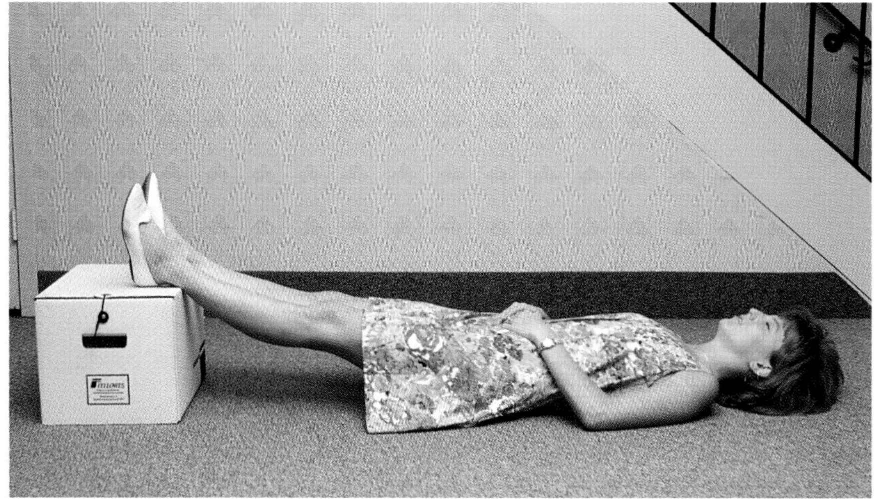

Fainting. *If someone faints, place the person on his or her back with feet elevated.*

Fainting may or may not be a symptom of a serious illness. Fainting is common in the first months of pregnancy. Some people faint easily from stress, fear, pain, or fatigue. Still others faint from the drop in blood pressure when standing up suddenly after sitting for a long time. Fainting may also indicate an obstruction in the arteries that serve the brain, an irregular heartbeat, or a neurological disorder.

If you are with someone who faints, make sure that person is on his or her back and elevate the legs to increase blood circulation to the brain (see illustration: Fainting). In most cases, the person revives within 1 or 2 minutes.

FIBROSITIS

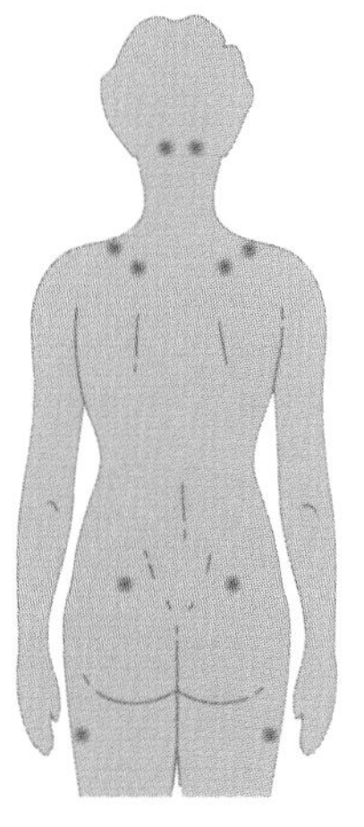

Trigger Points. *People with fibrositis may experience tenderness when pressure is applied to certain points on the body. The dots on the drawing indicate common tender points.*

Fibrositis is a chronic disorder characterized by muscle pain, fatigue, and tenderness at certain "trigger points" on the back, knees, hips, and neck (see illustration: Trigger Points). It is also called fibromyalgia or trigger-point syndrome. Fibrositis usually occurs in middle-aged people and affects women more often than men. It tends to come and go but does not get progressively worse.

There has been some controversy over whether fibrositis is a medically recognizable disorder because the symptoms—joint pain, weakness, and fatigue—are often vague. Fibrositis is also difficult to diagnose. There are no tests to detect it, so the physician must first rule out other disorders with similar symptoms.

Recent research suggests that fibrositis may be due to a lack of muscle fitness, compounded by sleep disturbances and stress. Underused or poorly developed muscles can become damaged and sore after only slight exertion from ordinary activities. In addition, people with fibrositis often suffer from SLEEP DISORDERS. It is believed that the lack of restful sleep may prevent the body from routinely repairing damaged muscles.

Exercising to strengthen muscles, improving sleep quality, and controlling stress can all help relieve the symptoms. Aspirin and hot baths are sometimes useful.

Foot Problems

Your feet are particularly susceptible to strains and pressures because they must support your weight and carry you around all day. Although most foot problems are minor, they can cause pain and affect mobility. Two of the most common foot disorders are BLISTERS, sores caused by pressure or friction on the skin, and *athlete's foot,* a fungal infection of the feet and toes. Other common problems include bunions, corns, ingrown toenails, flat feet, and gout.

A *bunion* is a condition in which the joint at the base of the big toe thrusts outward and the toe itself turns inward. The joint constantly rubs against the inside of the shoe, causing the skin to become rough, red, and swollen. The bursa, or fluid-filled sac surrounding the joint, often becomes inflamed as well.

Corns are areas of thickened skin that grow on toes as a result of pressure from tight, ill-fitting shoes. The word *corn* in this context refers to a hard, kernel-shaped mass of skin that grows downward and presses painfully on the nerves of the toe.

HEALTHY CHOICES

The main remedy for both bunions and corns is to wear properly fitting shoes. Some bunions, however, require surgery to correct the alignment of the toe bones. Corns often disappear on their own, but spongy pads may help relieve pressure on the growth. They can also be softened and rubbed off by using a commercial corn remover or by rubbing with a rough towel or pumice stone after bathing.

HEALTHY CHOICES

Ingrown toenails occur when the sides of the nail grow into the surrounding flesh of the toe, causing inflammation and infection. They usually affect the big toe. To prevent ingrown toenails, wear comfortable shoes, and cut the toenails straight across. In severe cases, minor surgery and treatment with an antibiotic may be required.

Flat feet is a condition resulting from collapsed arches in which the entire sole of the foot touches the floor. Almost everyone is born with flat feet, but most people develop arches in early childhood. However, some people never develop arches, while others become flat-footed in adulthood because their muscles and ligaments are too weak to support the arch. In many cases, people with flat feet suffer no symptoms, but some may experience foot pain and fatigue. The usual treatment is muscle-strengthening exercises and arch supports in the shoes.

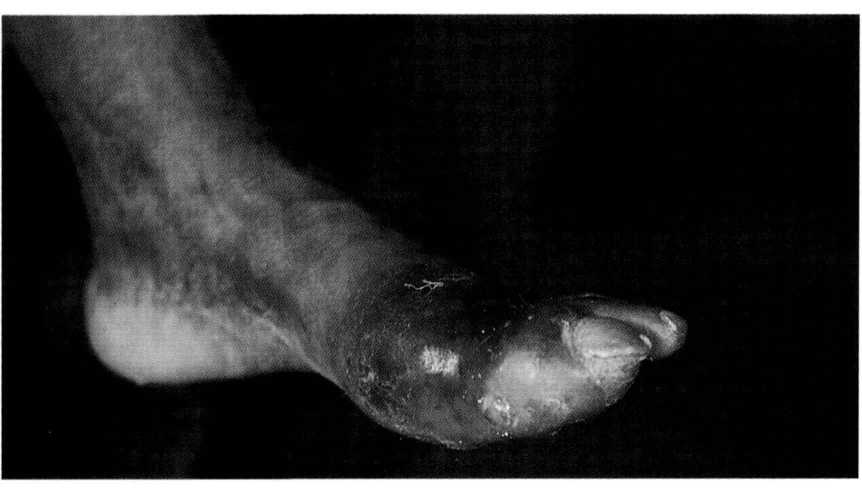

Gout. *In an attack of gout, an accumulation of uric acid crystals causes the joint to become red and swollen.*

Gout is a form of arthritis that can occur in any joint but usually affects the first joint of the big toe (see illustration: Gout). It is caused by a buildup of uric acid in the system. Uric acid crystals accumulate in the toe joint, causing it to become swollen and inflamed. An attack of gout strikes suddenly and lasts 1 to 2 weeks. Although often very painful, gout can be controlled with medication.

HEALTHY CHOICES

Many foot problems can be avoided by wearing shoes that fit properly. Very high heels and shoes with pointed toes should be avoided.

CONSULT A PHYSICIAN

Consult a *podiatrist* if minor foot problems become worse or fail to clear up on their own. (See also FOOT, 1; ATHLETE'S FOOT, 2; PODIATRIST, 9.)

GALLSTONES

Gallstones are lumps of solid matter that form in the *gallbladder,* a small abdominal organ in which bile is stored. *Bile* is a liquid produced in the liver that helps the body digest fats. A change in the chemical balance of the bile in the gallbladder may cause gallstones to form. The change may be the result of a high blood cholesterol level or obesity.

Gallstones usually consist mostly of cholesterol and range in size from tiny crystals to masses an inch (about 2.5 cm) across (see illustration: Gallstones). They are more common in women than in men and usually occur in older people.

RISK FACTORS

Symptoms In most people, gallstones produce few symptoms and are not a medical problem. However, if gallstones become very large or become lodged in the duct leading out of the gallbladder, they may cause severe pain and other complications. A person with a blocked duct may experience intense, constant pain in the upper right abdomen, accompanied by fever, nausea, vomiting, and loss of appetite. Severe gallstone attacks may result in inflammation of the gallbladder and JAUNDICE.

Treatment and Prevention For people with severe or chronic symptoms, the usual treatment is surgical removal of the gallbladder. Some relatively new techniques include removing the gallstones with a *laparoscope,* an instrument inserted through a small incision in the abdomen;

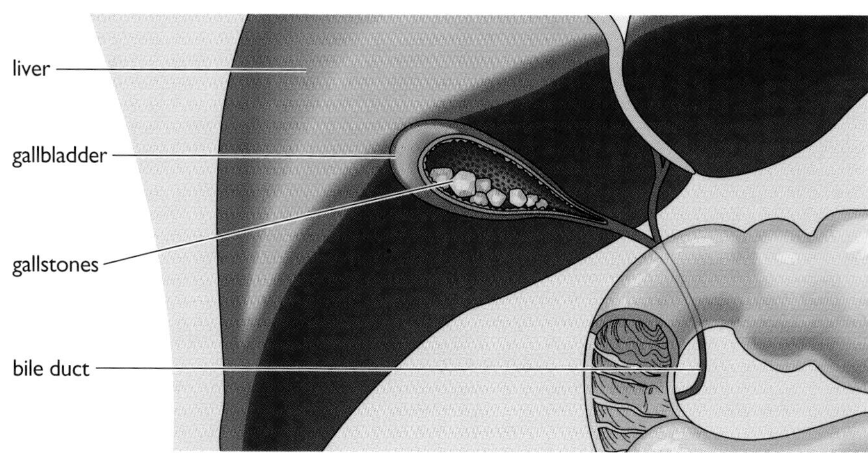

Gallstones. *Gallstones may form in the bile that is stored in the gallbladder. A painful attack may result if a gallstone blocks the bile duct.*

dissolving the stones with medication; or breaking them up with high-frequency sound waves.

HEALTHY CHOICES

Maintaining a diet low in fat and cholesterol and keeping to a healthy weight are the best ways to prevent the formation of gallstones. (See also DIGESTIVE SYSTEM, **1**; GALLBLADDER, **1**.)

GANGRENE

RISK FACTORS

Gangrene is the death of tissue due to a lack of blood circulation. It is caused by an injury to or blockage of an artery, and it usually affects arms, legs, fingers, and toes. Gangrene is most likely to occur in people with advanced DIABETES or ARTERIOSCLEROSIS (hardening of the arteries), but it can also develop as a complication of frostbite, a blood clot, a crushing injury to a limb, or a twisted intestine.

There are two forms of gangrene—dry and wet. A person with *dry gangrene* initially feels pain in the dying tissue before it becomes numb. The tissue eventually dries up, turns black, and falls off. Dry gangrene is not infected with bacteria and does not spread. In *wet gangrene,* dying tissue or a wound becomes infected by bacteria. The tissue swells, becomes hot to the touch, and blisters. Then it turns cold and blue. The bacteria will spread the gangrene to healthy tissue. One type of wet gangrene, gas gangrene, is caused by a virulent type of bacteria that forms a foul-smelling gas and spreads rapidly.

Treatment Treatment of dry gangrene consists of attempting to restore circulation. In wet gangrene, the only treatment is AMPUTATION, surgical removal of the dead tissue. Large doses of antibiotics are also necessary to prevent infection.

People with diabetes or arteriosclerosis must take good care of their feet and hands and treat even the most minor injuries immediately to prevent gangrene. (See also CIRCULATORY SYSTEM, **1**.)

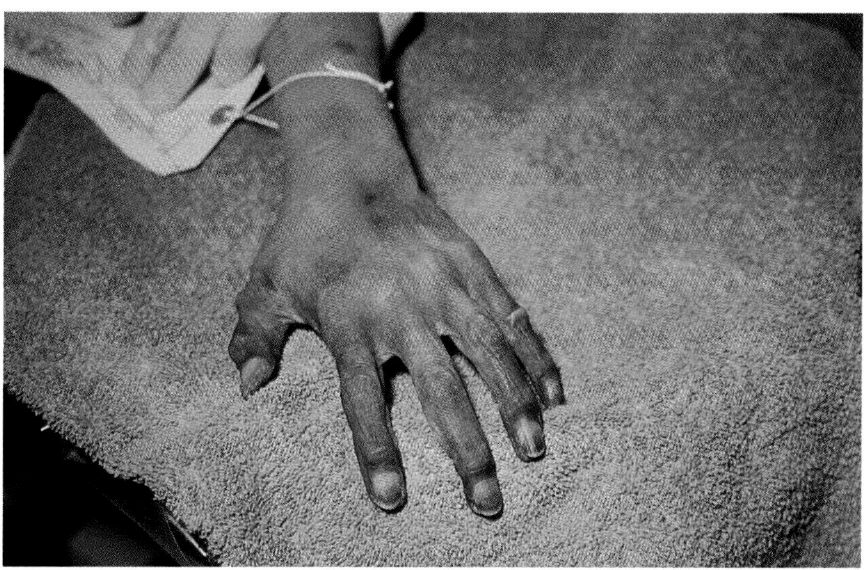

Dry Gangrene. *Pain is noticeable during the early stages of dry gangrene, but thereafter the area becomes numb and cold to the touch.*

Glaucoma

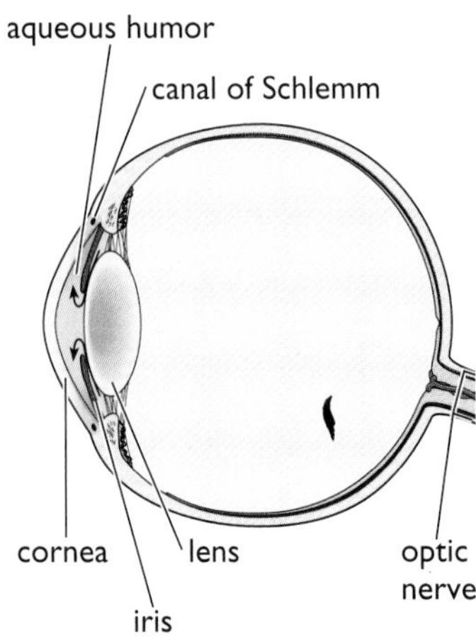

Fluid Drainage in the Eye. *In a healthy eye, the aqueous humor drains through the canal of Schlemm. In people with glaucoma, this canal is blocked, causing a buildup of pressure in the eye that damages the optic nerve.*

Glaucoma (glau KOH muh) is an eye condition in which a buildup of pressure within the eye leads to deterioration of the optic nerve and vision loss. Untreated, glaucoma can cause total blindness. In the United States, more than 2 million people over age 65 have glaucoma, and about 60,000 of these are legally blind. Glaucoma is rare among children and young adults.

Symptoms and Diagnosis Glaucoma can be either chronic or acute. *Chronic glaucoma* is more common and is characterized by a gradual loss of vision at the edges of the visual field (peripheral vision). Other than this gradual narrowing of vision, there are no early warnings and the disease may be undiagnosed for years. A simple, painless EYE TEST called a *tonometry test* allows an eye specialist to measure pressure in the eye and to diagnose glaucoma before damage occurs. People over age 40 should have this eye test regularly.

Acute glaucoma occurs when fluid that should drain from the eye is suddenly blocked. This causes pressure within the eye to rise quickly. Symptoms include pain in and above the eye, unclear vision, halos around lights at night, and redness of the eye.

Causes The abnormal pressure in the eye is caused by a buildup of a fluid, called the aqueous humor, that normally drains out of the eye (see illustration: Fluid Drainage in the Eye). If this drainage is blocked, pressure builds and pinches the blood vessels that supply the optic nerve, causing irreversible damage. CATARACTS, bleeding in the eye, and eye injuries can also cause glaucoma.

Treatment and Prevention Chronic glaucoma can usually be treated with eyedrops or oral medication, both of which help decrease pressure in the eye. Medication usually must be taken for life. Acute glaucoma is a medical emergency. It must be treated immediately with eyedrops, oral medication, or intravenous fluids to lower eye pressure. Both types of glaucoma may also be treated with surgery. A laser may be used to open blocked passages or create a new opening to allow drainage of fluid.

If glaucoma is detected and treated early, vision loss can be minimized. Getting regular eye tests and being aware of the risk factors for glaucoma are important means of prevention for this condition. These risk factors include age, a family history of glaucoma, African ancestry, and DIABETES. (See also EYE, 1.)

RISK FACTORS

Growth Disorders

A growth disorder is a condition that causes someone to be much shorter or much taller than normal height. When growth disorders are detected and treated early, they can often be minimized or reversed.

Gigantism, abnormal tallness, is usually caused by a tumor on the pituitary gland. The tumor prompts the gland to secrete abnormal amounts of growth hormone, causing the long bones of the arms and legs to grow to excessive lengths. Gigantism can be treated by removing the tumor surgically, by radiation therapy, or by administering a drug that blocks secretion of the growth hormone.

Growth Disorders. *A midget is a type of dwarf whose body proportions are normal.*

Dwarfism, abnormal shortness, occurs in two forms. One form consists of abnormally small people (commonly called midgets) whose arms, legs, and other body parts are in normal proportion to one another. The second type of dwarfism includes people whose head and body are of normal size but whose arms and legs are much shorter than normal. This form of dwarfism is usually inherited.

Dwarfism is often caused by undersecretion of the growth hormone (GH) by the pituitary gland. Malfunctions of the thyroid, adrenal, or pancreatic glands and chronic illness, such as HEART DISEASE, can also result in arrested growth. Malnutrition and physical or emotional abuse are other causes of dwarfism.

When malnutrition is the cause of dwarfism, it can be reversed if an adequate diet is provided early enough in life. Other causes of dwarfism may be treated by injecting growth hormone, by replacing other missing hormones, or by treating any underlying chronic illness. (See also GROWTH, 1; PITUITARY GLAND, 1; MALNUTRITION, 4.)

GUILLAIN-BARRÉ SYNDROME

Guillain-Barré (ghee lan bah RAY) syndrome is a disorder of the nervous system that causes sudden muscle weakness and, in extreme cases, temporary paralysis. This rare disorder often develops a few days or weeks after an attack of the flu or another viral infection. It is a serious condition that requires hospitalization, but it is rarely fatal.

The main symptom of Guillain-Barré syndrome is weakness in the limbs, usually spreading from the legs to the arms and sometimes the face. In severe cases of the disorder, the muscles that control breathing and swallowing may become weak or paralyzed, and the use of a respirator may be required.

Researchers believe that the syndrome is an allergic reaction to an infection. The antibodies produced by the body's *immune system* to fight the infection mistakenly attack parts of the *myelin sheath* that protects the nerves. Damage to the myelin disrupts the messages sent from the nerves to the muscles.

Most people with Guillain-Barré syndrome start recovering on their own a few weeks after the onset of the disease. But recovery can take months or years and is not always complete. Various treatments can limit the severity of the attack and shorten the recovery time. One procedure, called plasmapheresis, involves filtering the attacking antibodies out of the blood. A promising new therapy uses injections of gamma globulin, a blood protein that is important to the immune system. This seems to prevent the antibodies from attaching themselves to and destroying the myelin. Most people with the syndrome need physical therapy to retrain weakened muscles. (See also IMMUNE SYSTEM, **1**; NERVOUS SYSTEM, **1**.)

Gum Disease

Gum disease, or periodontal disease, is a major cause of tooth loss in adults over 35. It occurs when bacteria penetrate the gum line, destroying the underlying tissues. The process is usually painless and takes place over time. Eventually, the teeth become loose and either fall out or must be extracted. Gum disease affects many people—even those who take good care of their teeth. However, in most cases, the disease can be controlled or reversed.

Types of Gum Disease *Gingivitis* is the earliest stage of gum disease. It is caused by *plaque,* a sticky film of bacteria and food particles that builds up around the gum line. The plaque hardens into *calculus,* or *tartar,* a substance that irritates the gums, causing them to become red and swollen. Treatment includes thorough brushing and flossing as well as regular cleaning of the teeth by a dentist.

If gingivitis is not treated, it may develop into *periodontitis,* an inflammation of the teeth's supporting structures. Bacteria, plaque, and calculus build up under the gum line, eating pockets between the teeth and

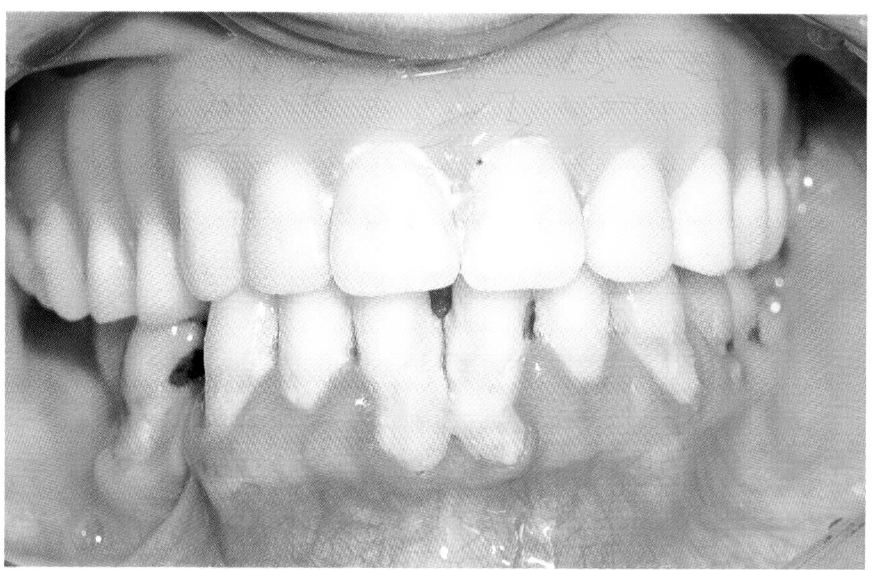

Periodontitis. *Advanced gum disease—periodontitis—results in red, inflamed, and receding gums and erosion of the ligaments and bone anchoring the teeth in the jaw.*

gums. The inflammation can spread to the periodontal ligaments, which hold the teeth in place, and to the bony tooth sockets. In the early stages, the dentist may be able to halt periodontitis by scraping away the plaque, calculus, and inflamed gum tissue. In more advanced stages of the disease, surgery may be required to correct gums and underlying bone damage.

Trench mouth, or Vincent's disease, is an infection of the gums that occurs most often in young adults. The gums become swollen and bleed easily, ulcers form on them, and the breath becomes foul. Trench mouth is treated with hydrogen peroxide or antibiotics and a thorough cleaning of the teeth and gums by a dentist.

HEALTHY CHOICES

Prevention Most cases of gum disease can be prevented or controlled by brushing and flossing the teeth daily and by visiting the dentist for checkups and cleaning once or twice a year. These measures stop the buildup of plaque before it can damage the teeth and gums. (See also DENTAL PROBLEMS; TOOTH, 1; DENTAL CARE, 9.)

Hair Loss

A person can experience hair loss (alopecia) for a variety of reasons. The leading cause is heredity, but illness and stress can also lead to hair loss. Hair loss is not a serious physical problem. A person could live a perfectly normal life without any hair at all. However, many people have a very strong reaction to the idea of baldness because they associate it with growing old and becoming less attractive.

Types of Hair Loss The most common kind of hair loss is *male pattern baldness,* which many men experience as they age. When, how, and to what extent baldness develops is determined by hereditary factors. Hair loss can begin at any time after adolescence and usually follows a set pattern at the hairline and on the crown of the head (see illustration: Male Pattern Baldness). Gradual hair loss in women, sometimes called *female pattern baldness,* is much less common and usually less extensive. The thinning of a woman's hair can also be caused by changes in hormones during menopause or pregnancy.

Most other kinds of hair loss are temporary. Certain illnesses, chemotherapy treatment for cancer, poor nutrition, the overuse of permanents or

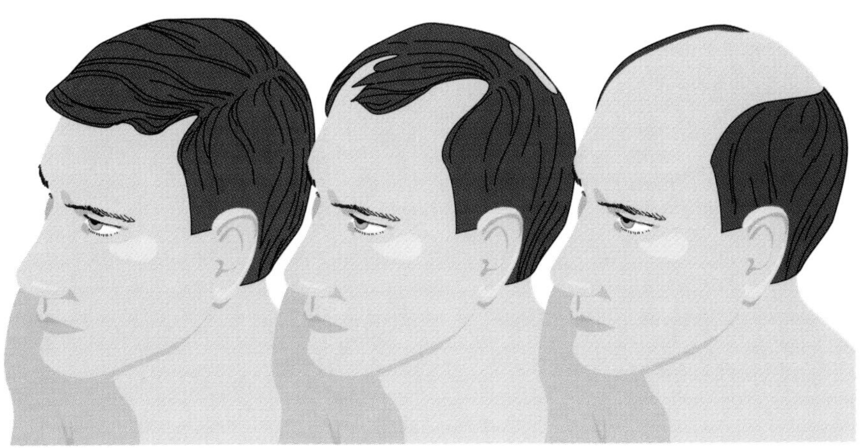

Male Pattern Baldness. *In male pattern baldness, the hairline typically recedes from the front in an M shape. Thinning also begins to form a characteristic "bald spot" on the crown of the head. The baldness at the front and back eventually meet, leaving only a fringe of hair at the sides and back.*

hair-straightening agents, and various other conditions can cause *temporary hair loss.* In most of these cases, the hair grows back when the cause is corrected.

Treatment There is no cure for male or female pattern baldness. Many people learn to live with it, but for those who wish to change their appearance, there are two avenues of treatment. The first involves hair pieces or hair weaving to conceal the loss. The second requires consulting a dermatologist about the approved methods for restoring hair—the drug *minoxidil* and hair transplants. Applying minoxidil to the scalp stimulates hair growth on some people, but the treatment is expensive. Replacing lost hair with *hair transplants* from other parts of the scalp is the most effective treatment, but it is also expensive and time-consuming. (See also MINOXIDIL, 7.)

Hay Fever

Seasonal Pollens. *The pollen responsible for most hay fever comes from the tiny flowers on common trees, grasses, and weeds—especially ragweed. These flowers produce millions of tiny grains that are blown from plant to plant by the wind. Although the cycle varies from region to region, trees generally release pollen in the spring, grasses in the early summer, and weeds in the late summer or early fall. During these times the pollen count can be very high.*

Hay fever (or allergic rhinitis) is a form of allergy caused by pollen, dust, molds, and other airborne substances. The allergic reaction is marked by nasal congestion and other coldlike symptoms. Hay fever usually occurs in the spring, summer, and fall, periods when plants produce the most pollen. It is a very common condition that affects about 20 million Americans annually. Although annoying and unpleasant, hay fever is not serious.

Most people experience no unpleasant symptoms when they inhale substances like the pollen from trees, grass, or weeds or the dander of a cat. For some people, however, these substances are *allergens*—that is, they induce an ALLERGY. When a person is sensitive to an allergen, the body reacts by producing antibodies to combat it. The antibodies trigger the release of a chemical called *histamine* that swells the mucous membranes in the nose. This produces the symptoms of hay fever: sneezing, coughing, watery eyes, and a runny, itchy, congested nose. Despite its name, fever is not a symptom of hay fever.

Treatment Mild attacks of allergic rhinitis can be treated with nonprescription decongestants and antihistamines (drugs that block the production of histamines). Many antihistamines cause drowsiness, so they must be used with care when operating machinery. Over-the-counter nasal sprays can provide relief from congestion, but they should not be used for more than a few days. Avoiding the allergens that have the most severe effect is the best way of preventing or minimizing the problem.

More severe or long-lasting allergies should be investigated by an *allergist,* a physician who specializes in treating allergies. ALLERGY TESTS are often used to identify the substances that cause allergic reactions. Treatment may include strong antihistamines or a corticosteroid nasal spray to prevent or ease congestion. In some cases the allergist will recommend a series of desensitizing injections, given over a period of years, to gradually condition the body to ignore the allergen. This provides long-term relief for some people. (See also ANTIHISTAMINES AND DECONGESTANTS, 7.)

HEADACHE

A headache is pain in the facial area or within the head. Headache pain may be felt in a specific place or all over the head; it may be dull or sharp, throbbing or constant. Headaches are caused by tension or inflammation in the outer lining of the brain; the skin or scalp; the facial muscles; or the sinuses, ears, or gums. Brain tissue itself cannot ache. Additional symptoms, such as nausea and vomiting, sometimes accompany a headache. Although headaches can be extremely uncomfortable, they rarely signal a serious disorder.

RISK FACTORS

Causes and Types of Headaches Common headaches are often the body's response to fatigue, stress, hunger, excessive consumption of alcohol, a noisy environment, or even a change in the weather. Such headaches usually clear up by themselves within a few hours. Certain

Headaches and Stress. *The stress produced by sitting in a traffic jam can result in the discomfort of a headache.*

foods and food additives; ear, tooth, and sinus infections; and head injuries may also cause headaches. More persistent and painful headaches include tension headaches, migraine headaches, and cluster headaches.

RISK FACTORS

A *tension headache* produces pain or pressure in the top or back of the head. Tension headaches may be caused by stress or by poor posture that strains related muscles.

MIGRAINE HEADACHES cause severe and often incapacitating pain and are often accompanied by nausea or vomiting, visual disturbances, and extreme sensitivity to light and noise. More women than men experience migraine headaches, which may involve a hormonal factor.

More men than women, however, have *cluster headaches*. Cluster headaches cause intense pain behind one eye. The eye may tear constantly and become reddened, and the nasal passages on that side may become congested. Cluster headaches often awaken a person at night and may continue for weeks or months.

In rare cases, a headache is a symptom of a serious condition requiring a physician's attention, such as a BRAIN TUMOR, high blood pressure (HYPERTENSION), or an ANEURYSM—a swelling of a blood vessel in the brain.

Treating Headaches Try to avoid situations that you know will trigger a headache. Once a headache has started, try relaxing, lying down, massaging the muscles of the head, neck, or shoulders, or taking a mild analgesic containing aspirin or acetaminophen. Seek medical help when a headache is severe and persistent or if it is accompanied by other symptoms, such as a fever or altered vision.

CONSULT A PHYSICIAN

HEARING LOSS

Hearing loss is the partial or complete inability to hear sounds. It can be temporary or permanent and can range from a mild condition to complete *deafness*. There are two kinds of hearing loss: conductive deafness and sensorineural deafness. In *conductive deafness*, the hearing loss

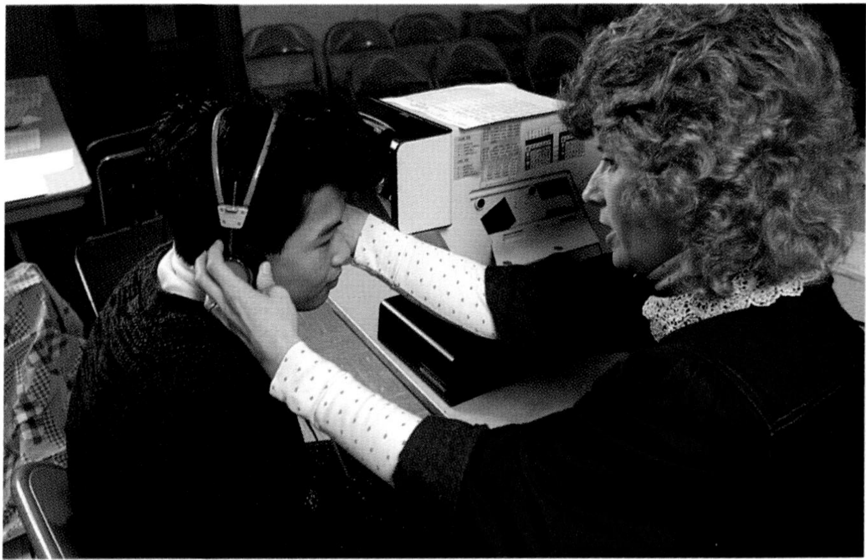

Hearing Tests. *Hearing tests are routinely given to children to detect early hearing problems or hearing loss.*

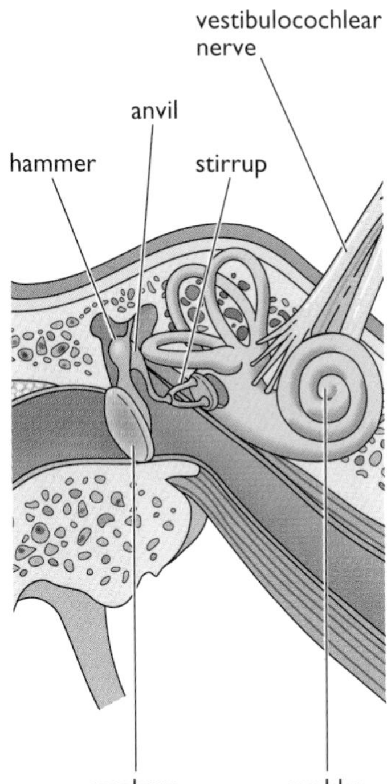

The Middle and Inner Ear. *The middle ear, which includes the eardrum, hammer, anvil, and stirrup, conducts sound to the inner ear. The inner ear—in particular the cochlea and vestibulocochlear nerve—translates sound into nerve impulses, which it sends to the brain.*

results from interference in the transmission of sounds through the outer and middle ear to the inner ear. *Sensorineural deafness* is the result of damage to the inner ear or to the auditory nerve, which conducts electrical impulses to the brain.

Conductive Deafness The buildup of earwax is one of the most common causes of conductive deafness. This wax, which is secreted by glands in the ear canal, may become hard and form a barrier that blocks out sounds. *Otosclerosis* is a form of conductive deafness in which an abnormal growth of bony tissue limits the mobility of the stirrup, or stapes. If the stirrup cannot move, it cannot transmit sound vibrations into the inner ear (see illustration: The Middle and Inner Ear). Both middle *ear infections* and damage to the middle ear from sudden changes in pressure can cause conductive deafness (See also EAR, 1.)

Sensorineural Deafness A common type of sensorineural deafness is *presbycusis*, or *age-related hearing loss*. Many people begin at about age 50 to experience hearing loss. This is usually caused by the deterioration of the cells of the cochlea, a cavity in the inner ear that converts sound vibrations to nerve impulses. Age-related hearing loss is sometimes accompanied by *tinnitus*, a ringing or buzzing in the ears. Younger people may experience sensorineural hearing loss from trauma, such as a blow to the ear, or continued exposure to loud noises. *Ménière's disease* produces recurring bouts of hearing loss, tinnitus, and vertigo (dizziness). It is caused by fluid buildup in the inner ear. Exposure to *rubella* (German measles) in the early stages of pregnancy can result in sensorineural deafness in the infant. Complications of other diseases, including chicken pox, influenza, meningitis, mononucleosis, and mumps, can damage hearing during childhood or later in life.

Treatment and Prevention Treatment of hearing loss depends on its causes and severity. If a buildup of earwax is dulling sounds, a physician can easily remove the excess material from the ear. Never try to remove it yourself, however, because you could puncture your eardrum. Otosclerosis can be treated by surgically removing the stirrup and replacing it with a fine wire substitute. *Hearing aids* help millions of people by amplifying the sounds that enter the ear, making them easier to distinguish. Modern hearing aids are very small, and many can fit entirely into the ear. A physician should be consulted to test and diagnose hearing loss before a hearing aid is purchased.

CONSULT A PHYSICIAN

Sensorineural deafness from birth is incurable, but deaf children can be taught to read lips, communicate in sign language, and sometimes speak vocally to some degree. Some forms of sensorineural deafness can be helped by an implant in the inner ear that stimulates the auditory nerve.

HEALTHY CHOICES

Hearing loss caused by prolonged exposure to excessively loud noise or music is preventable. People who work around loud machinery should wear ear protectors. It is also advisable to limit the volume when listening to music through earphones and to avoid standing too close to speakers at rock concerts. Finally, avoid inserting anything into the ears—it can puncture the eardrum and cause loss of hearing. (See also EAR INFECTIONS, 2; RUBELLA, 2.)

Heart Attack

In a heart attack, also called a myocardial infarction, a portion of the heart muscle suddenly dies. This tissue death is usually caused by a BLOOD CLOT in one of the coronary arteries—the vessels that supply oxygen-rich blood to the heart muscle. The clot cuts off blood supply to the heart. Heart attacks are fatal in about one-third of all cases. They are the leading cause of death in the United States.

Symptoms and Diagnosis The most common symptom of heart attack is sudden pain or pressure in the chest. Heart attack pain may range from mild to severe, but usually lasts at least 30 minutes and is not relieved by rest. Sometimes the pain is felt down the left arm, up into the jaw and back, or in the upper abdomen. It is also possible, however, for a heart attack to occur with no pain. Before the heart attack, a person may feel especially restless or apprehensive and during the attack may experience shortness of breath, cold and clammy skin, nausea or vomiting, and loss of consciousness. The initial attack may cause *congestive heart failure,* in which the heart cannot pump blood effectively, *arrhythmia* (irregular heartbeat), or damage to the valves of the heart.

A heart attack is diagnosed by considering the patient's history and symptoms. The physician is able to check the condition of the heart with an ELECTROCARDIOGRAM (ECG), a record of the heart's electrical activity.

Causes and Treatment The coronary artery blockage that causes a heart attack usually results from a blood clot that lodges in an artery already narrowed by a buildup of fatty deposits. This narrowing of the arteries, called ATHEROSCLEROSIS, may take many years to develop (see illustration: Elements of a Heart Attack). A number of factors are believed to contribute to atherosclerosis, including a diet high in salt, saturated fats, and cholesterol; obesity; cigarette smoking; stress; family

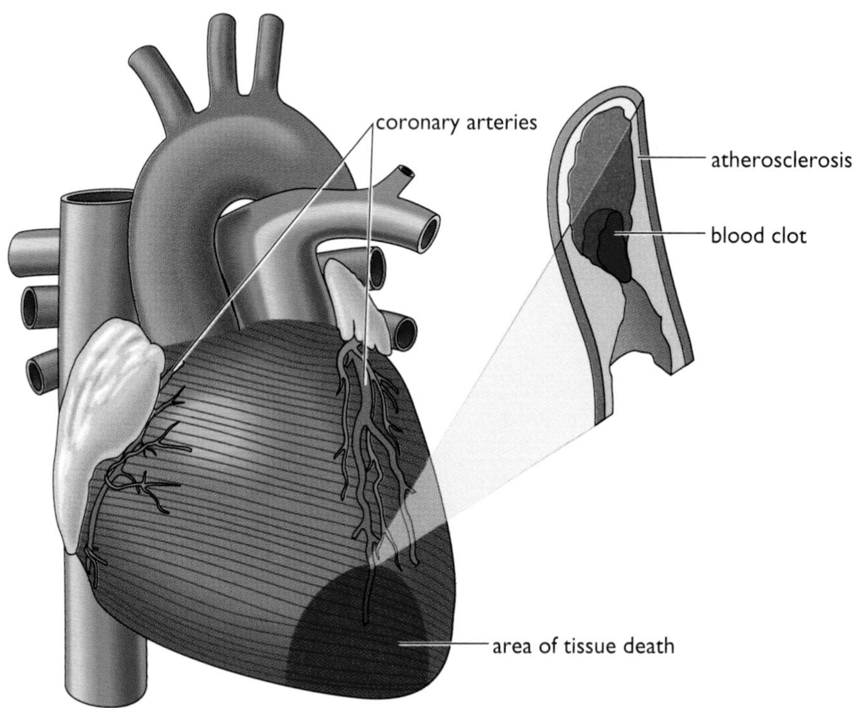

Elements of a Heart Attack. *In a heart attack, a coronary artery, already narrowed by atherosclerosis, becomes blocked by a blood clot. No longer supplied with blood and oxygen, the tissue on the other side of the blockage dies.*

history; and disorders such as HYPERTENSION (high blood pressure) and DIABETES.

When a heart attack is suspected, a person must receive immediate medical care. Treatment may include strong analgesics to relieve pain, oxygen therapy, and aspirin and drugs that dissolve blood clots. If the heart stops beating, the attending physician or paramedic will administer *cardiopulmonary resuscitation* (CPR).

To correct the problem that caused the blockage, *angioplasty* (a procedure to widen narrowed arteries) or coronary bypass surgery may be performed. *Beta-blockers,* drugs that make the heart slow down and use less oxygen, may be prescribed for long-term use after recovery.

HEALTHY CHOICES

Prevention You can help reduce the chance of heart attack by making these healthy habits part of your lifestyle: Exercise regularly; avoid smoking; try to manage stress; maintain ideal weight; and reduce consumption of foods high in salt, saturated fats, and cholesterol. (See also HEART DISEASE; HEART SURGERY; HEART, 1; BETA-BLOCKER, 7; CPR, 8.)

HEART DISEASE

Heart disease is the term used to describe a wide variety of disorders that affect the heart. Together these heart disorders are the leading cause of death and disability in the industrialized world. However, medical treatment and lifestyle changes have made it possible for millions of Americans with heart disease to continue to lead active lives.

RISK FACTORS

Heart disease affects men more frequently than women; it also tends to occur earlier in life in men. More women than men, however, die from heart disease each year—a phenomenon that is now being studied. The major types of heart disease are discussed below.

Coronary Artery Disease The heart muscle gets its supply of oxygen-rich blood from two coronary arteries. If the blood flow in these arteries is decreased, the heart may be damaged. Arteries may become less efficient because of ARTERIOSCLEROSIS, a hardening and thickening of artery walls, or be narrowed by ATHEROSCLEROSIS, a buildup of fatty deposits on the artery walls. Reduction of the blood flow to the heart muscle may cause *angina pectoris,* a pain in the chest during exercise.

A HEART ATTACK, or myocardial infarction, occurs when a coronary artery becomes completely blocked, resulting in the death of some portion of the heart muscle. A BLOOD CLOT in a narrowed artery can cause a heart attack. The most common symptom is sudden chest pain. Other symptoms include shortness of breath; a feeling of restlessness; cold, clammy skin; nausea; and loss of consciousness. It is possible, however, for a heart attack to occur with symptoms that are very mild or unnoticeable.

HEALTHY CHOICES

Treatment following a heart attack may include regular doses of aspirin and other drugs to dissolve blood clots, a procedure to widen narrowed arteries, or *coronary bypass* surgery. A drug called a *beta-blocker* may be prescribed to reduce the chance of a second heart attack by enlarging blood vessels. Lifestyle changes—modifying the diet, increasing exercise, quitting smoking, and reducing stress—are usually also part of the treatment plan. (See also BETA-BLOCKER, 7.)

Hypertensive Heart Disease The long-term effects of HYPERTENSION (high blood pressure) cause hypertensive heart disease, which causes the heart muscle to grow larger. If the high blood pressure is not adequately treated, the heart muscle will eventually fail. Hypertension also contributes to coronary artery disease. When diagnosed early, most hypertensive heart disease can be successfully treated with dietary changes and drugs that control hypertension.

Diseases of the Heart Valves The heart is made up of four chambers: a left and right atrium and a left and right ventricle. The four heart valves—the pulmonary valve, the mitral valve, the aortic valve, and the tricuspid valve—control the flow of blood between the chambers of the heart and the flow into and out of the heart (see illustration: The Heart). If a valve opening becomes narrowed, the reduced blood flow can result in enlargement of the heart chamber, congestive heart failure (see below), and atrial fibrillation (a type of irregular heartbeat). If a valve opening loses its shape and begins to sag, a condition called valve *prolapse,* blood flows backward instead of forward. Valve prolapse makes the heart work harder, which can eventually lead to heart muscle damage and congestive heart failure.

Treatment of heart valve problems involves diuretics, which reduce accumulation of fluid; medication to prevent blood clots; and drugs to control heart rate. In some cases, surgery may be necessary to repair or replace defective valves.

The Heart.

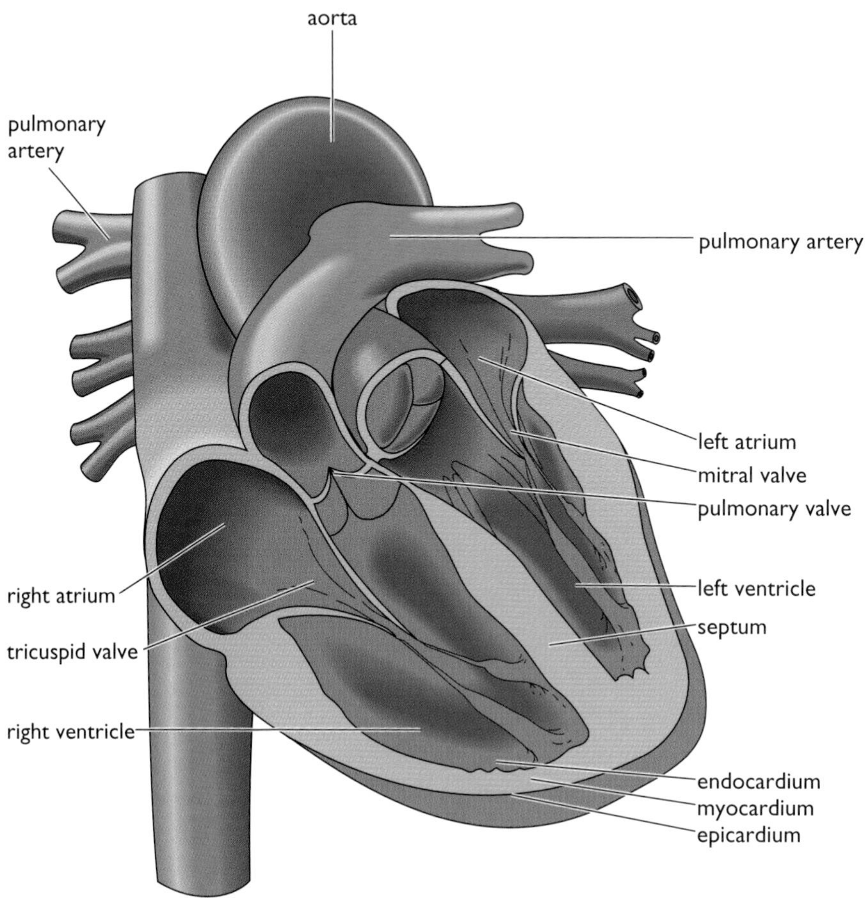

CONTROLLING RISK FACTORS		
Risk factors	**Effects on heart**	**Lifestyle changes**
Hypertension	Increases size of heart muscle; contributes to coronary heart disease; can result in heart failure	Modifying the diet, for example, by lowering the amount of salt; following drug therapy
Smoking	Increases heart rate and blood pressure; contributes to development of cholesterol in arteries	Quitting smoking
High blood cholesterol	Cholesterol deposits can clog arteries and possibly cause coronary artery disease, angina, and heart attack	Avoiding foods high in cholesterol and saturated fats
Obesity and sedentary lifestyle	Contribute to high blood pressure; increase heart rate; increase levels of fats in the blood	Exercising regularly; maintaining a well-balanced diet

Diseases of the Heart Tissue When the heart muscle itself is diseased, the condition is called *cardiomyopathy.* Some types of cardiomyopathy are inherited, and others are caused by nutritional deficiency, alcoholism, or certain prescription drugs.

RISK FACTORS ▶▶▶▶▶▶

Inflammation of the heart muscle, called *myocarditis,* is caused by viral infection, rheumatic fever, or exposure to certain chemicals or drugs. *Endocarditis* is an inflammation of the endocardium—the membrane that covers the inside of the heart. The condition can result in damage to the heart valves. *Pericarditis,* an inflammation of the tissue that encloses the heart, can be caused by a viral or bacterial infection. Treatment of diseases of the heart tissue involves treating the underlying cause with appropriate medications such as antibiotics and relieving symptoms. (See also ENDOCARDITIS, **2**; RHEUMATIC FEVER, **2**.)

Disorders of the Heart Rate and Rhythm Electrical impulses originating in a certain part of the heart control the heart rate. If these impulses are disturbed, the heart may beat too rapidly or too slowly. Such disorders are called *arrhythmias.* Treatment of arrhythmia may involve drugs, external electrical stimulus, or an implanted device called a *pacemaker.*

Sudden cardiac death is a heart rhythm disorder that can occur without warning and, for one out of four of its victims, without previous signs of heart problems. The most common cause of sudden cardiac death is *ventricular fibrillation,* rapid and irregular beating of the ventricle. Identifying those at risk of ventricular fibrillation may be the key to preventing sudden cardiac death. Treatment may include medication or having a device called a defibrillator implanted in the chest to restore normal heart rhythm with an electric shock when necessary.

Congestive Heart Failure In congestive heart failure, the heart's pumping ability becomes increasingly inefficient and the heart cannot maintain adequate circulation of the blood. The result is accumulation of blood in the liver, lungs, and intestines. Congestive heart failure is often a result of various kinds of heart disease, including coronary artery disease, heart attack, hypertension, heart valve disease, and arrhythmia.

Treatment for congestive heart failure includes lowering the amount of salt in the diet and using diuretics to reduce fluid accumulation and taking medication to strengthen the heartbeat or widen narrowed arteries. A *heart transplant* is a treatment of last resort for this serious heart condition.

Congenital Heart Disease This type of disease is present at birth, although diagnosis may not be made until later in life. About 1 in every 200 infants is born with some type of cardiovascular disease. Common congenital defects include a hole between the heart's chambers, narrowed heart valves, or a switch in the location of the two arteries of the heart. Often the cause of congenital heart disease is unknown, but certain genetic factors and viral infections (such as rubella) during pregnancy are known to play a role. (See also RUBELLA, 2.)

Symptoms of congenital heart disease include breathing difficulties, a bluish skin color, HEART MURMUR, and frequent respiratory infections. Surgical correction of many congenital diseases makes it possible for children to develop normally.

Diagnosis of Heart Disease The methods used to diagnose a specific heart disease include taking a detailed history of the patient's symptoms, listening to the heart with a *stethoscope* to detect any abnormalities in the heart's rhythm, and taking blood pressure readings. More specialized tests include an ELECTROCARDIOGRAM, also known as EKG or ECG, a recording of the electrical activities of the heart; a chest X ray; and an echocardiogram, a continuous image of the heart at work made by using sound waves.

Risk Factors for Heart Disease Some of the factors that contribute to heart disease, such as age, sex, and heredity, are beyond our control. Certain lifestyle habits are also risk factors, but lifestyle can be modified to help reduce the chance of developing heart disease (see chart: Controlling Risk Factors). A family history of heart disease or diabetes can also increase the risk of developing heart problems. (See also HEART SURGERY; TRANSPLANT SURGERY; HEART, 1; AEROBIC EXERCISE, 4; CHOLESTEROL, 4; FITNESS, 4.)

HEART MURMUR

A heart murmur is an unusual noise in the heart that a physician can hear through a stethoscope. A murmur may indicate an abnormal flow of blood through the chambers and valves of the heart. It may be caused by a congenital heart defect, such as a hole in the heart, or by inflammation of the membranes around the heart. Other causes include diseased heart valves that do not close tightly, and ARTERIOSCLEROSIS, hardening of the arteries. Not all heart murmurs indicate disease, and many require no treatment. However, a person with a heart murmur should always let the

surgeon or dentist know about it before any surgery or dental work is done, because precautions may need to be taken against endocarditis.

The cause of a heart murmur is diagnosed by determining the location and timing of the noise and by evaluating other symptoms experienced by the patient. A diagnosis may be confirmed with *echocardiography,* a device that uses sound waves to create a moving image of the heart as it works. (See also HEART DISEASE; HEART SURGERY; HEART, **1**; ENDOCARDITIS, **2**.)

Heart Surgery

Heart surgery includes a number of different operations performed on the heart. Just 40 years ago, surgery on the heart was very risky and, therefore, rare. Since that time, medical progress has made heart surgery safer and more effective.

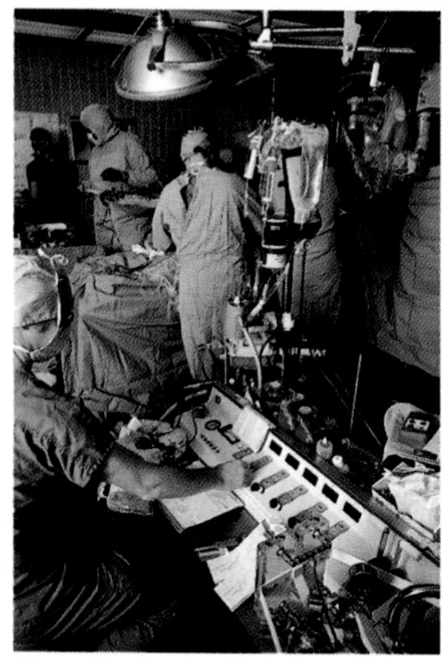

Open-Heart Surgery. *In open-heart surgery, a heart-lung machine pumps oxygen-rich blood through the body while the surgeons work on the patient's heart.*

Open-heart surgery is the general name for a group of procedures that involve opening the chest surgically to correct a defect or treat a serious heart condition. After the patient is placed under general ANESTHESIA, the heart is stopped and the patient is attached to a *heart-lung machine.* This machine keeps oxygen-rich blood circulating through the body while the operation is underway (see illustration: Open-Heart Surgery). Coronary artery bypass surgery, heart transplantation, artificial heart implantation, and some heart valve procedures are all types of open-heart surgery.

Certain other heart procedures, such as angioplasty and the insertion of wires for an artificial pacemaker, are performed through an opening made in a major vein or artery. They do not require open-heart surgery and are often carried out under a local anesthetic.

Coronary Artery Bypass Surgery First performed in 1967, bypass surgery is now used to treat over 300,000 Americans a year. The most likely candidates are individuals with one or more badly blocked coronary arteries. The procedure involves taking a segment of a healthy blood vessel, usually from a leg, and using it to create an alternate route for blood to flow around the blockage in the artery. Although bypass surgery significantly improves the patient's health, it is not a cure for heart disease. Lifestyle changes—including a low-fat diet and a regular exercise program—are necessary after the surgery to prevent the formation of new plaque deposits.

Heart Valve Surgery Heart valve surgery may be performed when a valve leaks or becomes narrowed (called valve *stenosis*). The valve is repaired or replaced with an artificial valve made of metal, plastic, or animal tissue. In some cases, a valve from a human donor is used. Long-term treatment with anticoagulant drugs is usually prescribed to prevent BLOOD CLOTS.

Heart Transplant In 1967, Dr. Christiaan Barnard of South Africa made history by performing the first human heart transplant. Early results were poor, however, because the patient's *immune system* rejected the transplanted heart. The operation is still very complicated and very risky, but advances in drugs that suppress immune response and reduce rejection have increased the life expectancy of transplant recipients. Heart transplantation is generally reserved for patients who have progressive, untreatable heart disease but whose other body systems are healthy. The donor heart usually comes from a person who has died from an illness or accident that did not damage the heart. (See also IMMUNE SYSTEM, **1**.)

Artificial Heart Implantation Medical researchers are still working to perfect an artificial heart, a mechanical substitute that can be implanted and take over or improve the heart's function. The Jarvik-7 artificial heart, first used in 1982, replaced both of the heart's ventricles, pumping blood to the lungs and body. In recent years, attention has turned to other types of artificial hearts that help the patient's own heart pump blood. They are used temporarily until a human heart transplant operation can be performed.

Artificial Pacemaker Implantation Surgical implantation of an artificial pacemaker can help patients with heart rate and rhythm disorders. The small battery-powered device is wired to the heart and produces electrical impulses that maintain a regular heartbeat. Most pacemakers are implanted under the skin of the chest. Other types, designed to be used for shorter periods, are carried outside the body.

Angioplasty Angioplasty is used to open arteries narrowed by ATHEROSCLEROSIS, the buildup of fatty deposits called *plaque* inside arteries. It may also be used to widen narrowed heart valves. Angioplasty involves threading a fine wire with an inflatable balloonlike top into a large artery; it is then guided through the arteries to the narrowed section. The balloon is then inflated, which flattens the plaque deposits and widens the artery.

Angioplasty, performed under local anesthetic, does have risks. During angioplasty an artery may break or some of the plaque may come loose from the artery wall and block the narrowed vessel farther along. In addition, plaque buildup frequently recurs, so angioplasty may be required again in 2 or 3 years. (See also HEART ATTACK; HEART DISEASE; TRANSPLANT SURGERY; HEART, **1**.)

HEMOPHILIA

Hemophilia is an inherited bleeding disorder in which the blood does not clot. Those affected are almost exclusively male; 1 boy in 10,000 is born with the disease.

Causes Hemophilia is caused by low levels of one of the proteins, or factors, involved in clotting blood—either factor VIII or factor IX. A blood test can show the levels of these factors.

In hemophilia a defective gene is usually passed from mother to son. A man with the disorder may also pass it on to some of his sons, and all of his daughters will become carriers. However, about one-third of those with hemophilia have no family history.

Symptoms Symptoms usually become apparent when a boy first begins to crawl and walk: He may develop bruises on the knees or hemorrhage into joints. Recurrent bleeding into the joints is common and quite painful. Unless treated, this can damage the joint. Bleeding may also occur spontaneously. Internal bleeding may be identified by blood in the stool or urine or by extensive bruising. Superficial injuries or minor surgery such as tooth extraction can produce excessive bleeding.

Treatment Fifty years ago, very few boys with hemophilia lived to adulthood. Today, however, bleeding episodes can be controlled by regular infusions of the missing clotting factor. Hospitalization is required for serious or unusual bleeding.

About 10 percent of those with hemophilia develop antibodies that resist the infusions of clotting factor. In these individuals treatment is especially difficult.

The risk of AIDS has become an issue of special concern among those with hemophilia. In the early years of the AIDS epidemic, much of the blood received through routine donations was untested. As a result, many people with hemophilia have contracted the AIDS virus (HIV). Blood used for transfusions is now tested, so the risk of becoming infected with HIV or some other communicable disease is minimal.

Precautions Most people with hemophilia can lead relatively normal lives. Extra precautions must be taken, however, to avoid injury. Activities such as football and rugby are unwise, but swimming and walking are encouraged. Genetic counseling is recommended for the relatives of those with hemophilia to determine who may be at risk of transmitting the disorder to their children. (See also BLOOD CLOT; GENETIC SCREENING, **6**; GENETIC COUNSELOR, **9**.)

HEMORRHOIDS

Hemorrhoids are swollen veins in the lining of the anus or rectum. They are caused by straining during difficult bowel movements or during childbirth. Hemorrhoids are common, especially among obese people and pregnant women. Although hemorrhoids can be painful and annoying, they are not serious.

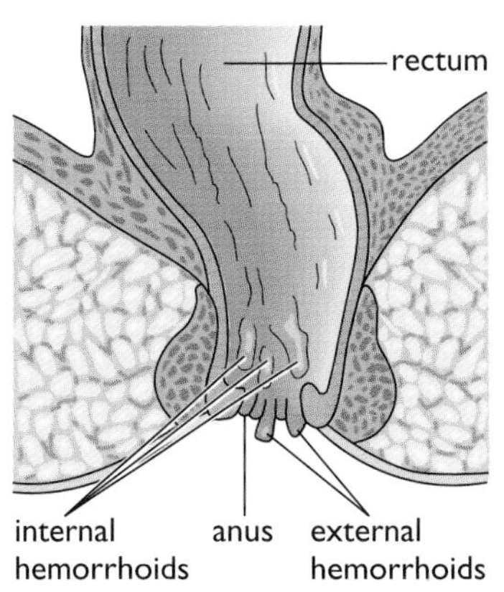

Internal and External Hemorrhoids. *This cross section of the lower rectum shows where hemorrhoids can occur internally and externally.*

Symptoms Hemorrhoids can be internal, in the wall of the rectum, or external, in the skin of the anus (see illustration: Internal and External Hemorrhoids). The main symptoms of hemorrhoids are pain during bowel movements, bright red blood in the stool or on toilet paper, and itching and burning around the anus. In some cases, a blood clot forms in the hemorrhoid, causing severe pain. Any person who has bleeding from the rectum or blood in the stool should consult a physician to make sure the cause is hemorrhoids and not intestinal polyps or COLORECTAL CANCER.

Treatment and Prevention Mild attacks of hemorrhoids can be treated using over-the-counter hemorrhoid creams and ointments to reduce swelling and itching. Warm baths may help relieve the pain of hemorrhoids. Physicians can remove large hemorrhoids by tying them off with rubber bands. After a few days, the hemorrhoids wither and fall off painlessly. Hemorrhoids can also be removed surgically.

Maintaining a high-fiber diet and drinking plenty of fluids may help prevent constipation and the straining that can cause hemorrhoids. Use of laxatives should be kept to a minimum, but occasional use of stool softeners may be helpful. (See also ANUS, **1**; RECTUM, **1**.)

HERNIA

A hernia, or rupture, occurs when an organ or other body tissue breaks through the thin sheet of muscle that normally contains it. Most hernias are in or near the abdomen and involve the intestine. They most commonly occur near the navel (*umbilical hernia*), in the groin (*inguinal hernia*), at the top of the thigh (*femoral hernia*), and through the diaphragm separating the chest and the abdomen (*hiatal hernia*) (see illustration: Two Common Types of Hernia).

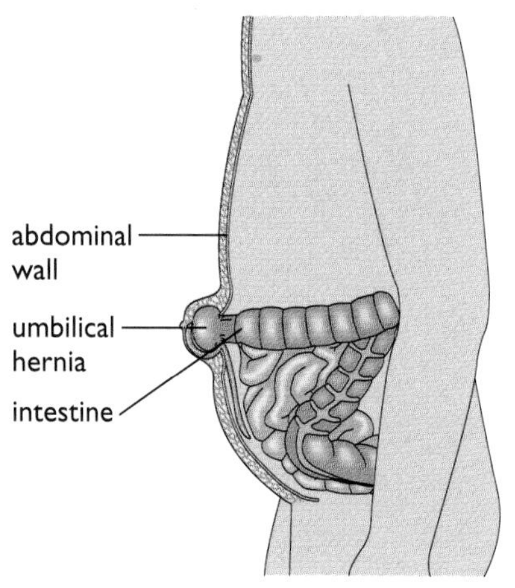

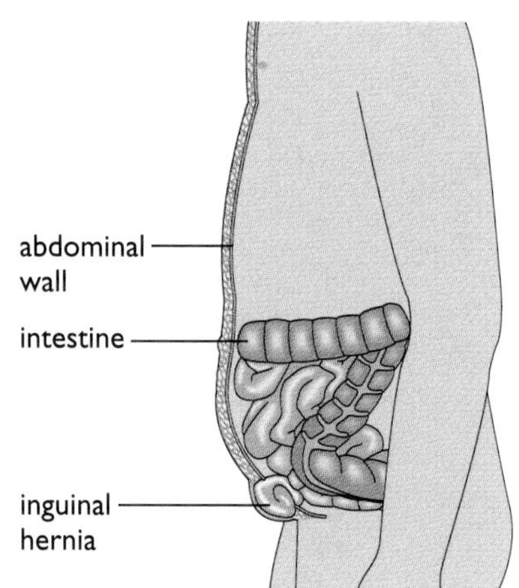

Two Common Types of Hernia. *Most hernias occur when a portion of the intestine pushes through the abdominal wall, which normally contains it.*

Causes and Symptoms Hernias usually occur as the result of a sudden strain, such as heavy lifting, a congenital weakness, or weakening due to abdominal surgery. Extreme weight gain or a long period of heavy coughing can also trigger hernias. Symptoms include discomfort when lifting or bending, sudden swelling under the skin, and tenderness.

Treatment In the case of a mild hernia, the intestine can sometimes be pushed back into place by a physician. Then the hernia can be held in place by a truss or special corset until it heals. In more serious cases, a section of bulging intestine may become pinched or twisted, blocking the intestine or its blood supply. This condition, called a *strangulated hernia,* can be extremely painful and eventually cause GANGRENE. This type of hernia requires surgery promptly to deal with the intestinal blockage and return the intestine to its proper place. The surgeon also repairs and reinforces the break in the muscle wall, in some instances adding a patch of synthetic material.

HEALTHY CHOICES

Prevention There is no sure way of preventing hernias. The best preventive measures are to stay fit and to use proper techniques when lifting heavy objects.

HICCUPS

Hiccups are sudden, repeated, uncontrolled contractions of the *diaphragm,* a muscle below the chest that aids breathing. When the diaphragm contracts abruptly, air is pulled through the vocal cords as the skin flap over them closes, causing the "hic" of the hiccups. Hiccups are rarely serious, but they can be annoying.

In most cases, the cause of hiccups is unknown. They may be caused by irritation of the nerve that controls the diaphragm as when a person has a minor stomach disorder or has eaten or drunk excessively. On rare occasions, persistent hiccups signal a more serious problem, such as a brain lesion or a tumor in the chest.

Most hiccups go away by themselves after a short time. Popular but unproven remedies include holding your breath or breathing into a paper bag. If hiccups continue for hours or days, a physician may prescribe a tranquilizer.

HODGKIN'S DISEASE

Hodgkin's disease, also known as Hodgkin's lymphoma, is a cancer of the lymphatic system characterized by enlargement of the lymph nodes. If untreated, Hodgkin's disease will spread throughout the body and interfere with the functioning of the *immune system.* It is a rare disease that occurs most frequently in young adults.

The first symptom of Hodgkin's disease is usually painless swelling of the lymph nodes in the neck, armpits, or groin. Other symptoms may include fatigue, fever, and weight loss. Diagnosis may be made through an X ray or through a lymph tissue or bone marrow BIOPSY, in which tissue is extracted for analysis.

The cause of Hodgkin's disease is not known. With early diagnosis and proper treatment, however, nearly 90 percent of patients can be completely cured. In the early stages RADIATION THERAPY is used. At a more advanced stage CHEMOTHERAPY (the use of anticancer drugs) may be used alone or with radiation therapy. (See also LYMPHOMA; LYMPHATIC SYSTEM, **1.**)

HYPERTENSION

Hypertension, also called high blood pressure, is a condition in which blood pressure is consistently above normal. Blood pressure is the force exerted by the blood on the walls of the arteries. Normal blood pressure for an adult is about 120/80. Measured in millimeters of mercury (120/80 mm Hg), the first number, the *systolic pressure,* is a reading of the maximum pressure as the heart pumps blood into the arteries; the second number, the *diastolic pressure,* measures the lowest pressure as the arteries are waiting for the next heartbeat. Consistent readings above 140/90 are generally defined as high blood pressure.

RISK FACTORS ▶ ▶ ▶ ▶ ▶ ▶

It is estimated that hypertension affects one in four American adults and is responsible for 30,000 deaths annually. Among those under the age of 50, men are more likely than women to have high blood pressure. The disease occurs among nonwhites two to five times more frequently than among whites.

Symptoms and Diagnosis Hypertension is often called the silent killer because it frequently has no symptoms. In fact, as many as half of those with high blood pressure do not know that they have it. Severe cases of high blood pressure may produce symptoms including headaches, dizziness, fatigue, vision problems, or heart failure.

THINGS YOU CAN DO TO CONTROL HYPERTENSION

- Do not smoke.
- Maintain ideal weight.
- Avoid alcohol consumption or drink in moderation.
- Exercise regularly.
- Learn to manage stress in your life.

It is easy to diagnose high blood pressure with a cuff and pressure gauge called a *sphygmomanometer* (sfig moh muh NAHM uh ter). However, blood pressure tends to vary, and a single high reading does not necessarily indicate hypertension.

Causes and Risk Factors Hypertension is either primary or secondary, depending on whether it is caused by another disorder. If the cause of hypertension can be traced to a specific disorder, such as ARTERIOSCLEROSIS or kidney disease, it is called *secondary hypertension.* In more than 90 percent of the cases, however, the cause of hypertension is unknown; this is considered *primary* (or essential) *hypertension.* Risk factors that have been linked to primary hypertension include a family history of the disease, obesity, cigarette smoking, extreme stress, lack of exercise, and excessive consumption of alcohol. For women, pregnancy or the use of birth-control pills may also increase the risk of hypertension. Too much salt in the diet has traditionally been associated with hypertension; recent research suggests that the effects of a high-salt diet may be less significant than was previously thought.

Complications Although hypertension is sometimes a result or symptom of another disorder, the condition itself can cause many complications over time. Untreated high blood pressure damages the cardiovascular system. The heart must work harder and becomes weaker. Subjected to constant elevated pressure, artery walls tend to thicken and lose their flexibility. Plaque can build up more quickly on damaged artery walls, causing ATHEROSCLEROSIS. Damage to blood vessels can also lead to loss of vision, KIDNEY DISORDERS, or STROKE, while severe high pressure can rupture an artery wall.

Treatment To reduce hypertension, physicians usually begin by recommending weight loss and lifestyle changes such as cutting down on salty foods, quitting smoking, reducing alcohol consumption, increasing exercise, and trying to limit the amount of stress (see chart: Things You Can Do to Control Hypertension). Sometimes these measures are enough to lower blood pressure to a normal range.

If medication is needed, however, there are several types of drugs to control hypertension (*antihypertensive drugs*). *Diuretics* help rid the body of excess fluids and salt. *Beta-blockers* reduce heart rate and the volume of blood pumped by the heart. *Vasodilators* relax the artery wall muscles so that arteries become wider. Once an effective drug or combination of drugs is found, the patient usually must take it for life. Once antihypertensive drugs are prescribed, it is important to take them daily as directed and not to stop them suddenly. (See also CARDIOVASCULAR DISEASE; HEART DISEASE; BLOOD PRESSURE, 1; STRESS, 5; STRESS-MANAGEMENT TECHNIQUES, 5; BETA-BLOCKER, 7.)

Hyperventilation

Hyperventilation is overly rapid or deep breathing that leads to a loss of carbon dioxide in the blood. It is a common reaction to anxiety or panic.

People who are hyperventilating cannot take in enough air and may feel faint or dizzy. Other symptoms may include headaches, chest pains, and numbness or spasms in the hands, arms, and feet. These symptoms can increase the anxiety or panic that a person feels, producing hyperventilation syndrome, a feeling of approaching disaster.

Hyperventilation. *A person who is hyperventilating can breathe into a paper bag to restore the proper balance of gases in the blood.*

Hyperventilation can also be caused by an increase in the body's metabolism, by DIABETES and certain other diseases, and by some drugs. Treatment involves getting the person suffering from hyperventilation to breathe more slowly or to breathe into a paper bag. Breathing into a bag forces the person to inhale the carbon dioxide that has been exhaled, which causes the carbon dioxide level in the blood to return to normal.

Immunotherapy

Immunotherapy is a means of fighting disease by chemicals that alter the response of the body's *immune system*. It is used to treat ALLERGIES as well as to fight certain kinds of CANCER.

Allergy Immunotherapy When used as a preventive treatment for allergies to substances such as pollen and bee venom, immunotherapy involves injecting increasingly larger doses of an *allergen*—the substance to which the person is allergic. The aim of this procedure is to get the body's immune system to build up tolerance to the allergen. Following any immunotherapy injection there is the risk of *anaphylactic shock*, an extreme and dangerous allergic reaction. Allergy immunotherapy is always, therefore, conducted under medical supervision.

Cancer Immunotherapy In people suffering from cancer, immunotherapy is sometimes used alongside traditional treatments to stimulate the body's immune response to *malignant* (cancerous) cells. One type of immunotherapy uses substances that stimulate the immune system in a general way. Another technique involves injecting the patient with tumor cells that have been taken from another person with the same disease and rendered harmless through irradiation. This causes the patient's immune system to produce its own antibodies to attack the tumor cells. Recently, tumor-fighting antibodies have been produced artificially through *genetic engineering*.

Sometimes cancer immunotherapy causes an allergic reaction in the person or interferes with—rather than helps—the body's fight against cancer. Although still in experimental stages, cancer immunotherapy holds great promise for the future. (See also IMMUNE SYSTEM, **1**; GENETIC ENGINEERING, **8**.)

INCONTINENCE

Incontinence is the inability to control the bladder or, less commonly, the bowels, resulting in the release of urine or feces. Incontinence is often a symptom of another disorder.

Symptoms and Causes of Incontinence The main symptom of urinary incontinence is an involuntary escape of urine from the bladder. Sometimes just a small amount of urine escapes when a person coughs, sneezes, or runs. Occasionally a person experiences a complete loss of bladder control. Incontinence is most common among the elderly and among women.

RISK FACTORS ▶▶▶▶▶▶

Urinary incontinence may be caused by a number of disorders, including *cystitis* (bladder infection), DIABETES, MULTIPLE SCLEROSIS, a STROKE, or enlargement of the prostate gland. Childbirth sometimes weakens the muscles that control the outflow of urine, causing incontinence.

With fecal incontinence there is an inability to control bowel movements. A common cause of fecal incontinence is *fecal impaction,* in which feces become lodged in the rectum. The rectum becomes irritated and some feces leak out. Other causes of fecal incontinence include surgery or an attack of severe diarrhea. Fecal incontinence sometimes occurs in elderly people.

Treatment Treatment of incontinence depends on the cause of the disorder. Cystitis, for example, can be treated with antibiotics. Special exercises for pelvic muscles can restore control to many women who experience incontinence after childbirth. A high-fiber diet may help prevent fecal impaction. When incontinence is untreatable, special undergarments may be worn to lessen discomfort and embarrassment.

INDIGESTION

see STOMACHACHE/INDIGESTION

JAUNDICE

Jaundice is a condition in which the skin and whites of the eyes become distinctly yellow. It is not actually a disease but a symptom of several diseases of the liver, gallbladder, and bile duct.

The yellow coloring is caused by an excess of a substance called *bilirubin* in the body. Bilirubin is a pigment produced by the liver during the breakdown of old red blood cells. Normally, the bilirubin is mixed with bile and excreted into the intestines. When anything interferes with this process, bilirubin builds up in the bloodstream and accumulates in the skin (see illustration: Causes of Jaundice).

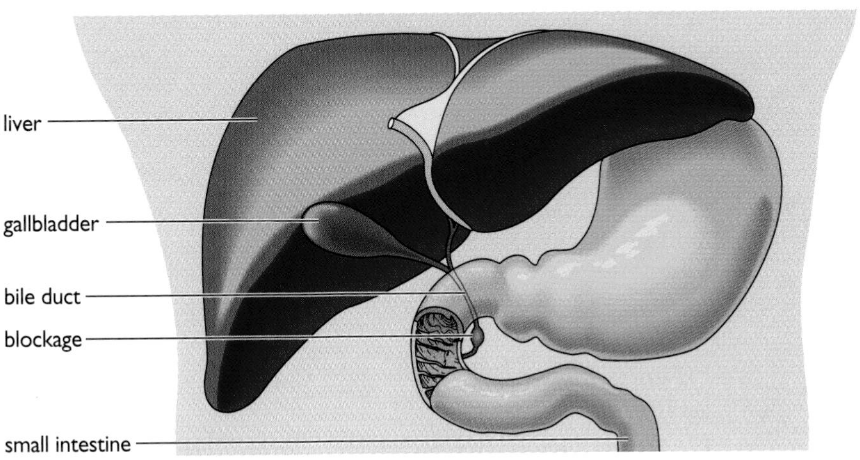

Causes of Jaundice. *Jaundice results from an excess of bilirubin, the bile pigments produced in the liver while breaking down red blood cells. The excess may be caused by an overproduction of bilirubin, a failure of the liver to process the bilirubin, or a blockage of the bile ducts connecting the liver, gallbladder, and small intestine.*

In adults, jaundice is often a symptom of a liver disease such as *hepatitis* or CIRRHOSIS of the liver, or a symptom of gallbladder disease or cancer of the bile duct. It can also indicate a type of ANEMIA or an infection such as *malaria*.

Neonatal Jaundice Jaundice occurs in more than 60 percent of full-term newborns. In most cases, this neonatal (newborn) jaundice is not a serious condition. It indicates that the infant's body is breaking down fetal red blood cells but that there is a deficiency in the enzyme that helps the liver excrete bilirubin. The problem usually corrects itself in a week to 10 days. In more serious cases, the newborn is placed under a high-intensity light that converts the excess bilirubin into a form that can be excreted from the body.

Diagnosis and Treatment When jaundice occurs, the physician may perform blood tests and examine the person's feces and urine to try to determine the cause. A liver BIOPSY, removal of a small sample of liver cells for examination, may also be necessary. When the underlying cause of the jaundice is identified and successfully treated, the skin and whites of the eyes return to normal color. (See also LIVER, **1**; HEPATITIS, **2**; MALARIA, **2**.)

KAPOSI'S SARCOMA

Kaposi's sarcoma (KAP uh zeez sahr KOH muh) is a condition characterized by cancerous skin TUMORS. A deadly form of this disease is now associated with *AIDS*.

Before 1981, Kaposi's sarcoma was a relatively rare disease, occurring mostly among elderly men or in organ transplant patients who were receiving drugs that suppressed their immune systems. With the emergence of AIDS, however, the disease has become more common and more serious. AIDS-related Kaposi's sarcoma is particularly dangerous because the damaged immune system is unable to fight the disease.

Symptoms and Diagnosis The first symptom of Kaposi's sarcoma is the appearance of red or purplish sores or lumps on the skin or on mucous membranes. Often the lesions begin on the feet and ankles but spread up the body to appear on the hands and arms. AIDS-related Kaposi's sarcoma often spreads rapidly through the gastrointestinal and respiratory tracts, causing internal bleeding. Diagnosis is made through a BIOPSY, the surgical removal and analysis of tissue from one of the skin tumors.

Treatment Milder forms of Kaposi's sarcoma are usually effectively treated with RADIATION THERAPY. In more severe cases, CHEMOTHERAPY (the use of anticancer drugs) may be needed to slow the spread of the disease. These drugs, however, have drawbacks because they can further weaken the immune system. (See also CANCER; IMMUNE SYSTEM, **1**; AIDS, **2**.)

KIDNEY DISORDERS

Kidney (or renal) disorders are abnormal changes in the functioning of the kidneys, the organs that filter extra water and waste substances from the blood. Unless both kidneys are affected, these disorders are rarely life-threatening because one kidney can perform the necessary functions. The symptoms of kidney disorders are often mild until the disease has progressed to a serious or irreversible stage.

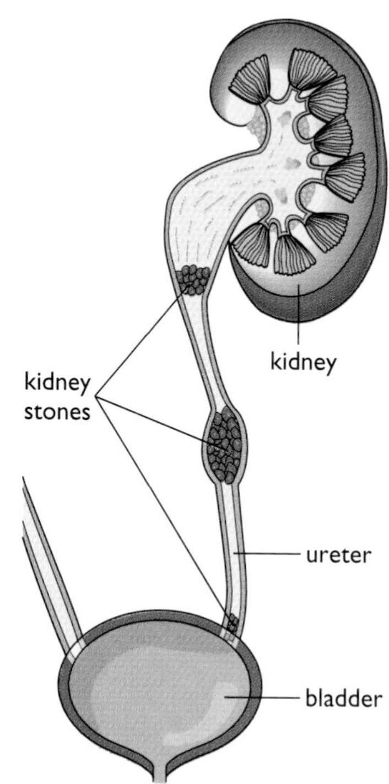

Kidney Stones. *Kidney stones can lodge in the ureter (the duct that carries urine from the kidney).*

Types of Disorders *Kidney stones* are the most common type of kidney disorder (see illustration: Kidney Stones). A kidney stone is a hard mineral deposit that forms in the kidneys and then travels down the urinary tract until it passes out of the body. A kidney stone can cause severe pain and even block the system, causing urine to back up in the kidneys. Treatment of such kidney stones usually consists of surgery to remove the stones.

Nephritis is an infection or inflammation of the kidneys. It often occurs as a reaction to a drug or a toxic combination of drugs. Nephritis can be symptomless and can lead to *kidney failure* (also called renal failure), a condition in which the kidneys are unable to filter waste. For that reason, physicians closely monitor the effects of drugs known to damage the kidneys.

Kidney failure may also occur suddenly as a result of injury, SHOCK, or illness. This is a life-threatening condition that requires hospitalization and DIALYSIS, the use of an artificial kidney machine to cleanse the blood of waste products. With care, the kidneys usually resume functioning on their own after a few weeks or months.

Chronic renal failure develops gradually. Symptoms include weight loss, vomiting, fatigue, headaches, and shortness of breath. HYPERTENSION (high blood pressure) and DIABETES are common causes of chronic renal failure. Untreated, chronic renal failure can develop into a life-threatening condition called *end-stage renal failure,* characterized by intense itching, vomiting, and lethargy. Without undergoing regular dialysis or a *kidney transplant,* the patient will lapse into a coma and die. People who undergo TRANSPLANT SURGERY have an excellent chance of complete recovery.

Treatment and Prevention To prevent kidney disorders, underlying diseases such as hypertension and diabetes need to be controlled. Treatment for all types of kidney failure involves following a low-protein diet, restricting salt intake, and controlling blood pressure. (See also KIDNEY, **1**; URINARY TRACT, **1**.)

LASER SURGERY

Laser surgery is the technique of using lasers to operate on areas of the body where precision is required and access may be difficult. *Lasers* are devices that transform and amplify light of various frequencies into small and intense beams of radiation. Laser surgery is often used in operations involving the eye and reproductive system and in the treatment of TUMORS or other abnormal growths in the eye and throat. It is also used to reduce pain in torn muscles, sprained ligaments, and inflamed joints and tendons.

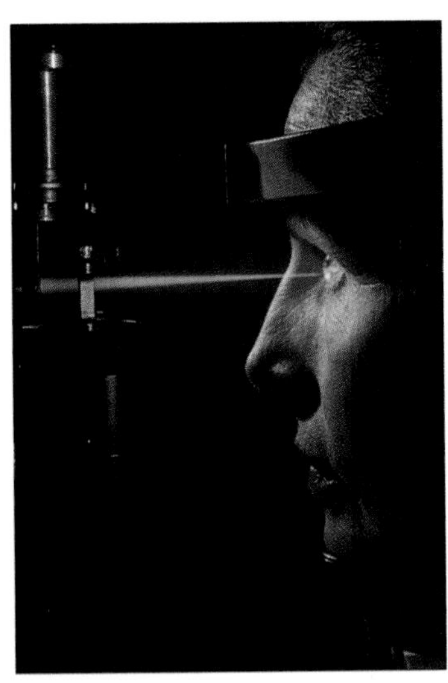

Laser Surgery. *Laser technology is used in the treatment of many eye problems.*

How Laser Surgery Works *High-intensity laser* beams cut through tissue and, at the same time, cause blood to clot. Because the beam destroys cells directly below it but does not damage adjacent cells, laser surgery is useful in the treatment of some tumors. *Low-intensity laser* beams reduce pain and swelling and stimulate healing by improving the flow of blood and lymph (clear liquid containing white blood cells) through the tissue. Lasers also reduce the production of certain chemical substances that stimulate inflammation and cause pain.

Uses of Laser Surgery Laser surgery is especially useful in treating EYE DISORDERS. It can reduce the pressure inside the eye caused by GLAUCOMA, repair tears in the retina, and remove tumors around the eye. Laser surgery is sometimes used to treat reproductive system problems, such as blocked fallopian tubes, and to remove small birthmarks.

Physicians hope to be able to use lasers to remove deposits of plaque from inside people's arteries, destroy bladder and kidney stones, and remove some tumors of the brain and spinal cord in the future. (See also SURGERY.)

LEUKEMIA

Leukemia is any of several types of CANCER that affect the blood-forming tissues of the body, including the *bone marrow* and the lymphatic system. The disease is characterized by an increase in abnormal white blood cells (*leukocytes*). These abnormal cells accumulate in the blood-forming tissue and interfere with the production of healthy red and white blood cells. This makes a person with leukemia highly vulnerable to infection, ANEMIA, and bleeding. The abnormal cells may also invade the bloodstream and affect the function of vital organs.

TYPES OF LEUKEMIA		
Type of leukemia	**Characterization by white blood cell type**	**People most commonly affected**
Chronic myeloid leukemia (CML)	Uncontrolled increase of abnormal granulocytes, a type of white blood cell produced in the bone marrow	Adults over 35
Acute myeloblastic leukemia (AML)	Uncontrolled increase of myeloblasts, or immature granulocytes	Adults over 35
Chronic lymphocytic leukemia (CLL)	Uncontrolled increase of abnormal lymphocytes, a type of white blood cell produced in the lymphatic system and bone marrow	Adults over 50
Acute lymphoblastic leukemia (ALL)	Uncontrolled increase of lymphoblasts, or immature lymphocytes	Children

There are several different types of leukemia, classified according to how quickly the disease develops (acute or chronic) and what type of abnormal white blood cell is causing the disease (see chart: Types of Leukemia). Without treatment, all forms of leukemia are fatal.

Symptoms and Diagnosis The first symptoms of leukemia may be a sudden fever and severe throat infection. Other symptoms include bleeding from the gums and nose, swollen lymph nodes, bruising without trauma or injury, fatigue, bone pain, and anemia. The onset of symptoms in chronic leukemia is usually slower than in acute leukemia; it may be marked by continuing fever and fatigue as well as progressive weight loss and may continue for years without showing major problems.

An initial diagnosis of leukemia may be based on a blood test. The diagnosis can be confirmed by examining bone marrow cells obtained through a BIOPSY.

Causes and Risk Factors The causes of leukemia are unknown. Several risk factors, however, have been identified, including exposure to radiation, drugs, and certain chemicals and viruses. The disease may also have a genetic component.

Treatment and Outlook The aim of leukemia therapy is to slow or stop the reproduction of abnormal cells and allow healthy cells to reproduce normally. Treatment usually involves transfusions of healthy blood cells as well as CHEMOTHERAPY (the use of anticancer drugs) and RADIATION THERAPY. A procedure known as *bone marrow transplantation,* in which healthy bone marrow cells are removed from a donor and injected into the bloodstream of the person with leukemia, has provided hope for many with leukemia. It does, however, carry great risks: Infections are common, and sometimes transplanted marrow is rejected by the body. A new, safer procedure involves removing marrow from the leukemia patient, treating it with anticancer drugs, and then returning it to the person.

The chances for surviving leukemia have improved significantly over the last 30 years, although certain types are still impossible to cure. (See also IMMUNOTHERAPY; BLOOD, **1**; BONE MARROW, **1**.)

Liver Disease see CIRRHOSIS

Lung Cancer

Lung cancer is a malignant TUMOR in the lungs caused by the uncontrolled growth and spread of abnormal cells. If not treated at an early stage, the CANCER may metastasize (muh TASS tuh size), or spread, to other parts of the body, including the liver, brain, and bones. Lung cancer occurs most frequently in people over 40. It is the leading cause of cancer death of both men and women in the United States.

Dangers of Smoking. *Smoking is the main cause of lung cancer. Just inhaling other people's smoke over a long period of time increases your chances of developing lung cancer.*

Symptoms and Diagnosis The most common symptom of lung cancer is a persistent cough, which may produce sputum (mucus) streaked with blood. There may also be hoarseness, chest pain, shortness of breath, and a loss of appetite. The disease may cause other lung problems such as pneumonia or a collapsed lung. As the cancer metastasizes to other organs, pain, weight loss, weakness, and other symptoms may occur.

Unfortunately, in many cases, the symptoms of lung cancer do not begin until the tumor is in an advanced stage. The disease is often discovered when a chest X ray reveals a shadow on the lung. A microscopic examination of the patient's sputum may confirm the presence of cancerous cells. A physician may also insert a special instrument down the airway to examine the lungs and collect tissue for a BIOPSY of the tumor.

Causes and Risk Factors Nearly 85 percent of all lung cancers are caused by *cigarette smoking.* Heavy smoking and smoking that began at a young age increase the risk of developing the disease. *Secondhand smoke,* or smoke you inhale from another person's cigarette, is also a risk factor. Other possible factors include prolonged exposure to asbestos, certain industrial chemicals, and radon gas.

Treatment and Prevention If lung cancer is diagnosed early—before it has metastasized to other parts of the body—removal of part or all of the lung is the usual treatment. For more advanced cancers, RADIATION THERAPY and CHEMOTHERAPY (use of anticancer drugs) may be used to contain the spread of the tumor or destroy cancerous cells.

HEALTHY CHOICES

The best way to prevent lung cancer is to stop smoking or not to start. People who do smoke should have annual chest X rays and periodic examinations of sputum. (See also SMOKING, 7; TOBACCO, 7; RADON, 8.)

Lung Disease

Lung disease refers to a variety of disorders that affect the lungs and reduce their ability to provide oxygen to and remove carbon dioxide from the blood. Major lung diseases described in separate entries include *bronchitis,* EMPHYSEMA, LUNG CANCER, PLEURISY, and *pneumonia.* Additional lung diseases include the following.

Pneumothorax Also called collapsed lung, pneumothorax is a condition in which air enters the space between the lungs and the chest wall.

The resulting pressure makes it difficult for the lungs to expand normally and can seriously hinder breathing. Pneumothorax can occur as a complication of another lung disease (especially emphysema), as the result of a rib fracture or other chest injury, or for no apparent reason. Its symptoms include shortness of breath and chest pain. A serious pneumothorax requires hospitalization and the suctioning of air from the cavity; a minor pneumothorax may require no treatment.

Pulmonary Embolism This life-threatening condition develops when an *embolism,* usually a blood clot, blocks the pulmonary artery or one of its branches in the lung. This condition, which causes roughly 50,000 deaths annually in the United States, causes sudden chest pain, shortness of breath, rapid pulse, sweating, and a cough that may produce blood-streaked sputum. A pulmonary embolism is diagnosed by X ray and treated with anticoagulant drugs or, in severe cases, by emergency surgery.

RISK FACTORS ▶▶▶▶▶▶

Occupation-Related Lung Diseases *Asbestosis* develops when asbestos fibers from insulation or other materials are inhaled and accumulate in the lungs. The lungs become irritated by the fibers, forming scar tissue, a condition called *pulmonary fibrosis.* As a result, the lungs lose their elasticity, which leads to increasing shortness of breath, dry cough, and possibly the development of tuberculosis or lung cancer. Symptoms may not appear until years after exposure to asbestos fiber. Although exposure to asbestos is now strictly controlled, more than 9 million workers are estimated to be at risk of the disease.

RISK FACTORS ▶▶▶▶▶▶

Other job-related lung diseases include coal worker's *pneumoconiosis* (black lung disease), which is caused by inhaling coal dust over prolonged periods (see illustration: Black Lung). *Silicosis,* the result of inhaling free silica (crystalline quartz particles) in industrial dust, may affect workers in mining, stonecutting, quarrying, blasting, and road and building construction. Both diseases have symptoms similar to asbestosis. No cure or specific treatment exists for occupation-related lung

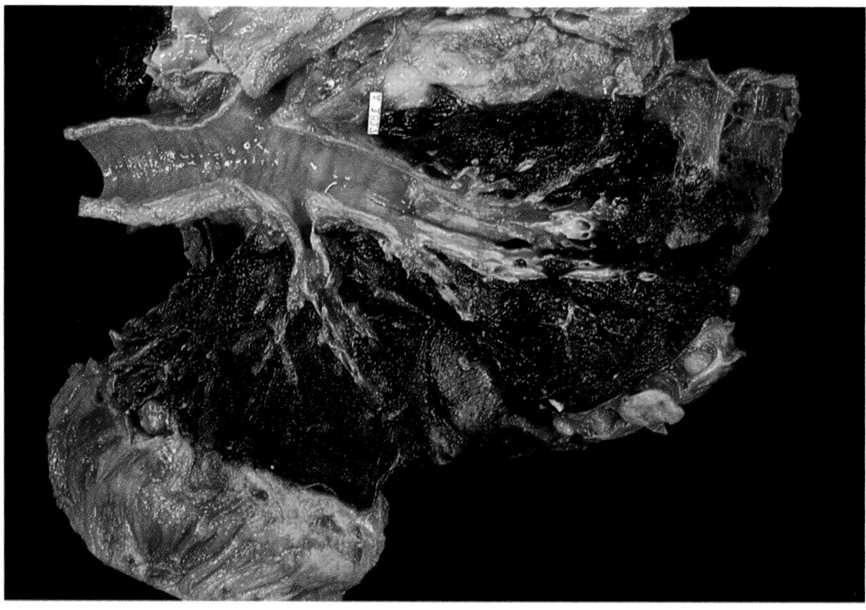

Black Lung. *This section of a lung was taken from a victim of black lung disease. The disease results from prolonged exposure to coal dust.*

disease. All are aggravated by cigarette smoking. (See also BRONCHITIS, **2**; PNEUMONIA, **2**.)

Lupus Erythematosus

Lupus erythematosus is a chronic disorder that affects the body's *connective tissue.* It is a lifelong disease that usually occurs in waves of attack and remission. Its most severe form, *systemic lupus erythematosus* (SLE), affects the skin and joints and can attack connective tissue and organs in any part of the body. A more common but less severe form of the disease, called *discoid lupus erythematosus* (DLE), affects only the skin.

A symptom of both types of lupus is a red rash on the face, often in a butterfly shape across the nose and cheeks. The rash is the only symptom of DLE; in SLE the rash is accompanied by various other symptoms, including pain and inflammation in the joints, fever, and a general feeling of sickness and fatigue. Attacks of lupus may be triggered by such things as exposure to sunlight, stress, and infections. Although they vary in intensity, the flare-ups can create life-threatening complications, especially when the kidneys are affected.

RISK FACTORS ▶▶▶▶▶▶

Systemic lupus erythematosus is believed to be an inherited AUTOIMMUNE DISORDER in which the body's immune system attacks the connective tissue. Its cause is unknown. Lupus usually appears first in young adults, affecting about nine times as many women as men. There is no cure, but the outlook for those with the disease has improved significantly in recent years. New drug therapies limit the damage to vital organs, suppress the immune system, and reduce inflammation. People with lupus are advised to keep out of the sun or wear strong sunscreen if sunlight brings on attacks of the disease.

Lymphoma

Lymphoma is any of a group of cancers of the lymph system. The two main forms of lymphoma are Hodgkin's lymphoma (HODGKIN'S DISEASE) and non-Hodgkin's lymphoma, the more common form. Untreated, the disease weakens the immune system, leaving the body extremely vulnerable to *opportunistic infections* or the spread of cancer.

The first symptom of lymphoma is usually painless swelling of the lymph nodes of the neck or groin. Sometimes the liver and spleen also enlarge. Other symptoms include headache, loss of appetite, fatigue, and fever. The cause of non-Hodgkin's lymphoma is unknown. Sometimes it may be related to the artificial suppression of the immune system following organ TRANSPLANT SURGERY. Certain viruses, including HIV, which causes AIDS, also seem to trigger the development of lymphoma. The disease may be diagnosed through blood tests or a BIOPSY in which lymph tissue or *bone marrow* is removed and examined.

Localized lymphoma can be treated with RADIATION THERAPY. More extensive forms are treated with CHEMOTHERAPY, or anticancer drugs. With early diagnosis of lymphoma, the chances of long-term survival are good. (See also LYMPHATIC SYSTEM, **1**; OPPORTUNISTIC INFECTIONS, **2**.)

Magnetic Resonance Imaging

Magnetic resonance imaging, or MRI, is a diagnostic procedure that uses the body's magnetic energy to create sharp, high-contrast images of internal organs and tissues. Magnetic resonance imaging is a relatively new and expensive technology. However, it is safer than a CAT SCAN or an X-RAY EXAMINATION because it does not use radiation.

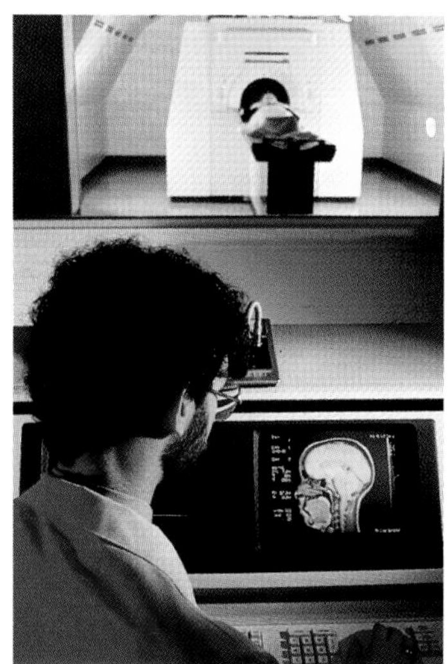

Magnetic Resonance Imaging. *A computer linked to a magnetic resonance imaging scanner converts the signals given off by a person's body into an image.*

MRI can produce cross sections of body tissues on any angle or plane. In addition, it can clearly show soft tissues, such as the brain, eye, heart, and blood vessels, that are difficult to examine using other diagnostic techniques.

An MRI scanner is a large cylinder of electromagnets. The person to be tested is placed on a table that slides into the center of the cylinder. The patient is then exposed to short bursts of powerful magnetic fields and radio waves. These bursts stimulate hydrogen atoms in the person's tissue to emit signals; different types of tissue produce signals of different strengths. The signals are converted to an image by a computer linked to the MRI scanner (see illustration: Magnetic Resonance Imaging). The patient will hear loud noises but will not feel anything. The whole process is painless and can be performed repeatedly. The only known risks are that the electromagnets can interfere with the operation of pacemakers, hearing aids, and other metal implants.

Magnetic resonance imaging is particularly useful in detecting disorders that do not show up well on X rays, such as TUMORS, infections, inflammations, STROKES, and hemorrhages.

Migraine Headache

Migraine headaches, or migraines (MY graynz), are intense, long-lasting HEADACHES that are usually more severe on one side of the head than the other. They can last from several hours to 2 days and may recur at intervals. Migraines are marked by severe, throbbing pain and are often accompanied by nausea, vomiting, visual disturbances, and extreme sensitivity to light and sound. Migraine headaches occur in about 10 percent of the American population, but women are three times as likely as men are to experience migraines. Although they are not life-threatening, migraines can be debilitating if they occur frequently and last for long periods of time.

RISK FACTORS

Symptoms Migraines usually follow one of two patterns, classic and common. A classic migraine is preceded by a set of symptoms called an *aura.* These symptoms may include feelings of elation, hunger for sweets, or thirst; dizziness, drowsiness, or irritability; or tingling and numbness on one side of the body. The victim may see flashing patterns of light followed by a slowly expanding blank area. In a common migraine, the headache comes on more suddenly with little or no aura preceding it.

Causes Migraines seem to run in families. They may be the result of a chemical imbalance in the brain that causes inflammation of blood vessels.

Migraine Triggers. *These are just a few of the foods that seem to trigger migraine headaches in some individuals. Learning to avoid the substances or conditions that trigger migraines is an important means of prevention.*

RISK FACTORS

Although it is not known exactly what triggers migraines, certain factors have been identified. These include stress; premenstrual tension in women; certain foods such as red wine, chocolate, and cheese; exposure to bright light or loud noise; and exercise. Recent studies have pointed to certain levels of hormones as possible migraine triggers.

Treatment and Prevention The standard treatment for migraines is a painkiller such as aspirin or acetaminophen and rest in a darkened room. Physicians may also prescribe antinausea medications and sedatives to help patients rest.

People who are prone to migraine headaches can sometimes learn to prevent attacks by keeping a diary to try to pinpoint triggering factors. If a certain food or a stressful situation sets off migraines, the individual can learn to avoid that trigger. Learning stress-management techniques may also be helpful. For those people who are subject to frequent migraines, physicians may prescribe medications, such as *beta-blockers,* to prevent the onset of an attack. (See also STRESS-MANAGEMENT TECHNIQUES, 5; BETA-BLOCKER, 7.)

MULTIPLE SCLEROSIS

Multiple sclerosis (MS) is a chronic disease of the central nervous system. It is characterized by the degeneration of the *myelin sheath* that covers and protects nerve fibers (see illustration: Myelin Sheath). The severity of MS varies greatly from person to person. Some people never experience disabling symptoms, while others may become unable to walk or maintain bladder control.

Symptoms and the Course of the Disease The first signs of MS usually occur between the ages of 20 and 40. Symptoms vary greatly, ranging from weakness, tingling, or numbness in a part of the body; to blurred or double vision; to trembling or loss of coordination; to INCONTINENCE. Generally, symptoms appear first as brief attacks that last for

Myelin Sheath. *Multiple sclerosis attacks the myelin sheath that protects nerve fibers; repeated attacks leave scarring (sclerosis). The damage prevents the affected nerve fibers from properly transmitting messages and impulses.*

days or weeks. These attacks are separated by periods of remission when the symptoms diminish or disappear. As MS progresses, however, the attacks may become longer and more severe, and the remission periods may be reduced accordingly. The attacks can cause a gradual deterioration of muscle control, which can lead to permanent disability. Complications may include painful muscle spasms, vulnerability to infections, and depression.

For many people with MS, the attacks create few problems or stop entirely after several years. On average, patients with MS will live more than 35 years after the start of the disease. In a few acute cases, however, the disease is fatal within the first year.

Causes and Treatment It is unclear what causes MS. It is thought to be an AUTOIMMUNE DISORDER, in which the body's defense system attacks and destroys scattered areas of the myelin sheath that protects the nervous system. Some researchers believe that this immune response may be triggered by a virus acquired in the first 15 years of life. Geographical or environmental factors may also play a part. The disorder is far more common in temperate areas of the world (such as the United States and Europe) than in the tropics. In addition, the risk of developing MS is much greater if a relative has the disease.

There is currently no cure for MS, but medical research is uncovering new clues about how the disease works and is developing better ways to treat it. The severity of attacks may sometimes be lessened by drugs that reduce inflammation (such as the hormone ACTH [adrenocorticotropic hormone]). Drugs that suppress the immune response are also being tested. Massage or physical therapy is often used to keep people with MS active and more comfortable. (See also NERVOUS SYSTEM, **1**.)

MUSCULAR DYSTROPHY

Muscular dystrophy is any of a group of inherited diseases in which the muscles progressively decrease in size and weaken. Duchenne (doo SHEN) muscular dystrophy is the most common and most severe type. All forms of muscular dystrophy are rare.

Duchenne muscular dystrophy affects only males. It is inherited through a recessive gene passed on by the mother. For reasons not fully understood, affected people lack a certain protein essential to muscle function. The symptoms usually appear before a child is 5 years old. These signs include increasing muscle weakness and problems with motor skills—lack of coordination, difficulty walking, and an inability to lift the arms over the head. Duchenne muscular dystrophy progresses rapidly during childhood: the muscles grow weaker, and people with the disease are usually unable to walk by their early teenage years. Most die before they reach adulthood.

There is no cure for Duchenne muscular dystrophy. Physical therapy will help keep patients active, independent, and comfortable for as long as possible. The only way to prevent this inherited disease is by identifying carriers. Any woman with a family history of muscular dystrophy should receive genetic counseling before becoming pregnant. (See also BIRTH DEFECTS, **6**; GENETIC SCREENING, **6**; GENETIC COUNSELOR, **9**.)

NEURALGIA

Neuralgia is a general term for pain along the course of a nerve. The sharp, severe pain of neuralgia often lasts for only seconds or minutes, but recurs for days or weeks. Although neuralgia is very uncomfortable, it is not life-threatening.

Neuralgia may affect many parts of the body. One form consists of severe spasms of pain that shoot along one side of the face. *Postherpetic neuralgia* is a constant burning pain that results from *shingles* (herpes zoster). The pain often continues for months or even years after the illness itself has disappeared. Another form of neuralgia affects the nerve endings around the eye and often occurs with a MIGRAINE HEADACHE. Neuralgia may result from injury to or irritation of a particular nerve, but in many cases the cause is unknown.

Mild neuralgia may be treated with painkillers such as aspirin, acetaminophen, or ibuprofen. In more severe cases, prescription drugs may be needed. (See also SHINGLES, **2**.)

NOSEBLEED

CONSULT A PHYSICIAN

A nosebleed is a common disorder characterized by sudden bleeding from one or both nostrils. In most cases, the bleeding is not serious and can be easily stopped. However, a nosebleed following a heavy blow to the head may indicate a serious injury and requires immediate medical attention.

Most nosebleeds begin on the *septum,* the cartilage that separates the two nasal cavities. The mucous membranes in the front of the septum are lined with fragile blood vessels. Bleeding occurs when these membranes are disturbed and the vessels are damaged. The most common causes of nosebleed include blows to the nose; irritation of the mucous membranes resulting from a cold, sinus infection, or dry air; and nose picking. In rare cases, recurrent nosebleeds may indicate a more serious underlying disorder such as HYPERTENSION or HEMOPHILIA.

Stopping a Nosebleed. *The proper position for treating a nosebleed is sitting upright and leaning forward slightly over a bowl. Holding the mouth slightly open, pinch the nostrils closed for 5 to 10 minutes while breathing through the mouth. Release the nose slowly and try not to touch or blow it. If the bleeding does not stop after 20 minutes, seek medical attention.*

A person with a nosebleed should be placed in a sitting position, with the head tilted *forward,* not backward, over a bowl. The soft part of the nose should be pinched firmly and held closed for 5 to 10 minutes, while the patient breathes through the mouth (see illustration: Stopping a Nosebleed). This pressure should stop the flow of blood. If a nosebleed does not stop easily or recurs frequently, a physician may need to cauterize (or burn) the affected blood vessels with chemicals or electricity.

One way to help prevent nosebleeds is to apply petroleum jelly to the inside of the nostrils once or twice per day. Increasing the humidity of the air by using a humidifier or vaporizer is also helpful. (See also NOSE, **1**.)

ORTHODONTIC DEVICES

Orthodontic devices, commonly called braces, are devices that help straighten and realign teeth. Their purposes are to improve a person's appearance and to correct any problems that interfere with talking, eating, or dental care. Braces are usually installed during childhood or adolescence, when the teeth and jaws have not yet fully developed and are easier to reshape.

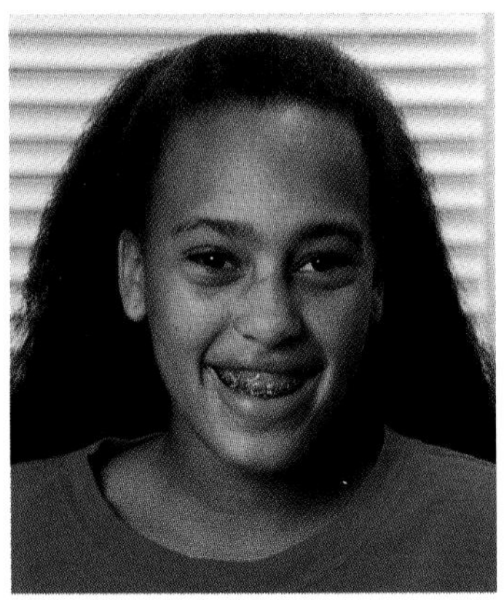

Fixed Devices. *Fixed braces consist of brackets and an arch wire that is adjusted to push and pull the teeth into their proper position.*

Orthodontic devices are used to correct malocclusion (an irregular bite between the upper and lower teeth), crooked or protruding teeth (buck teeth), and teeth that are improperly spaced. Dental specialists called *orthodontists* design each person's braces to correct his or her specific problems. When more than two teeth need correction, treatment often involves fixed devices that are worn for 1 or 2 years.

Fixed braces consist of brackets, which are cemented directly on the tooth or attached by a metal band around the tooth, and an arch wire threaded through the brackets. After the fixed braces are removed, the patient must usually wear a removable device called a retainer to hold the teeth in their new position until they become permanently fixed in place. Removable appliances are also used in cases when only a few teeth need to be moved.

Although wearing braces can be uncomfortable at times, the problems associated with them are usually minor. It is important to take extra care when brushing your teeth to clean around fixed appliances. (See also DENTAL CARE—ORTHODONTIST, **9**.)

OSTEOPOROSIS

Osteoporosis is a disease of the elderly caused by the loss of *calcium* and protein from the inner, porous layer of the bones. Everyone loses bone mass with age, but in people with osteoporosis the loss is substantial and causes the bones to become brittle and prone to fractures (see illustration: Disappearing Bone). The depletion of bone mass typically begins in middle age and is not noticed until years later when it is too late to reverse the process.

Symptoms and Causes The first symptom of osteoporosis is usually a wrist or hip fracture after a fall or back pain or a loss of height due to compression of the bones of the spinal column. Osteoporosis is more common in women than in men, affecting as many as 90 percent of all women over age 75. It is also more common in whites of northern European ancestry and in people who smoke or drink alcohol.

RISK FACTORS

Women may be more susceptible to osteoporosis because the healthy bones of women are less dense than those of men. In addition, bone loss in women accelerates after *menopause* when the body stops producing normal quantities of the sex hormone *estrogen*. Other causes of osteoporosis include overuse of corticosteroid drugs, a diet deficient in calcium and vitamin D, surgical removal of the ovaries, and certain hormonal diseases.

Prevention and Treatment Prevention of osteoporosis should begin early in life with a diet that provides adequate amounts of calcium. Some physicians recommend taking calcium supplements. Aerobic exercise, such as walking, biking, swimming, or jogging, at least three times a week can help prevent osteoporosis. The exercise should involve the weight-bearing bones of the legs and hips. Studies have shown that women who do heavy physical work throughout their lives are less likely to develop osteoporosis.

HEALTHY CHOICES

Many physicians recommend estrogen replacement therapy for women who have passed menopause. Such therapy has been shown to prevent or slow osteoporosis as well as to provide significant protection against heart disease. However, because estrogen can increase the risk of cancer of the lining of the uterus, its use must be monitored carefully by a physician. (See also CALCIUM, 4; VITAMIN D, 4; MENOPAUSE, 6; SEX HORMONES, 6.)

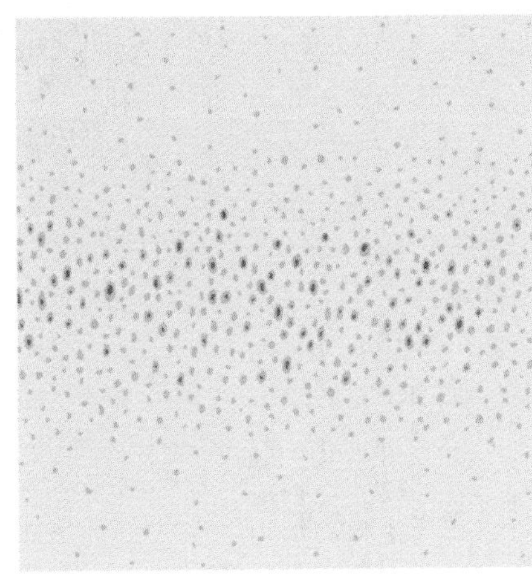

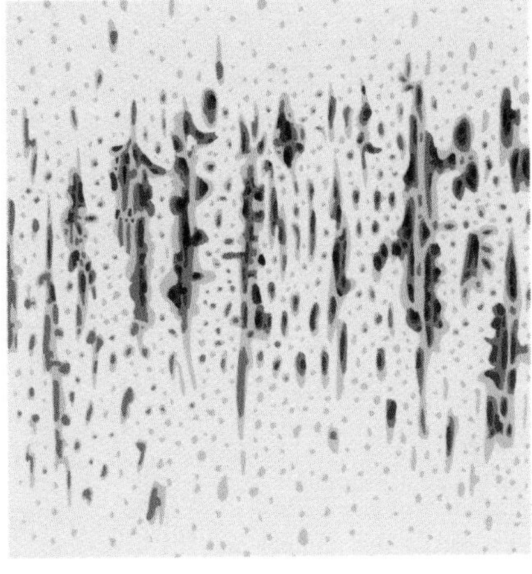

Disappearing Bone. *The density of the healthy bone at left gives it strength and makes it resistant to fracture. At right is the bone of someone with osteoporosis. It is less dense and therefore more brittle and susceptible to breaking.*

PAIN

Pain is a feeling of discomfort resulting from injury or irritation of the body tissue. It is an important part of the body's defense system because it signals that a part of the body has experienced an injury or become diseased. Pain causes you to take action to prevent further damage—to snatch a hand away from a hot stove, for example, or to see your dentist about an aching tooth. Pain can also indicate a serious emergency, as when chest pains signal a heart attack.

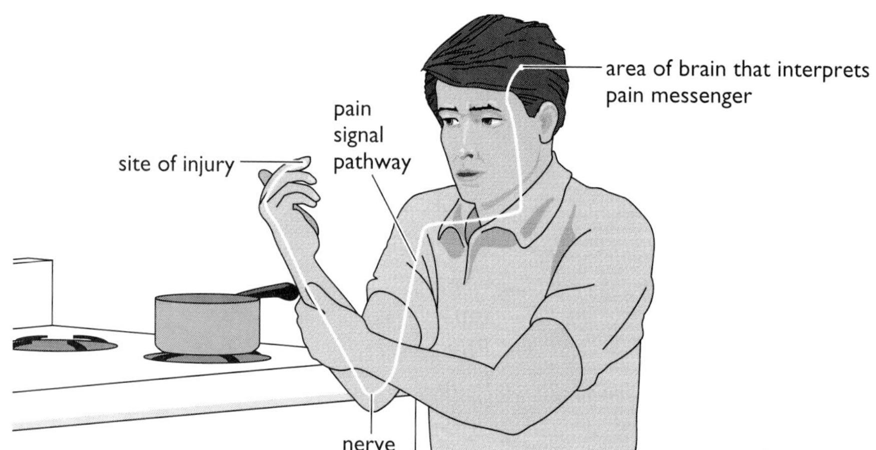

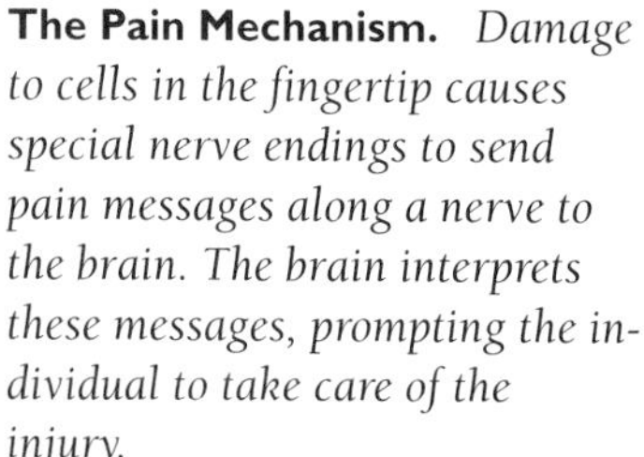

The Pain Mechanism. *Damage to cells in the fingertip causes special nerve endings to send pain messages along a nerve to the brain. The brain interprets these messages, prompting the individual to take care of the injury.*

Pain occurs when the damaged cells signal special nerve endings to send pain messages to the spinal cord and brain (see illustration: The Pain Mechanism). Pain may be felt in different ways. A cut finger may produce a sharp, intense pain; a pulled muscle may cause a dull soreness or tenderness. *Referred pain* is pain that is felt in a part of the body other than the diseased or injured part. It occurs because sensory nerves from various areas of the body draw together into larger nerves before entering the brain. It may not be clear to the brain exactly where the problem is located. The pain from an infected tooth, for example, may be felt as an earache.

Psychological factors can affect how pain is perceived or how well it is tolerated. Unexplained pain, for example, may be intensified by fear or anxiety about it. The tolerance of chronic pain may be lowered by psychological complications of a chronic illness, such as depression or insomnia.

Pain can be treated or controlled by taking *analgesics* (painkillers). The most widely used analgesics available without a prescription are aspirin, acetaminophen, and ibuprofen. Stronger prescription drugs are used to control severe or chronic pain. These include narcotics, such as morphine, which are often prescribed for serious injuries and for painful conditions such as kidney stones or cancer. Psychological treatments for managing chronic pain include *biofeedback,* in which a person learns to control unconscious body functions, and relaxation techniques. (See also BRAIN, 1; NERVOUS SYSTEM, 1; SPINAL CORD, 1.)

Paralysis

Paralysis is the complete or partial loss of the ability to move a muscle or group of muscles. Paralysis can be temporary or permanent, and it is usually accompanied by loss of feeling in the affected parts of the body. The three major types of paralysis are *paraplegia,* paralysis of the legs; *quadriplegia,* paralysis of all four limbs and the trunk; and *hemiplegia,* paralysis of one side of the body.

Most paralysis is caused by damage to the *nervous system.* This includes injury to the brain or spinal cord or to the peripheral nerves that connect the brain and spinal cord to the rest of the body. Paralysis can also result from diseases that affect the nervous system or muscles, such as BRAIN TUMOR, MULTIPLE SCLEROSIS, and MUSCULAR DYSTROPHY. A common cause of hemiplegia is STROKE, a hemorrhage or blood clot that damages a part of the brain. Quadriplegia and paraplegia are often caused by spinal cord injuries that occur in automobile, shooting, and diving accidents.

Treatment Treatment of paralysis depends on the underlying cause. Electrical stimulation has enabled some people with spinal cord injuries to walk with the aid of a walker, but in most cases, they are permanently confined to a wheelchair or bed. *Physical therapy* can help retrain and strengthen muscles paralyzed by diseases such as stroke and polio (see illustration: Physical Therapy). Physical therapy also helps prevent muscles and joints from freezing into rigid positions. Nerve transplants and tendon transplants have helped people who have paralysis caused by peripheral nerve or muscle damage. (See also NERVOUS SYSTEM, **1**; PHYSICAL THERAPIST, **9**.)

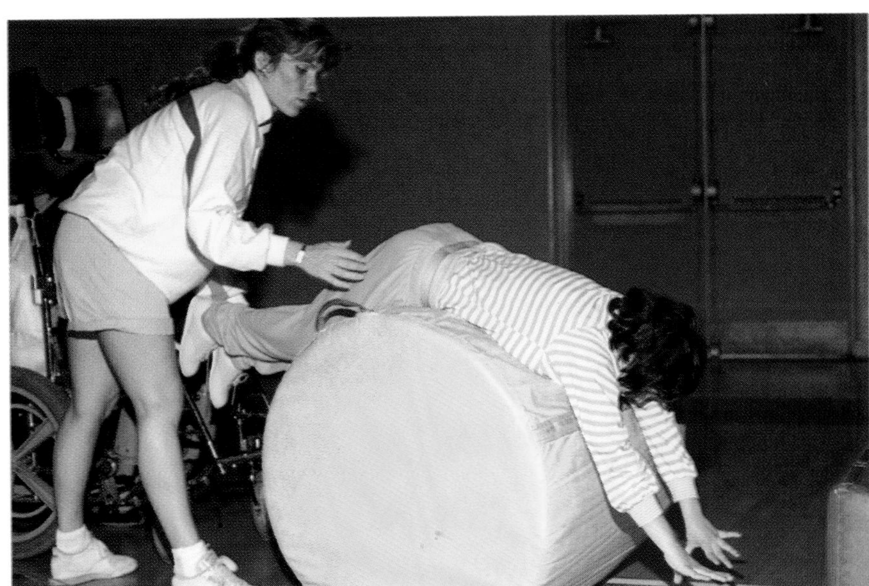

Physical Therapy. *Special exercise techniques used in physical therapy can improve muscle function and coordination impaired by some forms of paralysis.*

Parkinson's Disease

Parkinson's disease is a degenerative disorder of the nervous system marked by trembling, slow stiff movements, and problems with balance. It is caused by the death of cells in the part of the brain that controls muscle movement. These particular cells normally produce *dopamine,* a chemical that carries "messages" from one nerve cell to another. The lack of dopamine affects muscle control.

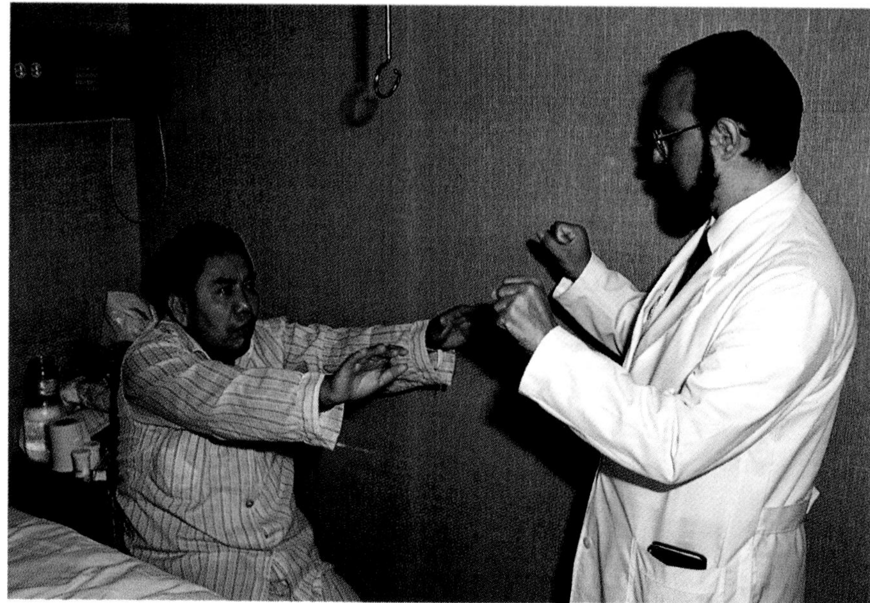

Parkinson's Disease. *Research continues into transplanting cells that produce dopamine into brains of patients with Parkinson's disease. People with Parkinson's have difficulty controlling their movements due to a failure in the production of dopamine.*

Causes and Symptoms Parkinson's is a disease of adults, usually striking between the ages of 50 and 65. It affects more than a million Americans. It is thought to result from a variety of conditions that can damage the brain, including CARDIOVASCULAR DISEASE, BRAIN TUMORS, *encephalitis*, blows to the head, and poisoning from drug overdose or carbon monoxide.

RISK FACTORS ▶▶▶▶▶▶

The first symptom of Parkinson's disease is usually a tremor (shaking) in one hand, often in the form of an uncontrollable pill-rolling motion between the thumb and fingers. In many cases, tremors progress to involve the entire arm and spread to other parts of the body. Muscle stiffness generally follows, making movement, particularly walking, difficult. Many people with Parkinson's become depressed.

In later stages of the disease, rigidity in the muscles of the face may result in a lack of facial expression, and speaking, swallowing, and chewing are often difficult. Problems with balance are common. Finally, a degree of paralysis may set in. Some of those with Parkinson's become mentally confused.

Treatment No cure exists for Parkinson's disease. Its progress can generally be slowed by eating well, exercising regularly, and getting adequate rest. Counseling and support groups can help those suffering from depression.

The drug *levodopa* (or L-dopa), which supplies additional dopamine to the brain, often provides relief of tremors and muscle rigidity. Occasionally, surgery is used to destroy certain brain tissues in an attempt to eliminate a patient's tremors.

Two recent treatments offer hope of halting the development of Parkinson's disease. One is the drug *selegiline* (trade name: Deprenyl or Eldepryl); recent studies suggest that it can delay the beginning of symptoms. The other is a surgical procedure that involves transplanting dopamine-producing cells (obtained from adrenal glands) to the brains of patients with Parkinson's disease. The procedure is still experimental. (See also ENCEPHALITIS, **2**.)

Periodontitis see GUM DISEASE

Peritonitis

Peritonitis is an inflammation of the peritoneum, the large membrane that lines the abdominal cavity. It is usually caused by the invasion of bacteria into the peritoneum as a result of an abdominal injury or disease. Peritonitis is rare in the United States. When it occurs, it is most often a complication of APPENDICITIS, a *peptic ulcer* that has eaten through to the peritoneum, DIVERTICULITIS, or, in women, an inflammation of the fallopian tubes.

The major symptom of peritonitis is severe abdominal pain. This may be accompanied by bloating, fever, nausea and vomiting, and a rapid pulse. Peritonitis is always a serious medical condition that requires immediate hospitalization and treatment to prevent death. Treatment usually involves surgery to repair the underlying disorder and large doses of antibiotics to fight the infection. (See also ULCER, PEPTIC.)

Plastic Surgery

Plastic (or reconstructive) surgery is a type of SURGERY that changes, replaces, or restores a visible part of the body. Most people use the terms *plastic surgery* and *cosmetic surgery* interchangeably. In fact, although the procedures employed in plastic and cosmetic surgery are similar, the purposes are quite different. Plastic surgery generally refers to operations that repair damaged or malformed tissue; cosmetic surgery refers to procedures that improve a healthy person's appearance.

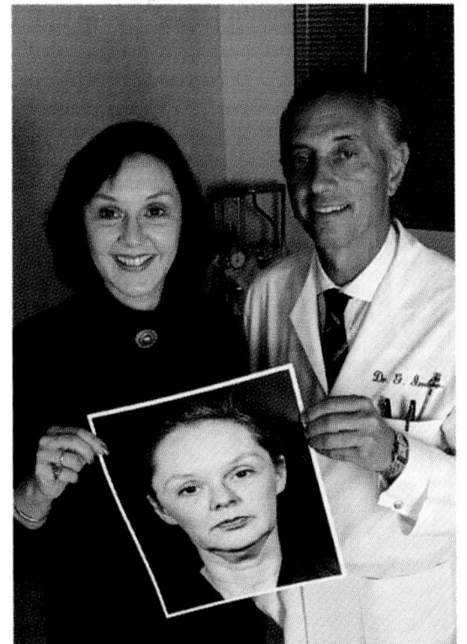

Plastic Surgery. *This woman had facial plastic surgery. She is holding a photo that shows how she looked before the operation.*

Plastic Surgery In plastic surgery, some part of the body is reshaped. Plastic surgery is used to repair such common birth defects as cleft lip and palate and to reconstruct injured body parts resulting from accidents or severe burns. Depending on the nature and extent of the injury, the surgeon may have to use skin grafts or skin and muscle flaps from other parts of the person's body to provide cover for damaged areas. A bone graft may also be necessary to provide support. The plastic surgeon's main objective is to restore normal use and appearance to the injured part.

Cosmetic Surgery Cosmetic surgery has become quite common in recent years. The most frequent operation is *rhinoplasty,* plastic surgery on the nose. *Face lifts,* the tightening of the facial skin to minimize wrinkles; breast enlargement; and liposuction are other popular procedures. In *liposuction* the surgeon removes fat cells from specific parts of the body, such as the hips, thighs, and buttocks, by a procedure involving suction. Cosmetic surgery can be painful and expensive, and it is seldom covered by medical insurance. And like any surgery, it is subject to complications.

One type of plastic surgery, the insertion of breast implants, has been the subject of considerable controversy in recent years. The controversy concerns the long-term health effects of silicon-gel implants used for breast enlargements or reconstructions. In 1992, a variety of reported problems led the federal Food and Drug Administration to ban their use until more research could be done on their safety. (See also BREAST IMPLANTS, 6; SURGEON, 9.)

Pleurisy

Pleurisy is an inflammation of the *pleura,* the membrane that covers the lungs and lines the chest cavity. In a healthy person, the surfaces of the pleura are moist, allowing the lungs to move smoothly over the chest wall as they expand and contract during breathing. In a person with pleurisy, the surfaces of the pleura are dry and rough.

Symptoms When dry, inflamed pleural surfaces rub together, sharp pain is felt, pain that worsens during deep breathing or coughing. This stage is called *dry pleurisy.* Chills, fever, coughing, and difficulty in breathing may also be present. As the illness develops, fluid may enter the chest cavity from blood vessels. This stage is called *wet pleurisy,* or pleural effusion. The fluid relieves pain and is eventually absorbed, but if too much fluid collects, the lungs become compressed, making breathing difficult. Complications of pleurisy may include bleeding or an accumulation of pus in the chest cavity. The symptoms of pleurisy are similar to those of lung cancer and tuberculosis.

Causes and Treatment Pleurisy is often a complication of an infection, such as pneumonia or tuberculosis. It can also be caused by the spread of a disease, such as cancer, from elsewhere in the body. Diagnosis and treatment of the underlying disease are necessary to cure pleurisy. This treatment may include antibiotics, heat applications, and anti-inflammatory and pain-relieving drugs. Wet pleurisy may also be treated with a surgical procedure that drains fluid from the chest. (See also LUNG, **1**.)

Psoriasis

Psoriasis (suh RY uh suss) is a chronic disease in which the skin erupts in red flaky patches covered by silvery scales. As many as 3 million Americans may suffer from psoriasis. It can range from a mild case affecting only a small area of skin to a severe condition that covers most of the body. No cure is known for psoriasis, but it can be treated and somewhat controlled.

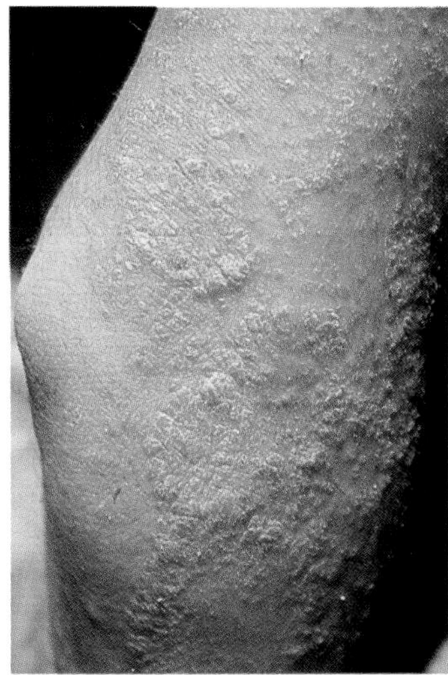

Appearance of Psoriasis. *The nature and extent of psoriasis outbreaks vary greatly. Most commonly, they appear as patches of dry, thickened skin covered by silvery scales.*

The cause of psoriasis is believed to be genetic. It occurs when the body produces new skin cells much faster than it can shed old ones. As a result, the dead cells accumulate in thick scales on the surface of the skin (see illustration: Appearance of Psoriasis). The condition typically flares up and then settles into a period of remission, the temporary lessening or disappearance of symptoms. Attacks of psoriasis can be triggered by injuries, sore throats, burns, certain drugs, and emotional stress. The first attack often erupts after a sore throat or streptococcal infection. (See also STREPTOCOCCAL INFECTIONS, **2**.)

Psoriasis usually occurs at the elbows, knees, arms, legs, trunk, and scalp. It can appear as small pimples, patchy flaking skin, or even pustules. Psoriasis can also affect the nails, causing pitting and in some cases separation of the nails from the nail bed. A small number of people with psoriasis develop a chronic form of arthritis as well.

Treatment Exposure to sunlight or artificial ultraviolet light is the most common treatment for psoriasis. Coal tar soaps and shampoos, corticosteroid creams, and moisturizing creams can also help calm a flare-up. Certain anticancer drugs and vitamin A derivatives have been effective in treating severe psoriasis, but they have serious side effects and must be used with care.

RADIATION THERAPY

Radiation therapy involves a carefully measured dose of radiation that is precisely focused to destroy localized cancer cells within the body. Also called radiotherapy, X-ray therapy, cobalt treatment, or irradiation, it is used as a partial or complete treatment for certain CANCERS.

How It Works The patient lies on a table in a specified position and an X-ray machine is programmed to deliver a strong dose of radiation to a particular cluster of cancer cells. As the radiation passes through the diseased tissue, it destroys or slows the growth of cancerous cells. Radiation technicians keep the destruction of normal tissue to a minimum by careful aiming and calculation of the radiation dose.

Radiation therapy is most effective when the cancer is limited to one area, in the vocal cords or on the skin, for example. It is also used after surgery to destroy any remaining cancer cells. In some cases, radioactive material is surgically implanted in a tumor to release continuous radiation to cancerous cells. Once cancer has spread throughout the body, however, radiation therapy is rarely useful. Radiation therapy may also be used to shrink noncancerous tumors to reduce the pressure or pain associated with their growth.

Side Effects Because radiation therapy can also damage healthy tissue, some side effects may occur. They include nausea, diarrhea, fatigue, hair loss, and skin irritation. Medications may be given before each treatment to lessen the severity of some side effects. Because of the potential dangers, the quality of the equipment used and the skill of the technician are both important to investigate before undergoing radiation therapy. (See also PHYSICIANS (M.D.'s)—RADIOLOGIST, 9.)

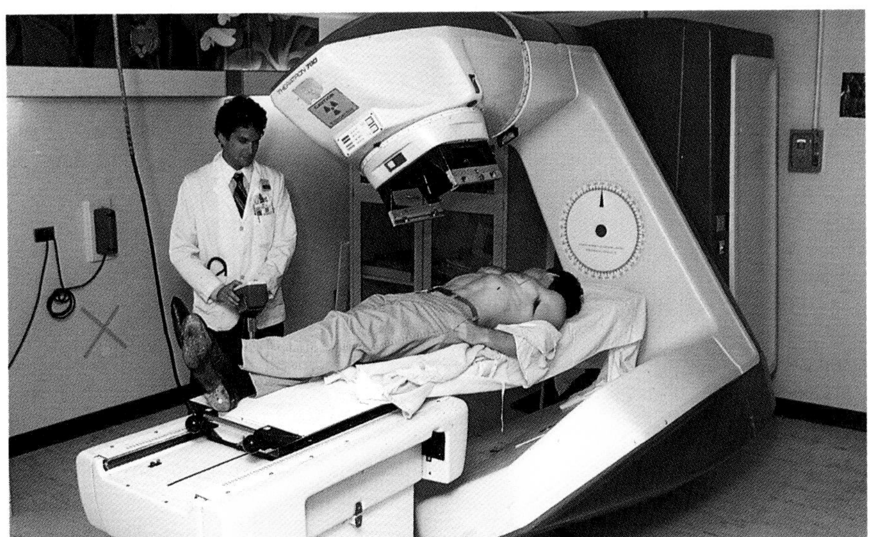

Radiation Therapy. *During radiation therapy, an X-ray machine emits radiation that destroys localized cancer cells. The machine can be tilted to send radiation from more than one angle.*

Raynaud's Phenomenon

Raynaud's (ray NOHZ) phenomenon and the related ailment *Raynaud's disease* are disorders in which the arteries in the hands and feet contract suddenly in response to cold temperatures. This cuts off blood flow, causing the skin of the fingers or toes to turn pale. Women are much more likely to be affected than are men. For most people, it is simply an uncomfortable condition, but in a few rare cases, people with Raynaud's have developed ulcers and GANGRENE in the fingers and toes.

Raynaud's Phenomenon. *Raynaud's phenomenon is common among people who operate vibrating machinery on their job or who frequently use their fingers on a keyboard.*

Physicians refer to the disorder as Raynaud's disease when the symptoms appear with no known cause and as Raynaud's phenomenon when the disorder is brought on by another underlying condition. Disorders such as ARTERIOSCLEROSIS, rheumatoid ARTHRITIS, or BLOOD CLOTS can cause Raynaud's phenomenon. It is also common among people who operate vibrating machinery, such as chain saws or jack hammers, in their jobs. Raynaud's phenomenon sometimes affects typists and pianists.

The standard treatment for both Raynaud's phenomenon and Raynaud's disease is to avoid all exposure to cold. This applies not only to dressing warmly or staying inside during cold weather but also to handling cold drinks or getting something out of the freezer. People with Raynaud's should also avoid smoking because it decreases blood flow to the hands and feet. Physicians sometimes prescribe drugs that help expand the blood vessels to treat the disorder. The treatment of Raynaud's phenomenon in particular also involves treating or controlling the underlying cause.

Reye's Syndrome

Reye's (RYZ) syndrome is a rare but life-threatening disease that follows an ordinary viral infection, such as influenza or chicken pox. The illness, which affects the liver, brain, and blood, usually strikes children between the ages of 2 and 15. The cause of Reye's syndrome is unknown, but giving children *aspirin* during a viral infection is believed to trigger it. Physicians now recommend that aspirin not be given to children under the age of 16.

RISK FACTORS ▶▶▶▶▶▶

Symptoms of Reye's syndrome include vomiting, nausea, lethargy, loss of consciousness, periods of agitation, and seizures. As the disease progresses, the blood chemistry becomes unbalanced, fat forms in the liver, and the brain swells. This can lead to loss of consciousness and COMA. Patients are usually hospitalized in intensive care units so that the blood chemistry can be stabilized and brain swelling can be monitored. About 10 percent of those with Reye's syndrome die. Most of those who survive recover completely, but some suffer brain damage.

Scoliosis

Scoliosis is a curvature of the spine to one side. It is a progressive disease that generally begins in childhood and becomes noticeable by early adolescence. The disease can cause pain and some disability. If left untreated, it can severely deform the body. The spine may rotate, forcing the ribs together on one side and apart on the other.

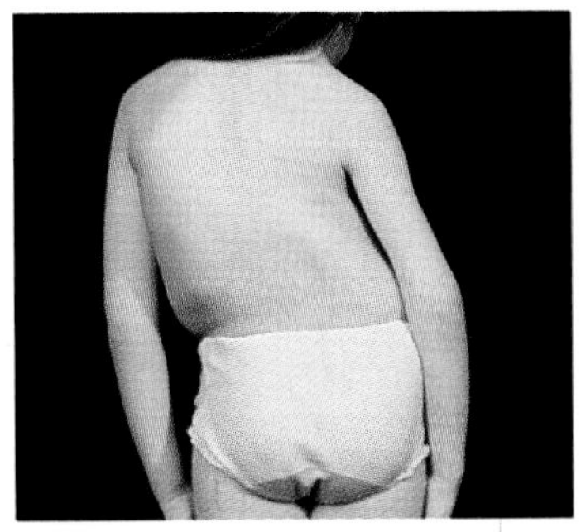

Scoliosis.

The typical S-shaped curve of scoliosis can usually be seen in a visual examination and can be confirmed through X rays (see illustration: Scoliosis). Many school districts examine students for the disease at regular intervals.

Scoliosis may be caused by genetic factors, poliomyelitis, or poor posture. In some cases, it is caused by the fact that one leg is longer than the other. In most patients, scoliosis can be treated by wearing a brace that straightens the spine gradually. Exercises to strengthen the back muscles may also be effective. However, surgery may be required in severe cases. Mild cases of the disease often do not require treatment but should be monitored periodically. (See also SPINE, **1**.)

SHOCK

Shock is the sudden reduction of blood flow throughout the body, which causes vital functions to slow down or stop completely. It is marked by an extreme drop in blood pressure. Shock is a dangerous condition that can lead to loss of consciousness, COMA, and death.

Shock is a common complication of severe bleeding, severe burns, and excessive loss of fluids (from prolonged vomiting or diarrhea, for example). Shock can also result from a HEART ATTACK, allergic reaction, or infection. *Anaphylactic shock* involves a severe allergic reaction to an insect sting or a drug. *Septic shock*, which may occur in BLOOD POISONING, is caused by the spread of an infection to the bloodstream. These types of shock are physiological—that is, they are related to major disruptions of the normal functioning of the body.

Mental "shock," which may follow emotional stress, and *electric shock* are quite different types of shock. However, a severe electric shock may cause the body to go into physiological shock.

CONSULT A PHYSICIAN

A person in shock or in danger of going into shock needs immediate care. A physician or ambulance should be called as soon as possible. If injury has caused shock, treatment includes stopping any bleeding, maintaining an open airway, and keeping the patient warm and lying flat until medical help arrives. Foods, liquids, or medication should not be given. Hospital treatment may include blood transfusions, intravenous fluids, oxygen treatment, and painkillers. (See also TOXIC SHOCK SYNDROME, **2**; BLEEDING, **8**; BURNS, **8**; ELECTRIC SHOCK, **8**; FIRST AID, **8**.)

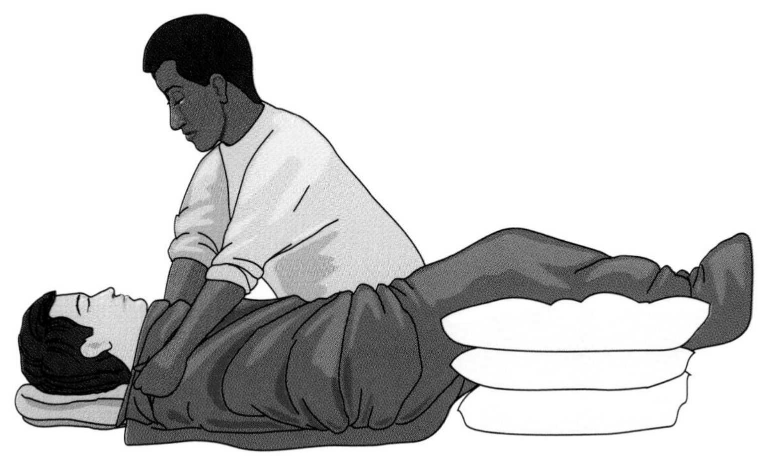

Until Medical Help Arrives. *A person in shock or in danger of going into shock should be lying down with legs and feet elevated. This increases the blood flow to the head and upper body. If raising the legs causes pain, leave the body flat. Keep the person warm and comfortable.*

SICKLE CELL ANEMIA

Sickle cell anemia is an inherited, chronic form of the blood disorder ANEMIA. The red blood cells of people with sickle cell anemia have an abnormal type of *hemoglobin* (the part of the blood that carries oxygen) called hemoglobin S. Normal red cells are round and flexible; hemoglobin S causes the red cells to become crescent-shaped and rigid (see illustration: Normal and Sickled Cells). The sickled cells are fragile and tend to break up, causing *hemolytic anemia.*

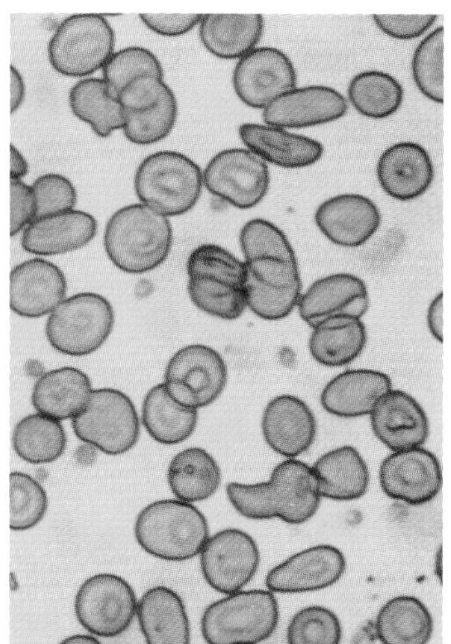

Normal and Sickled Cells. *Sickle cell anemia takes its name from the change of shape (sickling) that happens to normally round red blood cells. The disease affects African Americans most often, but it can occur in other ethnic groups.*

Sickle cell anemia occurs most frequently among African Americans. Someone with sickle cell anemia has inherited the gene for hemoglobin S from both parents. People who inherit the gene from just one parent become carriers; they may have abnormal red blood cells but normally show no symptoms. Blood tests are used to diagnose the disease or determine whether a person is a carrier.

Symptoms and Treatment Sickle cell anemia has symptoms like other anemias, including fatigue, breathlessness, and rapid heartbeat. In addition, affected people are prone to sickle cell crises, which are sometimes painful and life-threatening conditions. Crises occur when the deformed blood cells cannot pass through the smallest blood vessels. The blood vessels become blocked, depriving tissues of oxygen. Severe crises can cause chronic organ damage, especially to the bones, central nervous system, liver, lungs, and spleen.

There is no cure for sickle cell anemia, although antisickling drugs are being tested. Treatment during crises includes painkillers, drugs to prevent dehydration, and sometimes oxygen. Genetic counseling for people with a family history of sickle cell anemia is recommended to help them prevent passing the disease on to their children. (See also BIRTH DEFECTS, 6; GENETIC SCREENING, 6; GENETIC COUNSELOR, 9.)

SKIN CANCER

Skin cancer is the most common form of CANCER in the United States. It is characterized by malignant TUMORS on the skin and is usually associated with long-term exposure to sunlight. *Malignant melanoma,* which can metastasize (muh TASS tuh size), or spread, rapidly from the skin to other parts of the body, is the deadliest type of skin cancer. Most skin cancers, however, are of two nonmelanoma types: *basal cell carcinoma* and *squamous cell carcinoma.* These tend to remain in one area longer and are easier to treat. All three forms of skin cancer have a high rate of cure if detected early.

Symptoms and Diagnosis The first symptom of any type of skin cancer is a change in the appearance of the skin. These include the appearance of painless bumps or lesions; a wound that does not heal; a change in an existing birthmark, wart, or mole; or a new mole that shows up on the body after age 30. Most skin cancer lesions are painless at first, but any new or changed growths should be examined promptly by a physician. Diagnosis is usually made through visual examination of the area followed by a BIOPSY, in which samples of the tissue are removed and analyzed.

CONSULT A PHYSICIAN

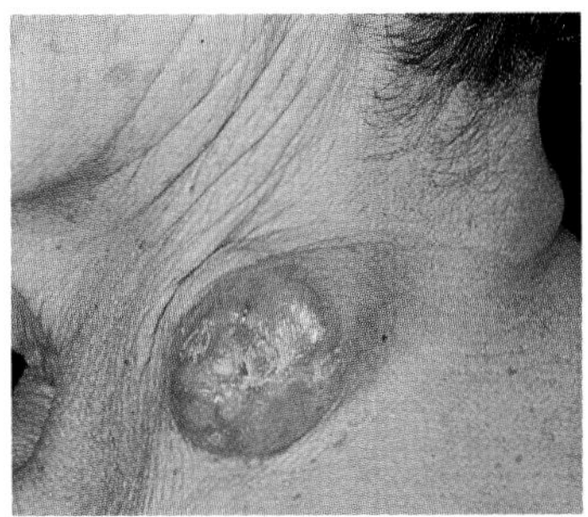

Basal Cell Carcinoma. *The most common type of skin cancer, basal cell carcinoma often appears on the face or neck. It begins as a small, flat nodule that eventually forms a shallow ulcer at the center.*

Causes and Risk Factors The primary cause of skin cancer is damage to the skin caused by excessive exposure to ultraviolet radiation from the sun. The people at the highest risk for skin cancer are those who are fair-skinned and those who spend a great deal of time in the sun. Other risk factors include exposure to certain industrial chemicals; also, heredity seems to play a role in susceptibility to skin cancer.

Treatment and Prevention Most skin cancer tumors can be removed surgically. Further treatment depends on the extent of the disease. It may include RADIATION THERAPY, CHEMOTHERAPY (treatment with anticancer drugs), and *cryosurgery,* the application of extreme cold to the affected area.

Many types of skin cancer can be prevented by limiting exposure to the sun. This can be done by wearing protective clothing and applying a sunscreen that blocks the sun's rays. If you have had skin cancer, you should have regular follow-up examinations to detect any recurrence of the disease. (See also KAPOSI'S SARCOMA; SUN DAMAGE, 8.)

Sleep Disorders

A sleep disorder is any significant disturbance in a person's normal sleeping patterns. Sleep problems, experienced by most people from time to time, become serious when they are chronic and interfere with daytime functioning.

Causes of Insomnia. *People who work on rotating schedules often experience insomnia because their sleeping and waking times are changed from week to week.*

Types of Sleep Disorders The most common sleep disorders are insomnia and sleep apnea. People who suffer from *insomnia* have difficulty falling asleep or staying asleep. Insomnia can be caused by a number of factors, including illness, anxiety, or some medications. Use of caffeine, alcohol, or certain drugs may also interfere with restful sleep. Shift workers, long-distance travelers, and others whose normal schedule is disrupted may also suffer from insomnia.

Sleep apnea (AP nee uh) is a condition in which a person's breathing is interrupted repeatedly during sleep. Interruptions usually last 10 seconds or more and occur many times a night. Sleep apnea may be caused by obstructions in a person's breathing passage and, sometimes, by obesity. The disorder may be responsible for reducing the supply of oxygen and damaging the heart and the lungs.

Narcolepsy (NAHR koh lep see) is another, less common sleep disorder. It is characterized by briefly falling asleep a number of times during the day. These uncontrollable "sleep attacks" often occur while the person is active—talking, laughing, or even driving. The cause of narcolepsy is not known, but its origin is probably neurological.

Treatment and Prevention People with insomnia are usually advised to eliminate all stimulants from their diet. Other recommendations include establishing a regular schedule for going to bed each night and getting up each morning, avoiding daytime naps, and exercising during the day (but not too close to bedtime). If sleeplessness strikes, getting out of bed and reading or doing some quiet activity until drowsiness sets in is often advised. Using sleeping pills for any length of time should be avoided because they can be habit-forming and may, themselves, disrupt sleep patterns.

If sleep apnea is caused by a physical abnormality, surgery may be required. A person with narcolepsy may be able to control the condition through planned naps or with special medications. (See also SLEEP, **1**.)

Speech Disorders

A speech disorder is any difficulty a person has in communicating vocally. Speech is a complex skill in which the brain, ears, larynx, mouth, and lips must all work together in a highly organized fashion. Damage to any of these parts of the body can cause a wide variety of speech disorders. Emotional problems may also affect a person's ability to speak clearly.

One of the most common speech disorders is delayed speaking. Most children start speaking by the age of 2½, but children who are mentally retarded, hearing-impaired, or autistic often start later and have great difficulty in learning to speak.

Other common disorders include stuttering and articulation disorders. *Stuttering* affects about 1 percent of adults. Some experts think it may be the result of brain damage or emotional problems. Stuttering in young children is often only a temporary condition. *Articulation disorders,* such as lisping, involve difficulty in pronouncing letters. This may result from a physical abnormality or improper placement of the lips or tongue in forming sounds.

Aphasia is the loss of the ability to comprehend language or to speak, write, or read. It is usually caused by a head injury, BRAIN TUMOR, or STROKE that damages the language centers of the brain.

Certain diseases and physical abnormalities can also lead to speech disorders. Cleft palate, CEREBRAL PALSY, MULTIPLE SCLEROSIS, and PARKINSON'S DISEASE may cause slurred or indistinct speech. People with larynx cancer who have had the larynx removed must learn to speak through the esophagus or by using an electronic device.

Treatment Speech therapists can often help people overcome minor speech disorders and can train many people with physical problems to

Speech Therapy. *Experts in speech therapy, called speech pathologists, help people with speech disorders that result from physical disabilities, learning problems, or hearing loss.*

speak more distinctly. Other forms of treatment include surgery to repair physical abnormalities, hearing aids for people with hearing loss, and drug treatment for problems that result from disorders of the nervous system or muscles. (See also SPEECH THERAPY, 9.)

STOMACHACHE/INDIGESTION

RISK FACTORS

Stomachache and indigestion are vague terms used to describe abdominal pain or discomfort. They are often caused by overeating, drinking too much alcohol, eating foods that the body does not tolerate well, eating contaminated food, taking medications that irritate the stomach lining, or by stress. In most cases, abdominal discomfort is not serious and clears up by itself.

There are four main types of minor stomach disorder: heartburn, indigestion, flatulence (intestinal gas), and gastritis.

Heartburn Heartburn is a burning sensation behind the breastbone, often accompanied by a bitter taste in the mouth. It is called heartburn because the pain is felt in the chest rather than in the abdomen, but it is not related to the heart. The most common cause of heartburn is a weak or defective muscle between the esophagus and the stomach that allows stomach acids to flow back into the esophagus.

Indigestion Indigestion (dyspepsia) results from poor or incomplete digestion of food. It includes a wide variety of symptoms such as vague abdominal pain, flatulence, burping, nausea, vomiting, a bloated feeling, and heartburn. Normally an attack of indigestion lasts only an hour or so, but chronic indigestion can last for days or weeks.

Flatulence *Gas* is produced in the large intestine as part of the normal digestive process. Flatulence, or excessive gas, is usually caused by foods such as beans and other legumes, by a high-fiber diet, or by an inability to digest the lactose in milk and dairy products.

Stomachache. *Overindulgence is one of the most common causes of minor stomach problems.*

Gastritis Gastritis is an inflammation of the lining of the stomach. It may be triggered by foods that are fatty or very acidic, or by caffeine, alcohol, and carbonated beverages. Other common causes include overeating, excessive consumption of alcohol, smoking, bacterial or viral infections, and stress. Certain drugs, such as aspirin and ibuprofen, cause a form of gastritis in which the stomach lining bleeds.

Treatment Antacids, which neutralize excess stomach acid, are often used to treat minor digestive problems. Identifying and avoiding foods that trigger digestive problems is usually helpful. People who get heartburn should not lie down after meals because that can cause acid to flow back into the esophagus.

Prolonged or severe stomach pain may be a symptom of a more serious problem such as a *peptic ulcer,* GALLSTONES, APPENDICITIS, or CANCER. If indigestion persists or if it is accompanied by prolonged vomiting, vomiting blood, or blood in the stool, a physician should be consulted. (See also ULCER, PEPTIC; ABDOMEN, 1; DIGESTIVE SYSTEM, 1.)

CONSULT A PHYSICIAN

STRESS TEST

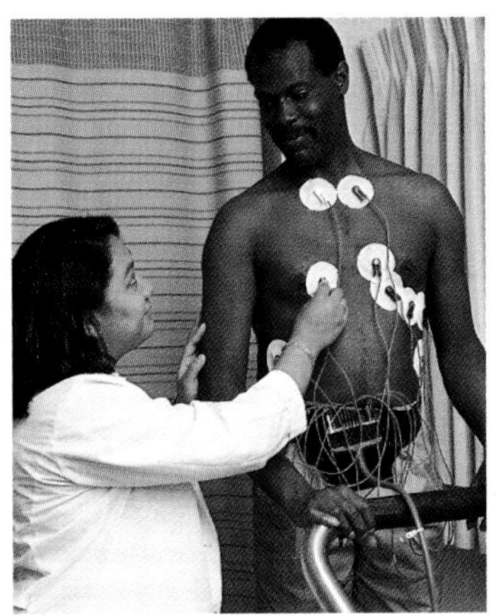

Stress Test.

A stress test, or exercise tolerance test, measures the functioning of the heart and lungs during exercise. The test is used to diagnose HEART DISEASE and evaluate the health of someone who has had a HEART ATTACK. It is also useful in establishing limits for a person beginning a program of vigorous exercise, especially if that person is over 40 and has a family history of heart disease.

A person taking a stress test walks on a treadmill or pedals a stationary bicycle while heart activity is recorded in an ELECTROCARDIOGRAM. Functions such as heart rate, blood pressure, and oxygen consumption by the lungs are monitored by a physician and technician, who evaluate the readings.

A new version of the test involves the use of a drug to stress the heart. This type of test enables a physician to evaluate the functioning of the heart of someone who is unable, because of disability or illness, to perform the exercise that is required in a normal stress test. (See also FITNESS, 4.)

STROKE

Stroke, also known as cerebrovascular accident (CVA), is a sudden loss of brain function caused by a reduced supply of blood to the brain. Like all organs of the body, the brain requires a constant supply of oxygen-rich blood. A reduction or loss of oxygen impairs or destroys brain cells. The resulting damage can be mild enough to cause temporary dizziness or severe enough to cause death within minutes. Stroke is the third leading cause of death in the United States, after heart attacks and cancer.

Causes and Risk Factors Three major conditions can produce a stroke (see illustration: Causes of a Stroke). A *cerebral thrombosis,* the most common, occurs when a BLOOD CLOT forms in a blood vessel leading to the brain, blocking the flow of blood. A *cerebral embolism* occurs when an artery in the brain is blocked by material (usually a blood clot) that has been carried in from another area of the body. A *cerebral hemorrhage* is a rupture of a cerebral blood vessel. All three conditions interrupt blood supply, and therefore oxygen flow, to a part of the brain. Occasionally, a brain tumor can also cause a stroke by pushing against an artery, cutting off the supply of blood to the brain.

Certain diseases and conditions increase the risk of stroke, including ATHEROSCLEROSIS, HYPERTENSION, irregular heartbeat, DIABETES, recent HEART ATTACK, and KIDNEY DISORDERS. Obesity, smoking, and, for women, the use of oral contraceptives are believed to increase the risk of stroke. Strokes are most common in people over the age of 65.

Warning Signs and Stroke Symptoms A stroke may be preceded by warning signs, called *transient ischemic attacks* (TIAs), that are caused by temporary interruptions of blood flow. TIAs typically last from a few minutes to a few hours. Symptoms include dizziness, dimness or loss of vision, slight weakness or numbness, problems with swallowing, and difficulty in speaking or thinking clearly. Although these symptoms are often ignored, recognizing and treating TIAs is important in preventing a fatal or disabling stroke. Anyone who experiences the symptoms of TIAs should have a physical exam and diagnostic tests, which may include an ELECTROENCEPHALOGRAM (EEG) and CAT SCAN.

Stroke symptoms depend on the extent of the damage and the areas of the brain affected. For example, an interruption of blood supply to the brain's speech center can produce speech difficulties; an interruption to areas that control motor coordination can cause symptoms ranging from numbness to permanent PARALYSIS. After a stroke, many patients become tired easily and suffer from memory loss, general confusion, and difficulty in concentrating.

Treatment and Rehabilitation *Anticoagulants,* which are blood-thinning drugs, may be prescribed to help prevent the formation of clots in narrowed arteries. A physician may recommend surgery to reduce the chance of future strokes. Surgery may involve removing *plaques* from the *arteries* that carry most of the blood supply to the brain. Blood flow to the brain can also be increased by rerouting superficial scalp arteries directly to the brain. If a stroke is caused by an ANEURYSM (the swelling of a blood vessel), surgery may be used to repair the torn blood vessel.

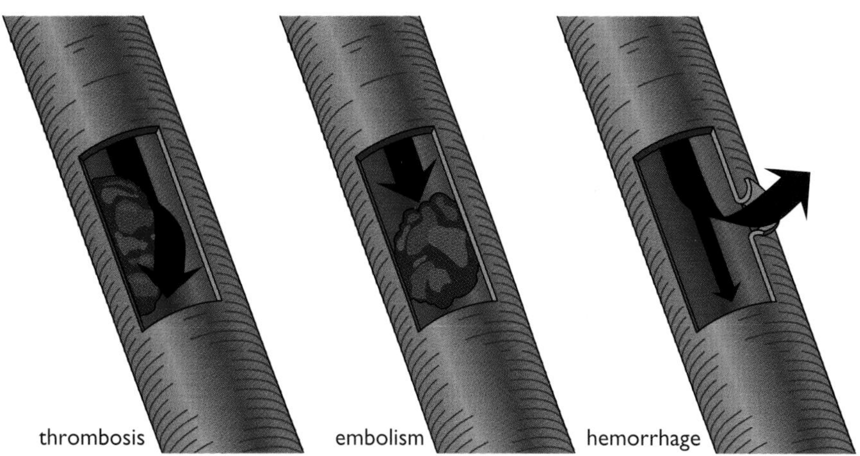

Causes of a Stroke. *Nearly all strokes result from damage to an artery of the brain. This damage may be caused in one of three ways: thrombosis, formation of a blood clot within the artery; embolism, blockage by material carried from another part of the body; or hemorrhage, rupture of the artery.*

Treatment after a stroke may also include diet and lifestyle changes to reduce the risk of another stroke.

The nature of *rehabilitation* for people who have had strokes depends on the severity and location of the brain injury. Rehabilitation is frequently a long and difficult process, requiring great patience and effort. Brain cells, unlike other body tissues, do not regenerate; however, with therapy, another part of the brain can sometimes "learn" to take over the function of an area damaged by a stroke. Long periods of physical therapy or speech therapy may be needed to recover movement and speech.

HEALTHY CHOICES

Prevention The chances of having a stroke can be reduced by controlling blood pressure, maintaining ideal weight, not smoking cigarettes, following a healthy diet, and exercising regularly. Recent research indicates that small daily doses of aspirin may help prevent stroke by reducing the blood's tendency to clot. A daily intake of potassium-rich foods (fruits and vegetables) may help reduce the incidence of stroke by reducing hypertension. (See also SPEECH DISORDERS; PHYSICAL THERAPY, 9; SPEECH THERAPY, 9.)

SUDDEN INFANT DEATH SYNDROME

Sudden infant death syndrome (SIDS) is the sudden, unexplained death of an infant. Typically, the parents put a seemingly healthy baby to bed at night only to discover the next morning that it has died in its sleep. SIDS, also called crib death, usually affects babies between 2 and 6 months old.

The cause of SIDS is unknown, but it does *not* result from choking or suffocation as many parents have believed. Certain babies are at higher risk than others. These include infants whose mothers smoked or took drugs during pregnancy, bottle-fed babies, and babies born prematurely or with low birth weight, especially boys. Babies who have had "near misses"—that is, who stopped breathing during sleep but were revived—are also at higher risk, as are infants with colds or respiratory infections.

HEALTHY CHOICES

Because sudden infant death syndrome strikes without apparent warning, one increasingly common practice is to attach a monitor to a high-risk infant. If the baby stops breathing during sleep, the monitor sounds an alarm. No one knows, however, whether monitors are effective in preventing SIDS. Other preventive measures include good prenatal health care and breast feeding. Babies who have colds should be watched closely until all symptoms disappear.

In their grief, the parents of a baby who has died from SIDS often blame themselves. Psychological counseling or special support groups may help them cope with their loss. (See also PRENATAL CARE, 6.)

SURGERY

Surgery is the branch of medicine that treats diseases, corrects deformities, or repairs injuries by procedures called *operations*. Surgeons perform operations for many reasons—to repair a damaged organ, remove diseased tissue, change a person's appearance, or deliver a baby, to name but a few. Many operations are undertaken by a team consisting of the

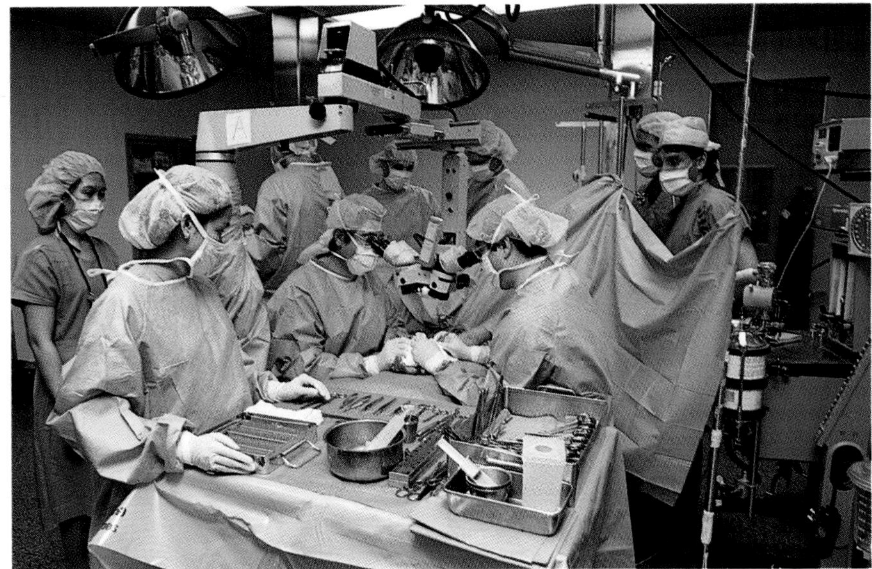

Surgery. *Surgery is often complicated, requiring many skilled persons, medicines, equipment, and specialized techniques.*

surgeon, a surgical assistant, a nurse, and an anesthesiologist. Minor operations are often handled as outpatient surgery, which requires only a day visit to a hospital, clinic, or physician's office.

Depending on the type of surgery, operations are performed under either local or general anesthetics (drugs that deaden sensation). The area of the incision is shaved and cleaned with antiseptics (substances that prevent the growth of germs that cause infection). After the operation is performed, the surgeon closes the area with sutures or staples. The patient then begins a period of recovery, or *convalescence,* which may last from a few days to several weeks. Years ago, surgical patients were kept in bed for many days. The trend today is to have them up and walking as early as possible—often on the same day the surgery is performed. Special care and instructions are given to help the patient regain strength and mobility as soon as possible.

Surgical Specialties Surgery is divided into a number of specialties. Some common areas of specialty include the following:

- *Cardiac surgery,* the treatment of heart conditions
- *Orthopedic surgery,* the treatment of bone and joint problems
- *Ophthalmic surgery,* the treatment of eye disorders
- PLASTIC SURGERY, surgery to repair, reconstruct, or replace damaged or unsightly tissue

Advances in Surgery At one time surgery was both dangerous and extremely painful. Today antiseptics and anesthetics have made surgery safer and easier on the patient. Among the newest surgical techniques are microsurgery and arthroscopy. *Microsurgery* involves the use of a special microscope that allows the surgeon to carry out delicate operations on very small body structures. Surgeons often use microsurgery to treat disorders of the eye, ear, or brain or to repair severed fingers, toes, hands, or feet. In *arthroscopy,* surgeons use a small flexible viewing tube to examine and operate on joints, especially the knee joint. Because the incision is so small, the joint heals quickly. (See also ANESTHESIA; LASER SURGERY; TRANSPLANT SURGERY; ANESTHESIOLOGIST, 9; SURGEON, 9.)

Tay-Sachs Disease

Tay-Sachs disease is a rare, inherited brain disorder that affects infants and young children. It is marked by progressive degeneration of the brain cells, resulting in death by the age of 4.

The first symptoms of Tay-Sachs disease appear 5 to 6 months after birth. These include loss of vision and hearing, convulsions, paralysis, and a deterioration of physical and mental abilities. The disease progresses rapidly, and by the second year, the child is left in a vegetative state.

RISK FACTORS

Tay-Sachs disease is caused by the deficiency of an enzyme that is essential for a healthy brain. The disease is passed on genetically if both the mother and the father carry a defective chromosome. The disorder is most common in families of eastern European Jewish descent. Although there is no treatment for Tay-Sachs disease, it can be prevented by careful parental screening. (See also BIRTH DEFECTS, **6**; GENETIC SCREENING, **6**; GENETIC COUNSELOR, **9**.)

Temporomandibular Joint Syndrome

Temporomandibular joint syndrome, also called TMJ syndrome, is a condition that affects the temporomandibular joint (see illustration: The Temporomandibular Joint). In TMJ syndrome, the joints of the jaw are not properly coordinated with the muscles that support and control them. The result is jaw and head pain. Some people also experience a clicking or grating sound when opening or closing their mouths and limited movement of the lower jaw.

Causes and Treatment Temporomandibular joint syndrome can have many causes. The most common is stress. People under stress often grind their teeth during sleep (*bruxism*) or keep their jaw muscles clenched for

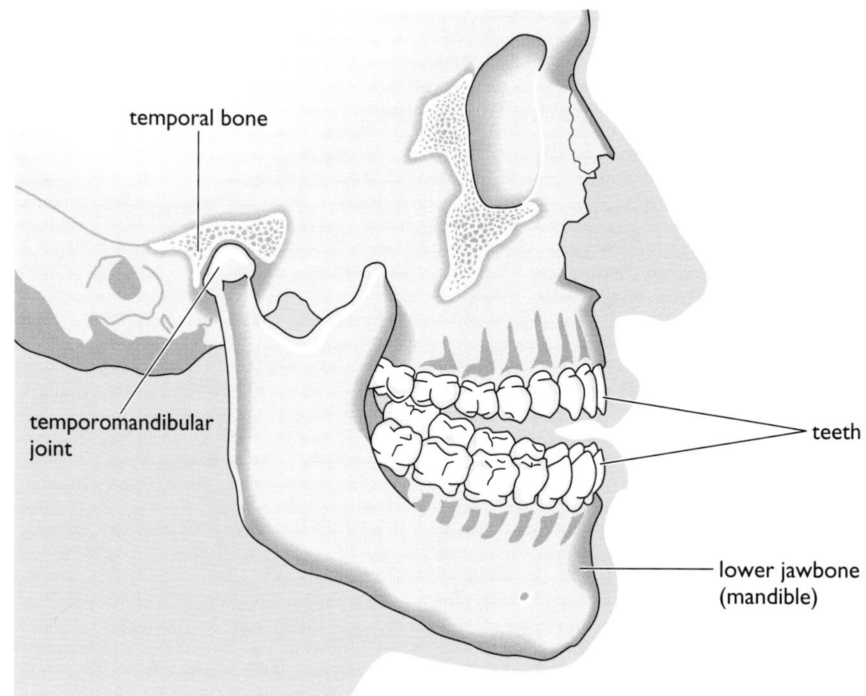

The Temporomandibular Joint. *The temporomandibular joints are the hinge joints that connect both sides of the lower jawbone with the temporal bone of the skull.*

long periods of time. These habits cause excessive tension in the jaw muscles. TMJ syndrome can also be caused by an injury to the jaw, weak jaw muscles, a misaligned bite, jaw muscle spasms, or ARTHRITIS in the joint.

Treatment of TMJ consists of relieving the pain and, when possible, eliminating the underlying cause. The pain can be treated with analgesics, along with heating pads and muscle-relaxing drugs. If the underlying cause is stress, a physician may recommend some form of stress management such as *biofeedback* or *relaxation training*. Dentists sometimes prescribe braces or other ORTHODONTIC DEVICES to realign a poor bite or to eliminate nighttime grinding of the teeth. In extreme cases, surgery may be required to repair the jaw or correct alignment. (See also JAW, 1; BIOFEEDBACK, 5; RELAXATION TRAINING, 5; DENTAL CARE, 9.)

TENDINITIS

Tendinitis is an inflammation of a tendon. The symptoms of tendinitis include pain and tenderness around the joint and, occasionally, restricted movement of the muscle attached to the injured tendon. The elbow and shoulder are most often affected.

Tendinitis is usually caused by injury to or excessive use of the shoulder or elbow. The pain results from inflammation or a small tear in the *tendon* that links the muscles to the bone. If the muscles and tendons are rested, the discomfort may disappear within a few weeks. However, in elderly people and those who continue to use the affected area, tendinitis often takes longer to heal. Over time, the ligaments and tendons in the shoulder may stiffen and scar, leading to loss of movement. If untreated, tendinitis can result in permanent damage to the tendons.

Rest is an essential part of any treatment for tendinitis. The affected area should not be used for several days. Elevating and applying ice to the area may help reduce the swelling, while analgesics, such as aspirin, can ease the pain. If tendinitis persists, a physician may inject corticosteroid drugs around the affected tendon.

Tennis Elbow. *A common form of tendinitis is tennis elbow, which causes pain and tenderness on the outside of the elbow and along the forearm. Nonathletic activities that involve repeated twisting of the forearm, such as house-painting and gardening, can also lead to "tennis elbow."*

HEALTHY CHOICES

The best way to avoid tendinitis is by warming up before exercising and cooling down afterwards. Muscle-strengthening exercises can help prevent further attacks. (See also CONNECTIVE TISSUE, **1**.)

THROMBOSIS

see BLOOD CLOT

THYROID DISORDERS

Thyroid disorders are malfunctions of the thyroid gland, an organ located at the base of the throat that secretes hormones affecting growth and development. Most thyroid disorders involve the overproduction or underproduction of thyroid hormones. Thyroid disorders are serious, long-term diseases, but they can usually be controlled through medication or surgery.

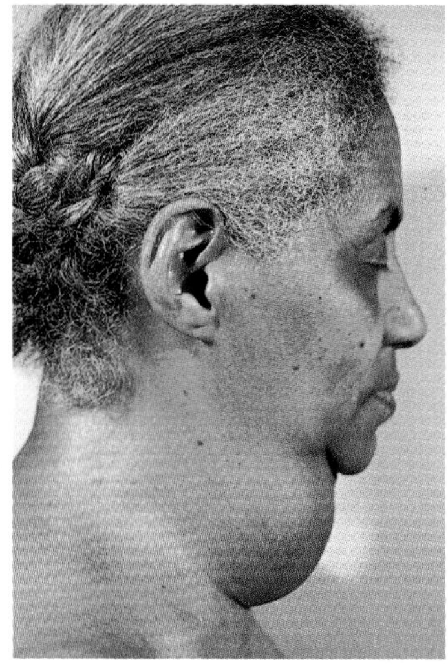

Goiter. *A goiter is an enlarged thyroid gland and can be a symptom of several different thyroid disorders.*

Types of Disorders *Hyperthyroidism* is overactivity of the thyroid gland that results in overproduction of thyroid hormones. The most common form is *Graves' disease,* an AUTOIMMUNE DISORDER in which the body produces an abnormal type of antibody that overstimulates the thyroid gland. The thyroid produces excessive amounts of hormones, which causes the metabolism to speed up, resulting in increased appetite but weight loss. Other symptoms include an increase in heart rate and blood pressure, sweating, muscle weakness, enlargement of the thyroid gland, and protruding eyes.

Hypothyroidism is the opposite of hyperthyroidism. Underactivity of the thyroid gland causes underproduction of thyroid hormones. It is also an autoimmune disorder, but in this case the body develops an antibody that attacks its own thyroid gland. Symptoms include fatigue, weight gain, decreased heart rate, hair loss, dry skin, and sensitivity to cold. Untreated hypothyroidism in children can cause mental retardation and stunted growth.

Goiter, an enlargement of the thyroid gland, is a symptom of most thyroid diseases including hyperthyroidism and hypothyroidism. In some parts of the world, goiters are caused by lack of dietary iodine, a mineral that is necessary for the production of thyroid hormone. This is rare in the United States, however, because most Americans use iodized salt.

Diagnosis and Treatment *Thyroid function tests* are medical procedures used to diagnose thyroid disorders. One such procedure is a blood test that measures the level of thyroid hormones in the blood. In the radioactive iodine uptake (RAIU) test, the patient swallows radioactive iodine, which is then measured by an instrument to determine how much is absorbed by the thyroid over several hours or a day.

In many cases, hyperthyroidism can be treated by administering radioactive iodine or special drugs to slow down hormone production. Sometimes surgery is necessary to remove part of the thyroid. Hypothyroidism is treated by administering thyroid hormones. The treatment must usually continue for the rest of the patient's life. The treatment of a goiter depends on the underlying thyroid disease. (See also THYROID GLAND, **1**.)

TRANSPLANT SURGERY

Transplant surgery involves the transfer of tissue or an organ from one person to another or from one place to another in the same person. It is used to replace a damaged organ or tissue with a healthy substitute. The transplantation of blood vessels, tendons, nerves, bones, and skin from one part of the body to another is quite common. Transplants of the heart, liver, kidneys, and bone marrow have been carried out between two people.

Organs or tissues for transplants are often taken from a person who has just died, or, in the case of kidneys, one of the two may be taken from a living relative of the recipient. The success of transplant surgery depends on the compatibility of the tissue or blood types of the donor and recipient. Some parts of the body—corneas (the clear part of the eye), tendons, and heart valves, for example—may be transplanted without the problem of *rejection,* the automatic attempt by the body's immune system to destroy foreign cells. However, people who undergo kidney, heart, and liver transplants usually require long-term treatment with drugs that reduce the risk of rejection of the new organ. These drugs suppress the *immune system,* which also prevents the body from fighting an infection. For people who receive transplants, therefore, even the mildest infection can be fatal.

PLEASE KEEP THIS CARD IN YOUR POSSESSION

In the hope that I may help others, I hereby make this anatomical gift, to take effect upon my death. The words and marks below indicate my desires.

For the purpose of transplantation, therapy, medical research or education, I give ☐ Any needed organs or parts
☐ Only the following organs or parts________

Signed by the Donor and two witnesses in the presence of each other.

Signature of Donor Donor's Birthdate

Witness________

Witness________

Date Signed________ City & State________

This is a legal document under the Uniform Anatomical Gift Act.

PLEASE KEEP THIS CARD IN YOUR POSSESSION

Transplant Surgery. *People who have chosen to donate their organs for use in transplants often carry donor cards. These cards are legal documents that state which parts of the body may be used after the donor dies.*

A technique known as *bone marrow transplantation* is used to treat people with potentially fatal blood and immune system disorders, including LEUKEMIA and severe aplastic ANEMIA. Bone marrow (soft tissue found inside bones) is removed from the hipbone of a healthy, compatible donor and injected into one of the recipient's veins. The new marrow then travels through the bloodstream to settle within the bones of the recipient where it produces new cells. (See also SURGERY; BONE MARROW, 1; IMMUNE SYSTEM, 1.)

Tumor

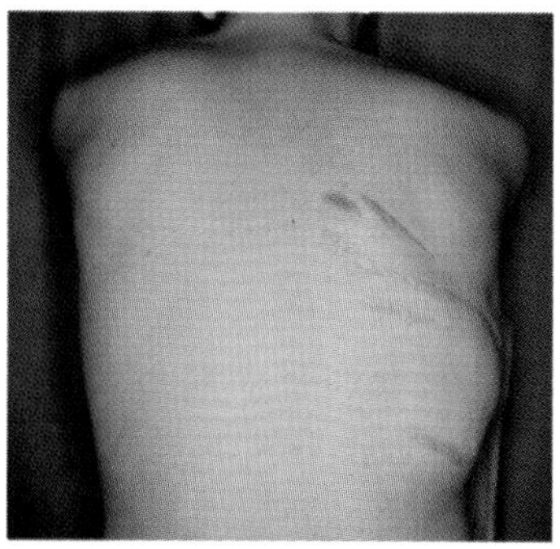

Tumor. *There are many types of benign tumors, including this hemangioma, a growth composed of blood vessels.*

A tumor, or *neoplasm,* is an abnormal mass of tissue in the body. There are two types of tumors. Tumors may be either *malignant* (cancerous) or *benign* (noncancerous).

Malignant tumors can grow rapidly, invading surrounding tissues. They may also spread through the bloodstream or lymphatic system and result in secondary growths, or *metastases,* elsewhere in the body. Benign tumors usually grow slowly and do not enter other tissues. They may, however, grow large enough to press on nearby structures and disturb body functions; in enclosed spaces such as the skull, this can be dangerous.

The effects and treatment of a tumor depend on its size and location. In some cases, both benign and malignant tumors can be removed completely through SURGERY. Other tumors can be removed only partially or not at all. Malignant tumors may also be treated with RADIATION THERAPY and CHEMOTHERAPY (anticancer drugs). (See also BRAIN TUMOR; CANCER; LYMPHATIC SYSTEM, **1.**)

Ulcer, Peptic

A peptic ulcer is a sore or hole in the digestive tract. There are two main types: *gastric ulcers,* which occur in the lining of the stomach, and *duodenal ulcers,* which occur in the duodenum (the part of the small intestine connected to the stomach) (see illustration: Peptic Ulcers). Ulcers can also be found in the lower esophagus. Peptic ulcers are a common disorder, affecting roughly 1 in 10 people in the United States sometime during their lives.

Symptoms and Diagnosis A gastric ulcer may produce burning, aching, or a feeling of hunger in the upper abdomen or lower chest. Additional symptoms include a bloated feeling after meals, nausea and vomiting, sharp abdominal pain, and black, tarry stools. The more common duodenal ulcer produces similar symptoms, although the discomfort is often felt in the upper abdomen, midback, or under the breastbone.

Diagnostic tests for ulcers include barium X rays of the esophagus, stomach, and intestine. If X rays show nothing, a physician may examine the area by inserting a small, lighted viewing tube (endoscope) through the esophagus and into the stomach.

Causes and Risk Factors The cause of ulcers is not fully known. They seem to occur when the normal balance between stomach acid and the protective *mucus* that lines the digestive organs breaks down. When this happens, the acid eats away at the unprotected linings, creating an ulcer.

Ulcers are commonly thought to occur in people who live stressful, hurried lives, but no clear evidence supports this theory. Stress can make an existing ulcer worse, however. Excess use of aspirin, alcohol, or certain other drugs can cause ulcers, and people with a family history of ulcers are more likely to have ulcers themselves.

Complications Ulcers can have several potentially dangerous complications. One is heavy internal bleeding, which is usually discovered when a person vomits bright-red blood. Ulcers can also eat a hole through the

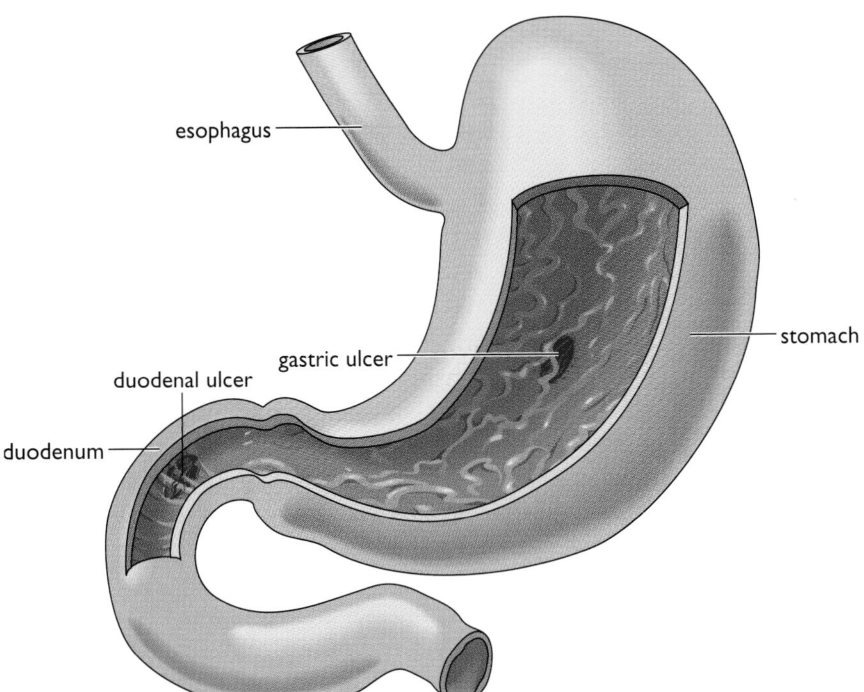

Peptic Ulcers. *Most peptic ulcers occur either in the stomach or the duodenum.*

wall of the stomach or duodenum into the abdominal cavity. This causes intense pain and sometimes results in PERITONITIS and often requires emergency surgery. Sometimes scar tissue produced by an active ulcer will block the exit from the stomach. Finally, the continuous, long-term bleeding from an ulcer can lead to ANEMIA.

Treatment Ulcers are treated with antacids to neutralize stomach acid or with drugs that reduce the production of stomach acid or that coat the stomach lining. Most ulcers respond well to these medications. Some physicians urge ulcer patients to avoid the consumption of alcohol and spicy food. Surgery is required only in rare cases and for serious complications.

Varicose Vein

Varicose veins are swollen and twisted blood vessels. They occur when valves in the veins do not function properly. Roughly 10 to 15 percent of the American population have varicose veins, and women are twice as likely as men are to develop them. In most cases, varicose (from the Latin word for "twisted") veins are not a serious medical problem.

Normal veins have one-way valves that keep the blood from flowing backward. When the valves are defective, blood floods back and forms pools in the veins, causing the veins to become distended and gnarled (see illustration: Varicose Veins). Varicose veins occur most frequently in the back of calves or on the inside of the legs. Veins in the esophagus, anus, and scrotum can also become varicose. Varicose veins often develop in people who are pregnant, obese, or who have inherited a tendency to the condition.

RISK FACTORS

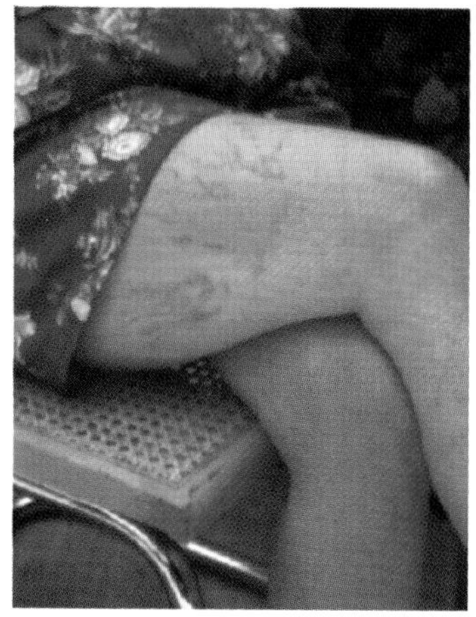

Varicose Veins. *Varicose veins typically appear gnarled and swollen.*

Symptoms and Treatment Because the veins just under the skin are most often affected, you can see the dark-blue, spidery lines of varicose veins through the skin. Some people experience mild to severe aching, itching, and ulcers (sores) in the area surrounding the veins. The skin may become brownish gray, hard, and dry. Swelling of the ankles and feet is another common symptom of varicose veins.

Most people are able to treat their varicose veins by wearing elastic stockings, exercising regularly, and elevating the legs above the heart after prolonged standing. Ulcers on the skin may be covered with a special dressing to promote healing, or they may be surgically removed. Although sitting or standing for long periods is not believed to cause varicose veins, it may aggravate the condition.

Physicians can remove varicose veins surgically using a technique called stripping. Another technique involves injecting each affected vein with an irritating agent that causes it to close off. Healthy veins then take over the function of carrying blood to the heart. (See also CIRCULATORY SYSTEM, 1; VEIN, 1.)

VISION PROBLEMS

Most vision problems are caused by irregularities in the cornea, the clear covering at the front of the eyeball; in the lens, the part that lies behind the cornea; or in the shape of the eyeball itself. These irregularities cause light rays to focus imperfectly on the retina, the light-sensitive area at the back of the eye. When this happens, the image the brain receives is no longer clear and distortion or blurring results. Vision problems are common, but most can be corrected with special lenses. (See also EYE, 1.)

Common Vision Problems. *In a normal eye, light rays are focused by the cornea and lens directly on the retina. When a person is nearsighted, the eyeball tends to be lengthened so that the rays are focused in front of the retina. A farsighted person's eyeball is usually too short, causing the light rays to focus at a point beyond the retina.*

Types of Vision Problems When the curve of the cornea is uneven, objects appear distorted or blurred. This condition is called *astigmatism.* Astigmatism may occur by itself or together with other vision problems.

A person who is *nearsighted* has poor distance vision. Nearsightedness, or *myopia,* most commonly occurs when the eyeballs are too long from front to back. Light rays from distant objects focus at a point in

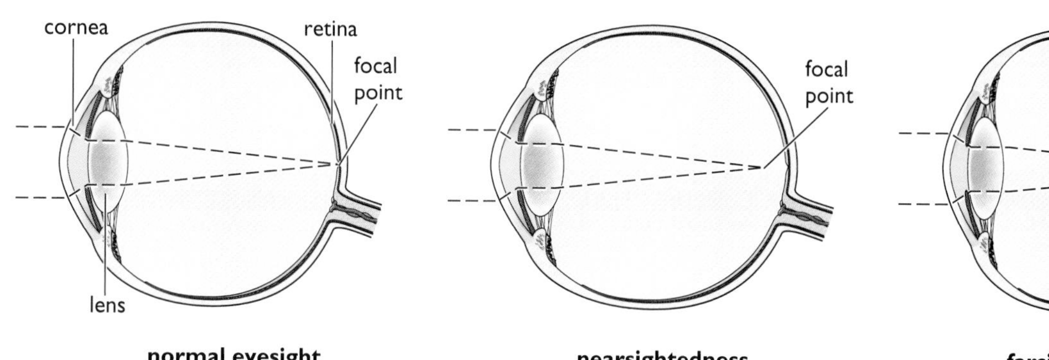

front of the retina rather than on the retina itself. Nearsightedness can develop or grow worse during adolescence, but it usually changes little after adolescence.

A person who is *farsighted* has the opposite problem. Farsightedness, or *hyperopia,* occurs when eyeballs are too short. This causes light rays from nearby objects to focus at a point behind the retina, which produces poor close vision.

In a normal eye, the lens changes shape slightly to focus light rays properly on the retina. During middle age, the eye's lens becomes less flexible, a condition known as *presbyopia.* This condition is characterized by an inability to focus on objects at close range.

Most vision problems can be remedied through the use of corrective lenses: eyeglasses or contact lenses.

Correcting Vision Problems All these vision problems can be remedied through the use of corrective lenses: eyeglasses or contact lenses. Astigmatism can be corrected with cylindrical lenses, which are shaped to correct the distortion of the cornea. Nearsighted people benefit from *concave* lenses, with the middle of the lens thinner than the edges. This causes incoming light rays to spread farther apart so that the image focuses on the retina rather than in front of it. Eyeglasses for farsighted people or those with presbyopia have *convex* lenses, which are thicker at the center than at the edges. These lenses pull the image forward onto the retina. People with conditions that affect both distant and near vision can use *bifocals,* in which the top part of the lens controls distant vision and the bottom part controls close vision.

Eyeglasses have been in use since the thirteenth century, although precision-ground lenses have been available only in the last 200 years. Contact lenses are a product of the twentieth century. The most popular type today is soft contact lenses. Because of their softness they cause little friction on the eyelids, and they allow some oxygen to reach the cornea. However, they tear easily and need careful cleaning. Hard contact lenses are more durable, and they can correct some problems, such as astigmatism, that soft lenses cannot.

In the last decade, several new surgical techniques have been developed to correct certain vision problems. *Radial keratotomy* involves making a series of cuts—resembling the spokes of a wheel—in the cornea. This procedure flattens the curve of the cornea and may help focus light rays closer to the retina. Some people with mild or moderate nearsightedness have been helped by this technique, although some physicians are concerned that the surgery may weaken the cornea. An even newer technique, used to correct both myopia and astigmatism, uses lasers to remove small portions of the cornea to correct vision. (See also CATARACTS; EYE DISORDERS; EYE TEST; GLAUCOMA.)

X-RAY EXAMINATION

An X-ray examination is a medical test used to diagnose injuries and diseases. X rays are a form of invisible energy released when electrons strike a heavy metal (such as tungsten). They are similar to light rays, but X rays can pass through dense materials that light cannot penetrate. For this reason, X rays can enter the human body and produce images of organs, internal tissues, and bones.

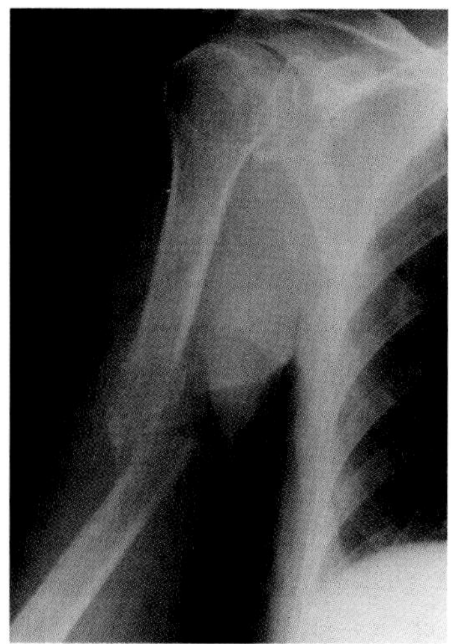

X ray of a Bone Fracture. *The fracture in this bone is easy to locate because it appears darker on the X-ray film than the bone does. This is because the X rays are absorbed by the bone but pass through the fractured area.*

X-ray Procedure Taking an X ray is very similar to taking a photograph. The X-ray machine is aimed at a body part and the rays pass through the body, leaving a shadowy image on film. Different parts of the body absorb varying amounts of X rays. Because bones are made of calcium, they absorb more X rays than do soft tissues and show up more clearly on X-ray film. To make soft tissues (such as blood vessels, organs, or muscles) stand out, the person to be X-rayed is given a dye or some other harmless substance that absorbs the X rays. A *barium X ray,* for example, is an X-ray image of the digestive tract that is taken after a person swallows barium sulfate.

Uses of X rays Barium X rays are very helpful in detecting TUMORS, ulcers, HERNIAS, and other disorders of the digestive system. *Mammograms* are X rays of the soft tissue of the breasts used to detect breast cancer. High doses of X rays are used in RADIATION THERAPY to attack cancer cells.

Although X rays are routinely used as a diagnostic tool, they have their drawbacks. Overexposure to X rays can damage living cells, especially rapidly dividing cells. For this reason, fetuses (unborn babies) are particularly vulnerable, and pregnant women should avoid X rays. In all examinations, parts of the body not involved in the X ray should be shielded with a lead apron. The most up-to-date X-ray equipment is designed to use the lowest possible dosage for diagnostic purposes; however, not all physicians or dentists may have such equipment, so it may be wise to ask questions about the level of exposure before having X rays taken. (See also CAT SCAN; MAMMOGRAM, 6; RADIOLOGIST, 9.)

SUPPLEMENTARY SOURCES

American Cancer Society. *Cancer facts and figures, 1992.* Updated annually.

American Diabetes Association. 1987. *Diabetes in the family.* Rev. ed. New York: Prentice-Hall.

Appleton, Nancy. 1991. *Healthy bones: What you should know about osteoporosis.* Garden City Park, N.Y.: Avery Publishing Group.

Arnold, Caroline. 1990. *Heart disease.* New York: Franklin Watts.

Bean, Constance A. 1989. *The better back book.* New York: William Morrow.

Brown, Fern G. 1987. *Hereditary diseases.* New York: Franklin Watts.

Check, William W. 1991. *Alzheimer's disease.* New York: Chelsea House.

Edelson, William. 1989. *Allergies.* New York: Chelsea House.

Fine, Judylaine. 1986. *Afraid to ask: A book for families to share about cancer.* New York: Lothrop, Lee & Shepard.

Mango, Karen. 1991. *Hearing loss.* New York: Franklin Watts.

McGoon, Dwight C. 1990. *The Parkinson's handbook.* New York: Norton.

McGowen, Tom. 1989. *Epilepsy.* New York: Franklin Watts.

Solomon, Seymour, and Steven Fraccaro. 1991. *The headache book.* Mount Vernon, N.Y.: Consumer Reports Books.

Subah-Sharpe, Genell. 1988. *Breathing easy: A handbook for asthmatics.* New York: Doubleday.

Tiger, Steven. 1986. *Understanding arthritis.* New York: Julian Messner.

University of California, Berkeley. 1991. *The wellness encyclopedia.* Boston: Houghton Mifflin.

ORGANIZATIONS

Alzheimer's Association
919 North Michigan Avenue
Chicago, IL 60611
(800) 272-3900

American Cancer Society, Inc.
National Headquarters
1599 Clifton Road, NE
Atlanta, GA 30329
Response System:
1-800-ACS-2345

American Dental Association
211 East Chicago Avenue
Chicago, IL 60611
(312) 440-2500

American Diabetes Association
1660 Duke Street
Alexandria, VA 22314
(703) 549-1500

American Foundation for the Blind
15 West 16th Street
New York, NY 10011
(212) 620-2000

American Heart Association
7320 Greenville Avenue
Dallas, TX 75231
(214) 373-6300

American Parkinson Disease Association
60 Bay Street
Staten Island, NY 10301
(718) 981-8001

American Speech-Language-Hearing Association
10801 Rockville Pike
Rockville, MD 20852
(301) 897-5700

Arthritis Foundation
1314 Spring Street, NW
Atlanta, GA 30309
(404) 872-7100

Asthma and Allergy Foundation of America
1717 Massachusetts Avenue
Washington, DC 20036
(202) 265-0265

Better Hearing Institute
Box 1840
Washington, DC 20013
(703) 642-0580
Hearing Helpline
(800) EAR-WELL

Better Vision Institute
1800 North Kent Street
Rosslyn, VA 22209
(703) 243-1508

Lupus Foundation of America
1717 Massachusetts Avenue, NW
Washington, DC 20036
(202) 328-4550

March of Dimes/Birth Defects Foundation
1275 Mamaroneck Avenue
White Plains, NY 10605
(914) 428-7100

Muscular Dystrophy Association
810 Seventh Avenue
New York, NY 10019
(212) 586-0808

National Association for Down Syndrome
P.O. Box 4542
Oak Brook, IL 60522
(708) 325-9112

National Diabetes Information Clearinghouse
Box NDIC
9000 Rockville Pike
Bethesda, MD 20892
(301) 468-2162

National Heart, Lung, and Blood Institute
9000 Rockville Pike
Bethesda, MD 20892
(301) 496-4000

National Kidney Foundation
30 East 33rd Street, 11th Floor
New York, NY 10016
(212) 889-2210

National Multiple Sclerosis Society
205 East 42nd Street
New York, NY 10017
(212) 986-3240

Office of Disease Prevention and Health Promotion
National Health Information Center
P.O. Box 1133
Washington, DC 20013
(800) 336-4797

United Cerebral Palsy Associations
7 Penn Plaza
New York, NY 10001
(212) 268-6655

INDEX

Italicized page numbers refer to illustrations or charts.

Abscess in tooth, 44–45, *45*
Absences (petit mal seizures), 54
Accidental amputation, 10
Acne, 4–5, *4*
ACTH (adrenocorticotropic hormone), 90
Acupuncture, 5–6
Acute glaucoma, 60
Acute lymphoblastic leukemia (ALL), *84*
Acute myeloblastic leukemia (AML), *84*
Adjuvant therapy for cancer, 27, 31
Age-related hearing loss, 67
Aging, cataract formation and, 35
AIDS, 25, 75, 81–82
Airborne allergens, 6
Alcoholism, cirrhosis and, 38, 39
Allergens, 6, 8–9, 64, 79
Allergic rhinitis. *See* Hay fever
Allergies, 6–8. *See also* Asthma; Eczema; Guillain-Barré syndrome; Hay fever
Allergy immunotherapy, 7, 79
Allergy tests, 8–9, 19
Alopecia. *See* Hair loss
Alternative health care, 5–6
Alveoli, 53, *53*
Alzheimer's disease, 9–10, 43, 44
American Cancer Society, 30, 40
Amniocentesis, 50
Amputation, 10–11, 59
Analgesics, 94
Anaphylactic shock, 6, 79, 101
Androgen, acne and, 4
Anemia, 11–12, 102, 113, 115
Anesthesia, 12–13, *13*, 109. *See also* Pain; Surgery
Anesthesiologist, 13, *13*
Aneurysm, 13–14, *14*, 107. *See also* Arteriosclerosis; Blood clot; Cardiovascular disease; Heart disease; Hypertension
Angina pectoris, 69
Angiography, 14, 19
Angioplasty, 19, 69, 74
Antacids, 106
Antibodies, 61–62, 64, 80
Anticoagulants, 24, 107
Antihistamines, 7, 65
Antihypertensive drugs, 78
Antiseptics, 109
Anus, hemorrhoids in lining of, 75
Aorta, aneurysm in, 13, 14
Aphasia, 104
Aplastic anemia, 12
Apnea, sleep, 103, 104
Appendectomy, 14
Appendicitis, 14
Appendix, 14, *14*
Aqueous humor, 60
Arches of foot, 57
Arrhythmia, 68, 71
Arteriosclerosis, 13, 15, 69. *See also* Atherosclerosis; Gangrene; Heart attack; Hypertension; Stroke
Artery, *19*
  diseases of, 13–14, 15, 19–20, 34
Arthritis, 15–17, 22, 58, 98
Arthroscopy, 109
Articulation disorder, 104
Artificial heart implantation, 74
Artificial limb, 10, *10*
Artificial pacemaker implantation, 74
Asbestosis, 86
Asbestos removal, 33, *33*
Aspirin, 100, 108
Asthma, 6, 17–19, *18*
Astigmatism, 116, 117
Ataxic cerebral palsy, 37
Atherosclerosis, 19–20, *20*, 68–69. *See also* Arteriosclerosis; Blood clot; Heart disease; Hypertension; Stroke
Athlete's foot, 57
Atrial fibrillation, 70
Aura, of migraine, 88
Autoimmune disorder, 20, 112. *See also* Anemia; Lupus erythematosus; Mononucleosis; Multiple sclerosis; Rheumatoid arthritis
Automatic responses, coma and, 40

Back problems, 21–22, *21*. *See also* Arthritis
Bacterial infections, cancer and, 30
Baldness. *See* Hair loss
Balloon angioplasty, 19
Barium enema, 39
Barium X ray, 40, 118
Barnard, Christiaan, 73
Basal cell carcinoma, 102, *103*
Benign tumor, 29, 114
Beta-blocker, 69, 78, 89
Bifocals, 117
Bile duct, blockage of, 58, *58*
Bilirubin, excess of, 81, *81*
Biofeedback, 94
Biological carcinogens, 33
Biopsy, 22–23, 26–27, 30, 38, 39, 77, 81
Blackheads, 4, *4*
Black lung disease, 86, *86*
Bladder problems, 80, *82*
Bleeding
  hemophilia and, 74–75
  iron-deficiency anemia caused by, 11
  nosebleeds, 91–92
  ulcers and internal, 114
Blindness, night, 54
Blisters, 23–24, 51, 57. *See also* Eczema
Blood blisters, 23
Blood clot, 24, *24*
  aneurysm forming, 14
  in coronary artery, 68, *68*, 69
  in hemorrhoid, 75
  pulmonary embolism caused by, 86
  stroke caused by, 106–7, *107*
  See also Arteriosclerosis; Atherosclerosis; Cardiovascular disease; Heart disease; Varicose vein
Blood poisoning, 24–25, 101
Blood pressure, normal, 77. *See also* Hypertension
Blood tests for anemia, 11
Blood transfusion, 25, 75
Body metabolism, epilepsy and, 54
Bone fracture, 93, *118*
Bone graft, 97
Bone marrow transplantation, 84, 113
Bowel movements, 41–42, 80
Braces. *See* Orthodontic devices
Brain
  Alzheimer's disease and, 9
  electroencephalogram of, 52
  epilepsy and electrical function of, 53–54
  interpretation of pain, *94*
  Reye's syndrome and, 100
  stroke and, 106–8
  Tay-Sachs disease and, 110
Brain damage, effects of, 36, 40–41
Brain tumor, 25–26, *26*, 43, 44. *See also* Cancer
Breast cancer, 26–28, *31*. *See also* Biopsy; Mammogram; Tumor
Breast examination, clinical, 26
Breast implants, 97
Breathing difficulties, 17–18, *53*, 79
Bridges (partial dentures), 46
Bronchial asthma. *See* Asthma
Bronchitis, asthma and, 18
Bronchodilators, 18
Bruxism, 110
Bunion, 57
Bursa, 28, *28*, 57
Bursitis, 28
Bypass surgery, 73

Calcium in bones, osteoporosis and, 93
Calculus, 62
Cancer, 29–32, *30*
  chemotherapy for, 31, 37
  radiation therapy for, 99, *99*
  warning signs, 30
  See also Biopsy; Brain tumor; Breast cancer; Carcinogens; Colorectal cancer;

Hodgkin's disease; Kaposi's sarcoma; Leukemia; Lung cancer; Lymphoma; Surgery; Tumor
Cancer cells, 29
Cancer immunotherapy, 31–32, 80
Canker sore, 32
Carbon dioxide in blood, 79
Carcinogens, 30, 33
Carcinoma, 29–30, 102, *103*
Cardiac asthma, 17. *See also* Heart attack
Cardiac (heart) surgery, 73–74, 109
Cardiomyopathy, 71
Cardiopulmonary resuscitation (CPR), 69
Cardiovascular disease, 34. *See also* Aneurysm; Arteriosclerosis; Atherosclerosis; Blood clot; Heart attack; Heart disease; Heart murmur; Heart surgery; Hypertension
Caries, dental, 44, 45
Carpal bones, *35*
Carpal tunnel syndrome, 34–35
Cataracts, 35–36, *35*. *See also* Eye disorders; Eye tests
CAT scan, 26, 36. *See also* Magnetic resonance imaging (MRI); X-ray examination
Cavity, dental, 44, *45*
Centers for Disease Control, 38
Cerebral embolism, 106–7, *107*
Cerebral hemorrhage, 107
Cerebral palsy, 36–37
Cerebral thrombosis, 106, *107*
Cerebrovascular accident (CVA). *See* Stroke
Chemical carcinogens, 33
Chemotherapy, 31, 37. *See also* Cancer; Radiation therapy; Surgery
Chicken pox, blisters of, 23
Cholesterol, 19, *20*, 58, *71*
Chromosome, extra, 49, *50*
Chronic fatigue syndrome (CFS), 38
Chronic glaucoma, 60
Chronic lymphocytic leukemia (CLL), *84*
Chronic myeloid leukemia (CML), *84*
Chronic renal failure, 82–83
Circulation, gangrene and lack of, 59
Cirrhosis, 38–39, *39*. *See also* Jaundice; Peritonitis
Cluster headaches, 66
Cochlea, 67, *67*
Colectomy, 40
Colitis, 39
Colon, diverticulitis in, 49
Colorectal cancer, 40. *See also* Colitis; Tumor
Color vision deficiency, 54
Colostomy, 40
Coma, 40–41. *See also* Brain tumor; Epilepsy; Stroke
Computerized axial tomography. *See* CAT scan
Conductive deafness, 66–67
Congenital cataracts, 35
Congenital heart disease, 72
Congestive heart failure, 17, 34, 68, 70, 71–72
Connective tissue, lupus and, 87
Constipation, 41–42, 49, 75
Contact dermatitis, 6
Contact lenses, 117
Convalescence, 109
Convulsions, epilepsy and, 53, 54
Cornea, vision problems and, 116, *116*
Corns, 57
Coronary artery bypass surgery, 19–20, 69, 73
Coronary artery disease, 34, 68, *68*, 69, 70
Cosmetic surgery, 97
Crib death. *See* Sudden infant death syndrome (SIDS)
Crohn's disease, 39
Cryosurgery, 103
CT scan. *See* CAT scan
Cyanosis, 18
Cystic fibrosis, 42–43
Cystitis, 80

Dandruff, 43
Deafness. *See* Hearing loss
Death, sudden cardiac, 71
Death syndrome, sudden infant, 108
Decongestants, 65
Defibrillator, 71
Degenerative joint disease. *See* Osteoarthritis
Delayed speaking, 104
Dementia, 9, 43–44. *See also* Anemia; Arteriosclerosis; Brain tumor; Hypertension; Stroke
Dental problems, 44–45, *44*. *See also* Dentures; Orthodontic devices
Dentists, 44
Dentures, 45–46
Dermatitis, 6, 43
Detached retina, 55, *55*
Diabetes, 10, 19, *20*, 46–48
Dialysis, 48–49, *48*. *See also* Kidney disorders
Diaphragm, hiccups and, 76–77
Diarrhea, diverticulitis and, 49
Diastolic pressure, 77
Diet
 constipation and, 41, 75
 diabetes treatment and, 47
Discoid lupus erythematosus (DLE), 87
Diuretics, 78
Diverticulitis, 49
Diverticulosis, 49
Donor cards for transplants, *113*
Dopamine, 95, 96, *96*
Double-blind food allergy test, 9
Down syndrome, 49–50, *50*
Drug allergies, 6
Dry gangrene, 59, *59*
Dry pleurisy, 98
Duchenne muscular dystrophy, 90, 91
Duodenal ulcers, 114, *115*
Dwarfism, 61
Dyskinetic cerebral palsy, 37
Dyspepsia. *See* Indigestion (dyspepsia)

Eardrum, *67*
Ear infections, hearing loss and, 67
Earwax, buildup of, 67
Echocardiogram, 72, 73
Eczema, 6, 51
Electric shock, 101
Electrocardiogram (ECG or EKG), 51–52, 72. *See also* Heart attack; Stress test
Electroencephalogram (EEG), 52, 54, *54*
Embolism, 14, 19, 24, *24*, 86
Embolus, 14, 24
Emphysema, 18, 53, *53*
Encephalitis, palsy and, 37
Endocarditis, 71, 73
Endorphins, acupuncture and, 5
Endoscope, *22*, 114
Endoscopic biopsy, 22–23
End-stage renal failure, 83
Enema, barium, 39
Environmental carcinogens, 33
Epilepsy, 53–54. *See also* Stroke
Epinephrine, 8
Epstein-Barr virus, 38
Essential hypertension, 78
Estrogen replacement therapy, 93
Exercise
 asthma and, *18*, 19
 diabetes treatment and, 47
 osteoporosis prevention and, 93
Exercise tolerance test. *See* Stress test
Eye
 fluid drainage in, 60, *60*
 yellow whites of, jaundice and, 81
Eye disorders, 54–55, *83*. *See also* Cataracts; Eye tests; Glaucoma; Thyroid disorders; Vision problems
Eyeglasses, 117
Eye tests, 54, 55, 60. *See also* Vision problems

Face lifts, 97
Fainting, 55–56
Farsightedness, *116*, 117
Fatigue syndrome, chronic, 38
Fecal impaction, 80
Fecal incontinence, 80
Feces. *See* Bowel movements
Female pattern baldness, 63
Femoral hernia, 76
Fiber, dietary, 32, 40, 41
Fibrositis, 56. *See also* Sleep disorders
Fingers, Raynaud's phenomenon and, 100
Fixed braces, 92, *92*
Flat feet, 57
Flatulence, 105
Flossing, 45, 63
Folic acid anemia, 12
Food(s)
 allergies to certain, 6, 7
 cancer and, 32
 fiber-rich, *42*

migraine triggered by, 89
stomachache/indigestion due to, 105–6
Food allergy test, double-blind, 9
Food and Drug Administration, 97
Foot problems, 57–58. *See also* Blisters
Fracture, bone, 93

Gallbladder, 58, 81
Gallstones, 58–59, *58*. *See also* Jaundice
Gamma globulin, 62
Gangrene, 10, 15, 59, *59*, 76. *See also* Arteriosclerosis; Diabetes
Gas, excessive, 105
Gastric ulcers, 114
Gastritis, 106
Gene, recessive, 42, 91
General anesthesia, 13
Generalized convulsive seizures (GCS), 54, *54*
Generalized nonconvulsive seizures (GNCS), 54
Genetic counseling, 42, 50, 75, 91, 102, 110
Genetic engineering, 80
Gigantism, 60
Gingivitis, 62
Glaucoma, 55, 60, 83. *See also* Cataracts; Diabetes; Eye tests
Goiter, 112
Gout, 17, 58
Grand mal seizures, 54, *54*
Graves' disease, 112
Growth disorders, 60–61
Growth hormone (GH), 60, 61
Guillain-Barré syndrome, 61–62
Gum disease, 45, 62–63. *See also* Dental problems

Hair follicles, 4, *4*
Hair loss, 63–64, *63*
Hair transplants, 64
Halitosis, 45
Hand, carpal tunnel syndrome and, 34–35, *35*
Hay fever, 6, 64–65
Headache, 65–66. *See also* Aneurysm; Brain tumor; Hypertension; Migraine headache
Hearing aids, 67
Hearing loss, 66–67
Heart, *70*
electrocardiogram of, 51–52, *52*
Heart attack, 15, 19, 24, 68–69, *68*. *See also* Atherosclerosis; Blood clot; Diabetes; Electrocardiogram (ECG or EKG); Hypertension
Heartburn, 105, 106
Heart disease, 34, 69–72. *See also* Congestive heart failure; Coronary artery disease
Heart-lung machine, 73
Heart murmur, 34, 72–73
Heart surgery, 73–74, 109
Heart transplant, 72, 73–74
Heart valve surgery, 73
Height, growth disorder and, 60–61
Hemiplegia, 95
Hemochromatosis, 38
Hemodialysis, 49
Hemoglobin, anemia and, 11
Hemoglobin S, 102
Hemolytic anemia, 12, 102
Hemophilia, 74–75
Hemorrhage, cerebral, 107
Hemorrhoids, 75, *75*
Hepatitis, cirrhosis and, 38
Heredity
Duchenne muscular dystrophy and, 91
Tay-Sachs disease and, 110
See also Genetic counseling
Hernia, 76, *76*
Herniated ("slipped") disk, 21–22
Herpes infections, blisters of, 23
Hiatal hernia, 76
Hiccups, 76–77
High blood pressure. *See* Hypertension
High-intensity laser, 83
Histamines, 6, 64
HIV, 25, 33, 75, 87
Hives (urticaria), 6
Hodgkin's disease, 77, 87. *See also* Lymphoma
Hormone therapy for cancer, 31
Hyperglycemia, 46
Hyperopia, *116*, 117
Hypertension, 77–78, *78*
cardiovascular diseases and, 13, 15, *20*, 34, 70, *71*
portal, 38–39
See also Kidney disorders; Stroke
Hypertensive heart disease, 34, 70
Hyperthyroidism, 112
Hyperventilation, 79
Hypoglycemia, 48
Hypothyroidism, 112

Ileitis. *See* Crohn's disease
Immune system
allergies and, 6
autoimmune disorder and, 20
chronic fatigue syndrome and, 38
Guillain-Barré syndrome and, 61–62
rejection of transplant, 73, 113
Immunotherapy, 7, 31–32, 79–80
Impacted teeth, 45
Impetigo, blisters of, 23
Incontinence, 80. *See also* Diabetes; Multiple sclerosis; Stroke
Indigestion (dyspepsia), 105
Infectious arthritis, 17
Inflammatory bowel disease, 39
Ingrown toenails, 57
Inguinal hernia, 76
Inner ear, *67*
Insomnia, 103
Insulin, 46, 48
Insulin-dependent diabetes mellitus (IDDM), 46, 47, 48
Iron-deficiency anemia, 11–12
Itchiness, eczema and, 51
Jarvik-7 artificial heart, 74
Jaundice, 38, 81, *81*
Jaw, temporomandibular joint syndrome and, 110–11
Joint(s)
of big toe, bunion on, 57
inflammation of. *See* Arthritis
temporomandibular, *110*
Juvenile rheumatoid arthritis, 17

Kaposi's sarcoma, 81–82
Kidney disorders, 82–83. *See also* Diabetes; Dialysis; Hypertension; Shock
Kidney failure, 48–49, 82–83
Kidney stones, 82, *82*
Kidney transplant, 83

Laparoscope, 58
Laser surgery, 83
Laxatives, 41
Lens implants, 36
Lens of eye
cataracts in, 35–36, *35*
vision problems and, 116, *116*
Leukemia, 83–84, *84*, 113. *See also* Anemia; Immunotherapy
Leukocytes, 83
Levodopa (L-dopa), 96
Lifestyle
cancer prevention and, 32
coronary artery disease treatment and, 69
hypertension treatment and, 78
sedentary, 19, *20*, *71*
See also Diet; Exercise
Life-support systems, 41
Liposuction, 97
Lisping, 104
Liver biopsy, 38, 81
Liver disease
cancer, 33
cirrhosis, 38–39, *39*
jaundice as symptom of, 81
Local anesthesia, 12–13
Low-intensity laser, 83
Lumpectomy, 27
Lung, cystic fibrosis and, 42–43
Lung cancer, *31*, *33*, 85
Lung disease, 85–87. *See also* Emphysema; Lung cancer; Pleurisy
Lupus erythematosus, 87
Lymphatic system, metastasis through, *27*, 29, *29*
Lymphoma, 87. *See also* Hodgkin's disease

Macular degeneration, 55
Magnetic resonance imaging (MRI), *26*, 88, *88*. *See also* CAT scan; X-ray examination
Male pattern baldness, 63, *63*
Malignant melanoma, 102
Malignant tumor, 29, 114
Malnutrition, 36, 61
Malocclusion, 45, 92
Mammogram, 26, 28, 118

Mastectomy, 27
Median nerve, 34, *35*
Melanoma, 102
Ménière's disease, 67
Meningitis, cerebral palsy and, 37
Menopause, bone loss in women after, 93
Mental retardation, cerebral palsy and, 36
Metacarpal bones, *35*
Metastasis, 26, 27, *27*, 30, *30*, 114
Metastatic tumor, 25
Microsurgery, 109
Middle ear, *67*
Midgets, 61
Migraine headache, 66, 88–89, 91
Minoxidil, 64
Mononucleosis, 38
Multiple sclerosis, 89–90. *See also* Autoimmune disorder
Murmur, heart, 34, 72–73
Muscle biopsy, 23
Muscle paralysis, 95
Muscles, Parkinson's disease and, 96
Muscle strains, 21
Muscular dystrophy, 90–91
Myelin sheath, 62, 89, *90*
Myocardial infarction. *See* Heart attack
Myocarditis, 71
Myopia, 116–17, *116*

Narcolepsy, 103, 104
Narcotics, 94
Nearsightedness, 116–17, *116*
Needle biopsy, 22, 26–27
Neonatal jaundice, 81
Neoplasm. *See* Tumor
Nephritis, 82
Nerve blocks, 13
Nerves, sensory, 94
Nerve transplants, 95
Nervous system
  paralysis and damage to, 95
  Parkinson's disease and, 95–96
Neuralgia, 91. *See also* Shingles
Neurons, 53
Night blindness, 54
Non-Hodgkin's lymphoma, 87
Non-insulin-dependent diabetes mellitus (NIDDM), 46, 47, 48
Nose, rhinoplasty on, 97
Nosebleed, 91–92, *92*. *See also* Hemophilia; Hypertension

Obesity, disease and, 19, *20*, *71*
Occupation-related lung diseases, 86–87
Open-heart surgery, 73, *73*
Operations. *See* Surgery
Ophthalmic surgery, 109
Ophthalmologist, 55
Ophthalmoscope, 55
Optometrist, 55
Organs, transplants of, 113
Orthodontic devices, 45, 92, 111
Orthodontist, 45, 92
Orthopedic surgery, 109
Osteoarthritis, 15–16, 22
Osteoporosis, 93, *93*
Otosclerosis, 67

Pacemaker, 71
  artificial, 74
Pain, 94, *94*
  abdominal, 14, 97
  anesthesia to prevent, 12–13
  of arthritis, 16
  headache, 65–66
  of heart attack, 68
  jaw and head, TMJ syndrome and, 110, 111
  neuralgia, 91
  phantom limb, 10
  of pleurisy, 98
  psychological factors in, 94
  of sciatica, 21
  of tooth decay, 44
  See also Back problems; Migraine headache
Pancreas, diabetes and, 46–48
Pap test, 32
Paralysis, 95, 107. *See also* Brain tumor; Multiple sclerosis; Muscular dystrophy; Stroke
Paraplegia, 95
Parkinson's disease, 95–96. *See also* Brain tumor; Cardiovascular disease
Partial seizure, 53
Peptic ulcer, 114–15, *115*
Pericarditis, 71
Periodontitis, 62–63
Peripheral vision, 55, 60
Peritonitis, 14, 19, 39, 97, 115
Pernicious anemia, 12
Petit mal seizures (absences), 54
Phantom limb pain, 10
Phlebitis, 24, 34
Physical therapy, 37, 95
Pituitary gland, growth disorders and, 60, 61
Placebo, 9
Plaque
  arterial, 19, 34, 74, 107
  dental, 44, 62, 63
Plasmapheresis, 62
Plastic surgery, 97, *97*, 109
Pleura, 98
Pleurisy, 98
Pneumoconiosis, 86, *86*
Pneumonia, asthma and, 18
Pneumothorax, 85–86
Pore, 4
Portal hypertension, 38–39
Postherpetic neuralgia, 91
Pregnancy
  amniocentesis during, 50
  fainting during, 56
  malnutrition during, 36
  rubella during, 35, 36, 67, 72
Presbycusis, 67
Presbyopia, 117
Primary hypertension, 78
Primary tumor, 25
Proctosigmoidoscopy, 40
Prolapse, valve, 70
Prosthesis, 10, *10*
Psoriasis, 98–99
Puberty, acne and, 4
Pulmonary embolism, 86
Pulmonary fibrosis, 86
Pustules, 4, *4*

Quadriplegia, 95

Radial keratotomy, 117
Radiation therapy, 31, 99. *See also* Cancer
Radical mastectomy, 27
Radioactive iodine uptake (RAIU) test, 112
Rash
  of allergies, 6
  of eczema, 51
  of lupus, 87
  seborrheic dermatitis, 43
RAST (radioallergosorbent test), 8, 9
Raynaud's disease, 100
Raynaud's phenomenon, 100. *See also* Arteriosclerosis; Arthritis; Blood clot
Recessive gene, 42, 91
Reconstructive surgery. *See* Plastic surgery
Rectum
  colorectal cancer in, 40
  hemorrhoids in lining of, 75, *75*
Red blood cells, 11, 12, 102, *102*
Referred pain, 94
Rehabilitation after stroke, 108
Rejection of transplant, 73, 113
Renal failure. *See* Kidney failure
Retainer, 92
Retina, detached, 55, *55*
Reye's syndrome, 100. *See also* Coma
Rheumatoid arthritis, 16–17
Rheumatoid nodules, 16
Rhinoplasty, 97
Root canal treatment, 45
Rubella, 35, 36, 67, 72

Sarcoma, 30, 81–82
Scaling, 51, 98
Scalp, dandruff and, 43
Scarring
  cirrhosis of liver and, *39*
  of multiple sclerosis, *90*
Schlemm, canal of, 60, *60*
Sciatica, 21
Scoliosis, 100–101
Screening of donated blood, 25, 75
Sealant, dental, 45
Sebaceous glands, 4, *4*
Seborrheic dermatitis, 43
Sebum, 4
Secondary hypertension, 78
Secondary tumor, 25
Secondhand smoke, 85
Seizure disorder. *See* Epilepsy
Selegiline (Deprenyl or Eldepryl), 96
Senility, 9
Sensorineural deafness, 67